Hypocrites or Heroes?

Hypocrites or Heroes?

The Paradoxical Portrayal of the Pharisees in the New Testament

ROGER AMOS

Foreword by Pieter Lalleman

WIPF & STOCK · Eugene, Oregon

HYPOCRITES OR HEROES?
The Paradoxical Portrayal of the Pharisees in the New Testament

Copyright © 2015 Roger Amos. All rights reserved. Except for brief quotations in critical publications or reviews, no part of this book may be reproduced in any manner without prior written permission from the publisher. Write: Permissions, Wipf and Stock Publishers, 199 W. 8th Ave., Suite 3, Eugene, OR 97401.

Wipf & Stock
An Imprint of Wipf and Stock Publishers
199 W. 8th Ave., Suite 3
Eugene, OR 97401

www.wipfandstock.com

ISBN 13: 978-1-4982-2027-9   03/26/2015

All scripture quotations, unless otherwise indicated, are taken from the Holy Bible, New International Version®, NIV®. Copyright ©1973, 1978, 1984, 2011 by Biblica, Inc.™ Used by permission of Zondervan. All rights reserved worldwide. www.zondervan.com The "NIV" and "New International Version" are trademarks registered in the United States Patent and Trademark Office by Biblica, Inc.™

Contents

Foreword by Dr Pieter Lalleman   vii

Preface   ix

Abbreviations   xi

1. Introduction   1
2. The Pharisees in the New Testament   11
3. "The Jews" in John's Gospel   90
4. The Pharisees in Josephus and the Rabbinical Literature   107
5. Historical Reconstruction 1—The Origin of the Pharisees   122
6. Historical Reconstruction 2—The Pharisees at the Time of Jesus   134
7. Historical Reconstruction 3—Jesus and the Pharisees   160
8. Hypocrites or Heroes?—Explaining the paradox   199

Appendix: Substitution of Synonyms   215

Bibliography   217

Index of Biblical References   219

Index of Names and Subjects   227

Foreword

MANY OF US WHO grew up in Christian homes will be familiar with the Pharisees as bad people. In countless stories which we were told from children's Bibles and other popular sources, they are the perennial adversaries of the Lord Jesus, always on hand to criticize him and to attack the good things he did for the people of Israel. In such stories there is normally not the faintest suggestion that some of the Pharisees might actually have had good intentions. Popular preachers are likely to misrepresent these contemporaries of Jesus in a similar way. Those of you who grew up outside the Christian tradition are not so likely to know these misleading stories but you will know the term "Pharisee" as a swearword.

In any case, the caricatures that are made of the Pharisees easily rub off on all Jewish people, first on Jesus' other contemporaries and then on all Jews anywhere. And regrettably this is what has happened: popular misrepresentations of the Pharisees have contributed to—and then in turn resulted from—the latent or open anti-Semitism which has characterized large sections of Christianity and of the western civilization in general for most of its history.

Part of the problem is that discussions among Jewish people can be sharp; sharper than we may find acceptable. Hence the New Testament itself is harsh about the Pharisees. Both sides of the divide, the Lord Jesus as well as his adversaries, call a spade a spade. In doing this, they simply follow conventions which we already find in the Old Testament, where the prophet Amos addresses the rich women of Samaria as "cows" (Amos 4:1) and Isaiah suggests that his contemporaries are less intelligent than an ox and a donkey (Isa 1:3), to give only two of many examples. In the Dead Sea Scrolls, texts written by Jews in the era just before the coming of the Messiah, this sharp tone is also found. For example, several texts refer to their own people as "children of light" and to their opponents as "children

Foreword

of darkness." In all these cases, the aim is to shock in order to gain attention and to call the addressees back to the fold. It is language Jews use among themselves.

We hear this same aggressive tone in many encounters of Jesus and the Pharisees. They are close to each other in their views and both have the best interest of the nation at heart—hence they speak with intensity. It is their very closeness that heightens the feelings and the tone. Hence they clash rather fiercely and mud flies through the air. British readers, who prefer to refer to total nonsense as "interesting" and have a friendly word for any lunatic, are likely to misunderstand this style and to be unnecessarily offended.

The present book by Roger Amos builds on contemporary scholarship about the Pharisees and takes it a step further. We can all be grateful to him for tackling the misunderstanding regarding the identity of the Pharisees effectively. I am glad to see that John's Gospel is taken as seriously as the other three gospels as a source of historical information. In addition to his clear discussion of the relevant material, the author might have drawn some attention to Acts 6:7, which tells us that many priests accepted Jesus as the Messiah of Israel; it is very likely that among them were many who would have seen themselves as Pharisees. This text then shows us that the breach between Jesus and the Pharisees was never too wide to be crossed.

This book can be read in conjunction with books that are drawing attention to the political aspects of the ministry of Jesus and to the fact that in the struggle against the Roman occupation of their country the Pharisees were aptly nationalistic whereas the Sadducees were collaborators. Although one can disagree with aspects of the argument and with some of Amos' conclusions, his rehabilitation of the Pharisees is appropriate and overdue. I fully agree with his words: "Jesus and the Pharisees usually agree on the fundamentals of their faith." Once again, it is the very closeness of these opponents that explains why the ultimate disagreement over Jesus' role and identity was so painful.

I sincerely hope that this book will help to eradicate the caricatures of the Pharisees and that it will contribute to a better mutual understanding of Jews and Christians, as well as of who the Lord Jesus is.

Dr Pieter Lalleman,
Academic Dean and Tutor of New Testament,
Spurgeon's College, London

Preface

DURING THE CLOSING YEARS of my pastoral ministry and the first years of my retirement I pursued the MA (by Distance Learning) course in Aspects of Biblical Interpretation from the London School of Theology. One of the concerns of my dissertation was a question which had engaged me for several years: precisely who were the "sinners" that the gospels mention in many places?

My research led to some unexpected discoveries. The pivotal episode is the feast in Matthew/Levi's house which prompted the Pharisees to criticize Jesus for dining with tax collectors and "sinners." Quite apart from the original question—who were those "sinners"?—another now raised its head: why did the Pharisees, so commonly regarded as Jesus' adversaries, expect Jesus and his disciples to behave as they themselves did?

There seemed only one logical explanation, but it so violently conflicted with traditional evangelical teaching that at first I relegated it to a tentative suggestion in a footnote: *that Jesus and his disciples were themselves Pharisees.* As my research progressed I was startled to find abundant corroborating evidence elsewhere in the gospels. Consequently that footnote grew steadily and eventually became so persuasive that I was compelled to move its content into the main body of text, where it became the turning point in the dissertation's argument. This was because of its implications for my original question: I concluded that the "sinners" were Jews outside the Pharisee movement; the gospels assume a Pharisaic environment, Pharisaism being the normative Judaism of first-century Palestine.

An internet search to discover whether any established scholars had reached similar conclusions led me to Professor Hyam Maccoby's book, *Jesus the Pharisee.* The closing date for submitting my dissertation was almost upon me and I had time to read and cite only a few of the passages most relevant to my argument. Not until after my dissertation had been

Preface

submitted did I read the book from cover to cover and find my attention drawn to further paradoxical elements in the New Testament's portrayal of the Pharisees. Of course, Professor Maccoby was a Jewish New Testament scholar, approaching the subject with presuppositions rather different to mine. On some points he won me over, while on others I still beg to disagree. I was sorry to learn that he had died a few years previously as I would have enjoyed corresponding with him and perhaps even meeting him.

It was reading his book that sowed the seeds of this one. Now there was a vacuum in my life: I had finished and submitted my MA dissertation; health issues had forced the suspension of my preaching ministry; I needed a new project and had been bitten by the theological research bug. What more natural than that I study for a PhD, my doctoral dissertation being to some extent a critique of Professor Maccoby's book? Because of family circumstances I decided against registering for a doctorate, but chose nevertheless to undertake the research and write the dissertation that I would have submitted (subject, of course, to the requisite approvals) had I opted to pursue that route. And, if the resulting document told a story that seemed to command sufficient interest, I would try to publish it.

In fact this work is far more than a critique of *Jesus the Pharisee*. It embodies some of the relevant material from my MA dissertation and seeks also to explain some of the other paradoxical elements in Jesus' ministry that have occupied my thoughts for some years. Whether readers will be convinced by my arguments remains to be seen, but I hope that they will be challenged to think more deeply about the issues involved.

I am indebted to John King, leader of the New Testament Greek Group at the Percival Guildhouse in Rugby, who read an early version of this book, spotted many errors and suggested many improvements, and to Dr Pieter Lalleman, Academic Dean at Spurgeon's College, who read a later version and not only provided the Foreword, but also spotted further errors and omissions.

Roger Amos,
Rugby, England, 2015

Abbreviations

EVV English versions
KJV King James Version
LXX Septuagint (Greek translation of the Old Testament, 3rd–2nd century BCE)
MSS Manuscripts
NIV New International Version
RSV Revised Standard Version

1

Introduction

THE PARADOX OF THE PHARISEES

IF THE NUMBER OF times the New Testament mentions a subject is a valid criterion of its importance, the Pharisees rank among its prime concerns. Not only does the Greek word *Pharisaios* occur 98 times, but it is supplemented by alternative terms such as *grammateus*, "scribe, teacher of the law," (63 times), *nomikos*, "lawyer," (9 times), and *nomodidaskalos*, "teacher of the law" (3 times), all of which are often used synonymously or nearly so with *Pharisaios*. Moreover, as will be demonstrated, in John's Gospel many of the 67 occurrences of *hoi Ioudaioi*, "the Jews," refer in fact to the Pharisees. This potential total of 240[1] mentions far surpasses that of such traditional Christian keywords as *stauros*, "cross," (28 times), *afesis*, "remission, forgiveness," (17 times), and *apolutrōsis*, "redemption," (10 times). In the gospels, in particular, the Pharisees dominate the social landscape.

The Pharisees, however, get a bad press. According to the *Chambers Dictionary*, "Pharisee" is recognized even in everyday English as denoting "a very self-righteous or hypocritical person." This is understandable in the

---

1. From this total may be deducted the occurrences of *grammateus*, *nomikos*, and *nomodidaskalos* that do not refer to the Pharisees and those instances where two of the keywords occur in conjunction, as in the frequently used phrase "teachers of the law and Pharisees." This, however, still leaves around 200 mentions.

Hypocrites or Heroes?

light of their description in some New Testament passages. For example, in Matt 23:13–29 Jesus addresses them as "hypocrites"[2] six times. But the New Testament makes more serious allegations concerning them. The synoptic gospels imply that the Pharisees plotted to kill Jesus (Matt 12:14; Mark 3:6). In John 8:40–44 a similar plot leads Jesus to brand them "children of the devil." It is not surprising that the late Professor Hyam Maccoby of the University of Leeds Centre for Jewish Studies describes these charges against the Pharisees as "a powerful ingredient in the formation of Western antisemitism."[3]

Recently scholars have begun to recognize that, where the Pharisees are concerned, our conventional understanding of the New Testament is often misleading. N. T. Wright, for example, points out that "traditional readings [of the gospels] have envisaged Jesus opposing the Pharisees, or they him, on the grounds that they supported a religion of outward observances and perceived him to be an antinomian threat . . . This double reading has recently been opposed . . . on the grounds of historical implausibility: Jesus did not 'speak against the law.' And what he did say would not have been particularly irritating to the Pharisees."[4] Although Wright is referring primarily to the supposed doctrinal differences between Jesus and the Pharisees, his observation applies over a broader spectrum. All references to the Pharisees in the New Testament need careful interpretation in the light of the picture that they paint as a whole. For in that overall picture there are some surprising details which are easily overlooked, but nevertheless significant.

For example, the New Testament also contains passages that show the Pharisees in a favorable light. In Matt 5:20 Jesus acknowledges that they have righteousness of a kind, although he demands higher standards of his own disciples. When, in Matt 9:10–13, Pharisees criticize Jesus for dining with tax collectors and "sinners," Jesus' response implies that he regards the Pharisees as "healthy" and "righteous" and therefore, by implication, not in need of the attention that he is giving to those who do need it. In the same speech in which he six times declares the Pharisees hypocrites Jesus acknowledges their authority as interpreters of the law and enjoins obedience to them (Matt 23:2f). At times Jesus enjoyed friendly relations with them:

---

2. For a detailed discussion of the Greek word *hupokritēs*, which is transliterated as the English word "hypocrite" see later under *Hypocrisy*, p. 146.

3. Maccoby, *Jesus*, 84.

4. Wright, *Jesus*, 372.

Introduction

Luke, who of the evangelists seems the least antagonistic towards the Pharisees, records three occasions on which Jesus accepted dinner invitations from Pharisees;[5] although all three occasions formed part of their official surveillance of him, nevertheless their very nature presupposes a degree of congeniality between those concerned. Luke 13:31 describes another friendly act towards Jesus on the part of some Pharisees: far from attempting to kill him, they warn him that Herod Antipas is seeking his death and they advise him to leave Antipas' territory in order to save his life. Finally, in Acts 5:27–41 when Peter and some other apostles are on trial before the Sanhedrin for preaching about Jesus, it is "a Pharisee named Gamaliel, a teacher of the law, who was honored by all the people" who addresses the Council and persuades it to release the apostles on the grounds that "if their purpose or activity is of human origin, it will fail. But if it is from God, you will not be able to stop these men; you will only find yourselves fighting against God." What the author of Acts omits to mention is that this "Gamaliel was not just an individual Pharisee, but the leader of the whole Pharisee movement. We learn this information from the rabbinic literature . . . As the leader of the Pharisees, Gamaliel naturally carried all the other Pharisee members of the Council . . . with him when the matter came to a vote, and Peter was duly rescued from death."[6] So here is the leader of the Pharisee movement persuading its representatives on the Sanhedrin to release the apostles of the same Jesus whom Pharisees were allegedly plotting to kill not long previously.

It was probably inconsistencies such as these that led Professor Roland Deines of the University of Nottingham to describe the Pharisees as "Good Guys with Bad Press."[7] The inconsistencies raise a number of questions. Not least of them: precisely who were the Pharisees? What is known about them from the New Testament and other ancient sources? Were they really the murderous hypocrites that some New Testament passages claim? If not, why do those passages portray them as such? What was Jesus' relationship with them? Do the gospels' contrasting depictions of that relationship indicate that it changed over time? If so, what precipitated those changes? Another question that raises itself when we begin detailed study of the Pharisees in the New Testament is this: if, as the scholars convincingly demonstrate, Pharisees visited Galilee only rarely, why do the gospels record so many

5. Luke 7:36; 11:37; 14:1.
6. Maccoby, *Jesus*, 5f.
7. Deines, 'Good Guys,' 22.

occasions on which Jesus encountered them there? Indeed this disparity has led some scholars to question the reliability of the gospel accounts.

Intriguing as these questions are, they are of more than academic importance. Much of what the gospels record of the actions and teachings of Jesus falls within the context of his encounters with the Pharisees. An essential prerequisite to understanding Jesus, then, is some knowledge of the people with whom he so frequently interacted. This study's attempt to answer the questions raised above should therefore provide not only a clearer picture of the social and religious environment in which the Christian faith originated, but also a deeper understanding of Jesus, who is its very center.

PREVIOUS SCHOLARSHIP

The first volume of N. T. Wright's study of Christian origins, *The New Testament and the People of God*, provides a useful overview of scholarship on the Pharisees as it stood at the time of its publication in 1992.[8] He first considers the source texts and then the identity of the Pharisees, but devotes most space to their agenda and influence. He emphasizes the difficulty of researching the Pharisees:

> At no point in these sources are we able to read a picture of the Pharisees straight off the text. But at no point are we forced, as some reconstructions have been, to eliminate altogether, or for that matter to elevate to a position of infallible "objectivity," any one strand of the evidence. The Pharisees remain a complex and elusive group. But this has not prevented us from sketching in some basic historical probabilities about them, which will enable us . . . to show how their worldview and belief system formed an important variation within the broad spectrum of options open to first-century Jews.[9]

Wright's fourth volume in the series, *Paul and the Faithfulness of God* published in 2013, updates the earlier account.[10] Wright is now more confident about his sources: "Despite the difficulty in using these sources, we can construct a relatively clear picture of the Pharisees in the first half of the first century AD, not least by building out from the certainties which these texts provide to others which speak of the same beliefs and practices

---

8. Wright, *New Testament*, 181–203.
9. Ibid., 202f.
10. Wright, *Paul*, 80–90.

but without using the word 'Pharisee' itself."[11] This implies recognition that Pharisaism was a broad movement which did not always use that name. The second volume in the series, *Jesus and the Victory of God* published in 1996, also contains material on the Pharisees, but dispersed throughout the volume. Particularly useful is a section overviewing Jesus' encounters with the Pharisees.[12]

Until recently most scholars considered that at the time of Jesus Pharisaism was just one of a number of competing varieties of Judaism. The view of Giorgio Jossa in his 2006 monograph *Jews or Christians?* is typical: "Judaism was not yet what would become, after 70, the rabbinic (and normative) Judaism of the Mishnah and of the Talmud, with its absolutely prevalent insistence on the observation of the law, but . . . it included a great variety of positions and orientations: the apocalyptic currents and the authority of the priests were no less important than the Pharisaic groups."[13]

Jossa may have been influenced by A. J. Saldarini who wrote what is perhaps the best known reference work on the subject: *Pharisees, Scribes and Sadducees in Palestinian Society*, first published in 1988 and republished in 2001 as part of Eerdmans' *Biblical Resource Series*. He claims that, "In the Hasmonean and Herodian periods the Pharisees were one, but only one, well known group, characterized by a distinctive way of living Judaism and constant social involvement."[14] However, because of the contradictory source materials he concludes that, "Data on the Pharisees is so sparse and difficult to evaluate that any historical reconstruction must remain incomplete and uncomfortably hypothetical. Many attempts have harmonized very different and contradictory sources and others have placed great weight on single texts and minor details; the results have been very speculative."[15] Saldarini uses a sociological approach to overview Palestinian society, concentrating on social classes and groups, including a fascinating analysis of the place of the Pharisees in that society and of relationships within the movement.

In his survey of the literary sources—Josephus, the New Testament and the Rabbinic literature—Saldarini devotes a chapter to the Pharisees,

---

11. Ibid., 82.
12. Wright, *Jesus*, 371–383.
13. Jossa, *Jews*, 46f.
14. Saldarini, *Pharisees*, 278.
15. Ibid., 277.

scribes and Sadducees in Mark and Matthew,[16] another to these groups in Luke-Acts and John[17] and another on what can be gleaned about the Pharisees from Paul.[18] His analysis of the authors' usage of the terms is meticulous, perhaps inordinately so as he attaches variant meanings to each keyword and these vary from author to author—this study concludes from the tendency of the evangelists to use "Pharisees" and "scribes" interchangeably that they are sometimes synonymous, although they often carry distinct nuances that must be discerned from the context. Saldarini also attaches great significance to the locations in which the groups are encountered, ignoring the wealth of evidence in the gospels that at least one delegation of officials was sent from Jerusalem to Galilee to investigate Jesus. It is a pity that he relegates "the Jews" in John' Gospel to little more than a footnote. Finally in a section dedicated to interpretation and synthesis he describes the social roles of scribes, the place of the Pharisees, and the leadership role of Sadducees.

Another eminent scholar in this field whose views are similar to Saldarini's is E. P. Sanders, whose prodigious literary output covers many aspects of the New Testament and Judaism in New Testament times. He describes his *Judaism: Practice and Belief 63BCE–66CE*, published in 1992, as "the book I always wanted to write, or at least close to it."[19] This comprehensive study devotes two chapters to the Pharisees: one to their history[20] and one to their theology and practice.[21] The former usefully includes a detailed study of the first century BCE. The whole of the volume, however, is helpful to students of the New Testament, as it also describes other Jewish groups such as the Sadducees and Essenes. While some recent scholarship disagrees with Sanders' evaluation of the Pharisees' importance, he has made a major contribution to Jewish studies through his emphasis on "Common Judaism," to which he devotes ten chapters. This embraces those aspects of Judaism which were common to all its divisions and which made it one religion rather than a collection of several.

Some 15 years after the first publication of Saldarini's book and 11 years after Sanders', in 2003 Hyam Maccoby published *Jesus the Pharisee*,

16. Ibid., 144.
17. Ibid., 174.
18. Ibid., 134.
19. Sanders, *Judaism*, ix.
20. Ibid., 380.
21. Ibid., 413.

revealing views which in many respects are the antithesis of Saldarini's and Sanders'. He finds no lack of data on the Pharisees, although well aware of the many paradoxes in this subject. He eloquently expresses one of these when he states that "It is an extraordinary fact that while Jesus is portrayed in the gospels as a strong opponent of the Pharisees, he himself is the most recognizable Pharisee in the whole of first-century Jewish literature."[22] He supports this claim with evidence from the rabbinic literature[23] including a comparison of the teaching content and methods used by Jesus and the rabbis of the second century and later. That rabbinical movement, he asserts, was a continuation of the Pharisee movement of Temple times; he offers evidence to support this claim too.

Another difference from Saldarini and Sanders is Maccoby's contention that Pharisaism was not only the most influential religion of first-century Israel, but indeed the normative Judaism of that period: "The Gospels, together with the similar testimony of Josephus, are our chief source for the prominence of the Pharisees as far more than a sect, but on the contrary the representatives of normative Judaism, the grouping to which ordinary Jews automatically belonged."[24] While this study accepts Maccoby's conclusions enumerated above and offers further evidence from the New Testament that Jesus and many of his disciples were themselves Pharisees, it disagrees with some of his other assertions. For example, to explain the presence in the gospels of contradictory pro-Pharisee and anti-Pharisee passages Maccoby resorts to a complex theory involving multiple stages in the editing of the gospels, the later anti-Pharisee redactors conveniently neglecting to remove or tone down some of the work of their pro-Pharisee predecessors.[25] This study offers a simpler explanation that not only preserves the integrity of the gospel texts, but also explains other paradoxical elements in the evangelists' accounts of the ministry of Jesus.

Maccoby was strongly influenced by Roland Deines' essay *The Pharisees between "Judaisms" and "Common Judaism"*, published in English translation in 2001,[26] which he claims "outstrips all previous work in

---

22. Maccoby, *Jesus*, 141.

23. Maccoby claims that Jesus is mentioned in the Babylonian Talmud and some other rabbinic sources and was regarded by the rabbis for a short time as a "fully fledged member of the rabbinic movement known in his day as the Pharisees," albeit a disgraced member (Maccoby, *Jesus*, 144, 148).

24. Maccoby, *Jesus*, 74.

25. Ibid., 156f.

26. Deines, "Pharisees," 443.

careful analysis of the sources."[27] It is probably from Deines that Maccoby adopted the idea that the Pharisees were not a sect, because they existed for the people as a whole and laid down no exclusive conditions of entry. Deines' work is indeed masterly, providing a feasible explanation of the situation portrayed in the New Testament. He concludes, "Pharisaism can be called *normative*, because whatever was *integrated and thus legitimated* by its recognized representatives . . . over time became the possession of all of Israel. In the consciousness of the majority of the people, the Pharisees were the religious group that determined the boundaries of what was still and what was no longer Jewish."[28]

An earlier work that inspired Maccoby—he describes it as "essential reading"[29]—is Ellis Rivkin's *A Hidden Revolution*, published in 1978. Unlike Saldarini, Rivkin confines his attention to the Pharisees and teachers of the law, but like Saldarini he struggles with the sources: "Yet the sources . . . are few in number, contradictory, highly subjective, and scanty in details. No source defines the name, pinpoints the origin, tells the story, describes the institutions, or pens the lives of the leading Pharisees."[30] Nevertheless he devotes a chapter to each of the three main sources: Josephus, the New Testament, and the Tannaitic (rabbinic) literature. Despite the alleged inadequacy of these sources, he concludes that, "The hitherto discordant sources are now seen to be in agreement. Josephus, Paul, the gospels, and the Tannaitic Literature are in accord that the Pharisees were the scholar class of the twofold Law—nothing more, nothing less."[31] It is Rivkin's contention that the twofold (written and oral) law was the feature that distinguished the Pharisees from other movements, such as the Sadducees, who accepted only the Pentateuch, understood literally, as authoritative. The Pharisees' oral law attempted to identify the principles underlying the written law and apply them in situations that the written law did not cover explicitly.

Rivkin proceeds to deliver two chapters of historical reconstruction. One of these, which dramatically explores the obscure origins of the Pharisee movement, concludes, "The Pharisaic Revolution has remained a hidden revolution, but it was a revolution nonetheless."[32] But of particular

27. Maccoby, *Jesus*, 76.
28. Deines, "Pharisees," 503.
29. Maccoby, *Jesus*, 80.
30. Rivkin, *Revolution*, 27.
31. Ibid., 179.
32. Ibid., 215.

interest to both New Testament interpretation and the understanding of Christian origins is the third part of the work in which Rivkin claims that the Pharisees were the first to *internalize* the written and oral law. Further extending the principles that gave rise to the oral law, they taught that what God demands of humanity is not just outward observance of the commandments, but conformity in the individual's inner life as well; the twofold law is binding upon a person wherever in the world he or she may be, quite independently of the laws of the local city or state. The reward for keeping these internal commands is felicity in the world to come, resurrection being a Pharisee belief. "Internalization of the divine will as the ultimate, the most certain, and the only enduring reality—this was the grand achievement of the Scribes-Pharisees. And it was this achievement that served as the bedrock of the emergent Christianity."[33] Indeed, many of the ethical principles which western civilization inherited from the Christian faith had in fact originated amongst the Pharisees.

Lastly, although Stephen Motyer's *Your Father the Devil?* may not seem relevant to the present study, its subtitle *A New Approach to John and "the Jews"* indicates otherwise. Published in 1997, its primary aim is to reach an understanding of John 8:31–59 (in which Pharisees are not mentioned), but any exploration of John's use of the term "the Jews" (see the start of this chapter) is bound to consider the extent to which the group so designated overlaps with the Pharisees. Moreover, Motyer's investigation of the relationship of the Fourth Gospel to its audience in the world of post-Temple Judaism reveals the polemical nature of the document and polemics explains the sharp language that has sometimes led to accusations that this gospel is anti-semitic.

THE APPROACH TAKEN IN THIS STUDY

In this study we attempt to build a coherent picture of the Pharisees and, in particular, Jesus' relationship with them. Building our picture is, however, like solving a jigsaw puzzle. The pieces of the puzzle are, of course, the passages in the New Testament and other ancient sources that refer to the Pharisees. But at the outset we do not know how the pieces fit together; moreover, we may expect to find that some pieces are missing, leaving us guessing at the content of parts of the picture. We shall return to this analogy later.

33. Ibid., 302f.

Hypocrites or Heroes?

First we examine every verse in the New Testament that contains the word *Pharisaios* or one of its synonyms mentioned earlier. A separate chapter explores the occurrences of *hoi Ioudaioi* in John's Gospel, many of which are shown to refer to the Pharisees. A chapter briefly overviews the references to the Pharisees in Josephus and the Rabbinic literature, assessing the extent to which these confirm or conflict with the picture given by the New Testament.

There follow three chapters of historical reconstruction drawing upon the sources considered earlier. The first probes the obscure origin of the Pharisee movement. The second examines the main features of the movement at the time of Jesus. The third analyses the ministry of Jesus with special reference to his dealings with the Pharisees and seeks to explain some of the apparent contradictions in the New Testament's portrayal of the movement and of Jesus himself.

A final overview chapter seeks to draw conclusions from the foregoing and, above all, to answer the question posed in the study's title: hypocrites or heroes? Were the Pharisees self-righteous murderers as popular Christian piety sometimes portrays them? Or were they unsung heroes whose beneficial influence upon Jesus and the Christian community and—through them—upon western civilization remains largely unrecognized?

2

The Pharisees in the New Testament

MUCH OF WHAT IS known today about the Pharisees is derived from what the New Testament, which contains most of the pieces of the jigsaw puzzle, says about them. It is important to remember, however, that the writers of the New Testament had a specific agenda. They were not historians documenting the Pharisee movement; their principal purpose was to promote Jesus, his teaching, and the exploits of his earliest followers. They did not wish to expend any more precious time and papyrus describing the Pharisees than was strictly necessary to achieve their purpose.

Moreover, they may not have been as concerned about the accuracy of their portrayal of the Pharisees as they were about that of Jesus; they considered themselves answerable to Jesus! It is even possible that they blackened the Pharisees somewhat in order to show Jesus and his teachings in a better light. To some extent the gospels are polemical documents and, in the Graeco-Roman world, polemics allowed authors a license that would be unacceptable in the western world today. Perhaps this is what Wright has in mind when he concludes that 'The plethora of references in the gospels . . . is hard to use . . . because of the multiple questions that have been raised about their historical value, especially in the light of the writers' obvious agendas.'[1] This study contends, nevertheless, that useful information about the Pharisees can be gleaned from the New Testament, including

---

1. Wright, *Paul*, 81.

the gospels, but the texts must be subjected to critical scrutiny and cannot always be accepted at face value.

Furthermore, it is an established hermeneutical principle that readers' presuppositions influence their understanding of a text.[2] Most people who read the New Testament do so in order to learn more about Jesus, his teaching or the earliest Christian communities. Although they may be unaware of it, these aims, often motivated by Christian beliefs and molded by Christian experience, inevitably color their reading of the text. Reading the New Testament in order to learn about the Pharisees turns a different spotlight on the text, sometimes causing details that previously seemed insignificant to stand out in sharp relief. No reader can ever be completely free from bias, but when studying the New Testament's references to the Pharisees, it is important that so far as possible readers set aside their presuppositions—especially any previous prejudice about the Pharisees—and allow the text to speak for itself.

The 98 occurrences of *Pharisaios* in the New Testament are made up of 29 in Matthew, 12 in Mark, 27 in Luke, 20 in John, 9 in Acts, and 1 in Philippians. To these, however, must be added the occurrences of three other words which are often used synonymously or nearly so with *Pharisaios*: *grammateus* and *nomodidaskalos*, both usually rendered "scribe" or "teacher of the law" in EVV, and *nomikos*, "lawyer." *Grammateus* occurs 63 times in total, made up of 22 in Matthew, 21 in Mark, 14 in Luke, 1 in John,[3] 4 in Acts, and 1 in 1 Corinthians. *Nomikos* occurs 9 times: once in Matthew, 6 times in Luke, and twice in Titus. *Nomodidaskalos* occurs only 3 times in the New Testament: once each in Luke, Acts, and 1 Timothy.

All three of these words sometimes appear in conjunction with *Pharisaios*. Although sometimes they have no connection with the Pharisees, for the sake of completeness all occurrences of each are included in the following analysis.

Ultimately *grammateus* denotes someone who could read and write; it appears in conjunction with *Pharisaios* 19 times in the New Testament.[4]

---

2. As Graham Stanton has observed, "Presuppositions are involved in every aspect of the relationship of the interpreter to his text . . . different conclusions . . . arise from the prejudice of the individual interpreter" (Stanton, "Presuppositions," 61f).

3. This solitary instance (John 8:3) occurs in the passage concerning the woman caught in the act of adultery, which many scholars consider out of place in John's Gospel and belonging properly in the synoptics.

4. Matt 5:20; 15:1; 23:2, 13, 15, 23, 25, 27, 29; Mark 2:16, 7:1, 5; Luke 5:21, 30; 6:7; 11:44, 53; 15:2; John 8:3.

When used in conjunction with it, both nouns are always plural, *grammateis* always preceding *Pharisaioi* except in Mark 7 and Luke 15; it is as though "teachers of the law and Pharisees" was a phrase in regular usage; the two go together naturally. To complicate matters, however, of the other 44 occurrences of *grammateus* no fewer than 24 are in conjunction with the chief priests who were Sadducees.[5] These particular *grammateis* were probably administrative assistants or legal advisors to the chief priests; despite the number of references to them, they were probably relatively few in number, as the chief priests themselves were a small group. *Nomikos* is associated with *Pharisaios* in two of its nine New Testament occurrences: Luke 7:30 and 14:3. *Nomodidaskalos* is associated with *Pharisaios* in two of its three New Testament appearances: Luke 5:17 and Acts 5:34.

This chapter examines every occurrence of each of these keywords, working through the New Testament books in canonical order, except that the synoptic gospels are considered together, to facilitate the comparison of parallel texts. Occurrences in John which appear to parallel synoptic passages are considered with those synoptic parallels, others separately. The NIV text of each passage is given; following renderings of *grammateus*, *nomikos*, and *nomodidaskalos* the transliterated keyword is shown in square brackets to indicate which keyword occurred. The following chapter considers the occurrences of *hoi Ioudaioi* in John's Gospel; evidence will be given that John often uses this term as a synonym for *hoi Pharisaioi*.

THE SYNOPTIC GOSPELS
Herod enquires concerning the Messiah's birth

> When he had called together all the people's chief priests and teachers of the law [*grammateis*], he asked them where the Christ was to be born. (Matt 2:4)

Although it is possible that these *grammateis* were administrative staff in the service of Herod himself or of the chief priests, it is inherently more likely that they were indeed "teachers of the law," most of whom belonged to the Pharisee party. It is unlikely that Herod convened a meeting of the Sanhedrin, even though this might be inferred from the reference to the "chief priests and teachers of the law." The elders of the people who formed

---

5. Matt 2:4; 16:21; 20:18; 21:15; 26:3, 57; 27:41; Mark 8:31; 10:33; 11:18, 27; 14:1, 43, 53; 15:1, 31; Luke 9:22; 19:47; 20:1, 19; 22:2, 66; 23:10; Acts 4:5.

Hypocrites or Heroes?

the third of the three constituent bodies of the Sanhedrin are not mentioned and, as R. T. France observes, "relations between Herod and the Sanhedrin were not cordial, and it may be that Matthew has exaggerated the formal nature of an ad hoc consultation with selected experts."[6] This certainly seems plausible. The Pharisees and teachers of the law had a reputation as experts in the Hebrew scriptures and it was this expertise which Herod (whose own Jewish orthodoxy was suspect) wished to tap in order to learn the expected birthplace of the Messiah. Matthew records that in reply they quoted the prophecy of Micah (Mic 5:2) referring to Bethlehem in Judea.

Pharisees and Sadducees visit John the Baptist

> But when he saw many of the Pharisees and Sadducees coming to where he was baptizing, he said to them: "You brood of vipers! Who warned you to flee from the coming wrath?" (Matt 3:7)
> Now this was John's testimony when the Jews of Jerusalem sent priests and Levites to ask him who he was . . . Now some Pharisees who had been sent . . . (John 1:19, 24)

Both Matthew and John report a deputation of officials sent from Jerusalem to investigate the activities of the Baptist. If, as is almost certain, John 1:19 and 24 refer to the same deputation as Matthew and if by priests John means the chief priests who were Sadducees, both evangelists attest that it included Sadducees as well as Pharisees. The Sadducees were a small sect consisting of the chief priests and their families and a few other prominent landowners. Their influence was political rather than religious and they were strongly pro-Rome. Rarely did the Pharisees and Sadducees act in concert, as each group regarded the other as heretical. The significance is that here is evidence that the deputation was sent at the instigation of the Sanhedrin—as the Sanhedrin included members of both groups it is understandable that representatives of both were included in this deputation. Moreover John refers to the senders as "the Jews of Jerusalem," which is a typically Johannine appellation for the Sanhedrin.

Since John's ministry at that time was making a major impact, it was natural that the leaders of Judaism would wish to discover his message, actions, and intentions. Deines offers an explanation of the Pharisees' interest in John: "It [Pharisaism] includes everything that belongs to the Torah

---

6. France, *Matthew*, 71.

tradition, and everything that is new can be integrated by the representatives of this movement, as long as it does not conflict with the principle of the normativity of Torah tradition as understood by the Pharisees."[7] The Pharisees' main interest, then, would have been to discover to what extent John's ministry conformed to Torah.

The meaning of *epi to baptisma* in Matt 3:7 is debated, as evidenced by the contrast between the RSV's "for baptism" and the NIV's "to where he was baptizing." Both are valid translations, but, in the light of Matt 21:25–27 where another deputation from the Sanhedrin declines to say whether or not John had divine authority, it seems unlikely that this first deputation was seeking baptism; its mission was purely investigative. It is true that John's words in Matt 3:7 suggest that he thought that these people had come for baptism, but at that stage he may not have ascertained the purpose of their visit. According to Matt 3:5 large numbers from Jerusalem were coming to him for baptism and he may have assumed that this was the intention of this group too.

Higher righteousness

> For I tell you that unless your righteousness surpasses that of the Pharisees and the teachers of the law [*grammateōn*], you will certainly not enter the kingdom of heaven. (Matt 5:20)

This is the first of the 19 conjunctions of *grammateis* and *Pharisaioi* in the New Testament. The translators of the NIV have transposed the two groups. This saying forms part of the Sermon on the Mount which Matthew presents as addressed by Jesus to his disciples.

There are two possible interpretations. The first understands the saying literally so that it could be paraphrased: "The teachers of the law and the Pharisees are excellent examples of righteousness, but you must do even better than they." The alternative understands it ironically so that it could be paraphrased: "The teachers of the law and Pharisees may set themselves up as examples of righteousness, but they are a sham; you, on the other hand, must exhibit the genuine article." The weight of evidence favors the first, literal interpretation. For example, other passages such as Matt 23:2–7 demonstrate that at that time the teachers of the law and Pharisees were indeed popularly regarded as models of righteousness; Josephus offers similar

---

7. Deines, "Pharisees," 503.

testimony.[8] Moreover, there is evidence, which will be considered later (see *The earlier pro-Pharisee phase of Jesus' ministry*, p. 173), that in this early part of his ministry Jesus aligned himself with the teachers of the law and Pharisees; so that he may indeed have genuinely admired them. On this basis, then, the injunction is almost a counsel of perfection, his disciples being required to outperform the acknowledged champions in righteousness. There are other similar counsels of perfection in this sermon, such as Matt 5:48. Support for the alternative, ironical interpretation is the fact that Jesus castigates the teachers of the law and Pharisees as play-actors who pretend their piety in such passages as Matt 23. But those sayings probably belong to the later period of his ministry when Jesus had become disillusioned with the Pharisees; when Jesus uttered the saying in Matt 5:20, he meant it literally and sincerely. Either interpretation assumes that Jesus' hearers, presumably in Galilee, were familiar with Pharisees and their reputation.

According to Benno Przybylski, many scholars consider this verse to form an introduction to the Antitheses which follow it, contrasting Jesus' interpretation with traditional Pharisaic understanding of Torah.[9] The Antitheses exemplify the ethical standards surpassing those of the Pharisees and teachers of the law which Jesus demands of his disciples. The interpretation of 5:20 is therefore influenced by what follows. It is also influenced by the sayings immediately preceding it, which show Jesus upholding typically Pharisaic support for the law:

> Do not think that I have come to abolish the Law or the Prophets; I have not come to abolish them but to fulfill them. I tell you the truth, until heaven and earth disappear, not the smallest letter, not the least stroke of a pen, will by any means disappear from the Law until everything is accomplished. Anyone who breaks one of the least of these commandments and teaches others to do the same will be called least in the kingdom of heaven, but whoever practises and teaches these commands will be called great in the kingdom of heaven. (Matt 5:17–19)

Maccoby's observation that, "As for Matthew, it is clear that his own opinions were in accordance with Matt 5:21–48, not with Matt 5:17–20, which sticks out from his Gospel like a sore thumb"[10] reveals a misunder-

---

8. "The cities testify to their devotion to their ample goodness which is superior to everything in lifestyle and teaching." (Josephus, *Antiquities*, 18:1)

9. Przybylski, *Righteousness*, 80.

10. Maccoby, *Jesus*, 163.

standing of the two passages. There is no discrepancy between them; far from abrogating the law, the Antitheses (Matt 5:21–48) intensify it; for example, Jesus pronounces God's judgment not only upon the outward acts of murder and adultery, but also upon the innate urges, anger and lust, that give rise to them.

Jesus taught with authority

> because he taught as one who had authority, and not as their teachers of the law [*grammateis*]. (Matt 7:29)
>
> The people were amazed at his teaching, because he taught them as one who had authority, not as the teachers of the law [*grammateis*]. (Mark 1:22)

Matthew places this tradition at the conclusion of the Sermon on the Mount. Maccoby explains the evangelists' claim that Jesus had an authority which the teachers of the law lacked as follows:

> we here glimpse something that was true about the Pharisees: the modest claims they made for themselves. Though they "sat in Moses' seat," they by no means claimed the authority of Moses or any other prophet. When one steps from the atmosphere of the New Testament to that of the rabbinic writings, one is struck by a huge difference. In the Gospels, there is really only one figure, that of Jesus, to whom all others are infinitely subordinate. If anyone disagrees with him, that can only be through malice, not from genuine difference of viewpoint. In the rabbinic writings, however, there is no dominant figure. All the rabbis are equal and constantly disagree with each other, in an amicable way.[11]

Maccoby often compares the gospels with the Rabbinic literature, which is not always helpful as they serve different purposes and came into existence through dissimilar processes—they are not comparable in any significant manner. What Maccoby seems to be saying here is that the difference between Jesus and the Rabbis is that Jesus made absolute claims. Asked what one should do in particular circumstances, the Rabbis who taught observant Jews in the synagogue every Sabbath would have given a reply like the following: "*I* say that *this* is what you should do, but Rabbi A says *that* is what you should do and Rabbi B says something altogether

---

11. Ibid., 54f.

different is what you should do." This kind of reply would have left many ordinary Jews confused, since they were now presented with several conflicting expert opinions from which they were required to choose one. In contrast, Jesus would give a single definitive response: "*This* is what you should do." Thus Jesus behaved as though he alone carried divine authority. The passage demonstrates that even in "Galilee of the Gentiles" Jesus' hearers were familiar with *grammateis*.

A would-be disciple

> Then a teacher of the law [*grammateus*] came to him and said, "Teacher, I will follow you wherever you go." Jesus replied, "Foxes have holes and birds of the air have nests, but the Son of Man has nowhere to lay his head." (Matt 8:19f)

This fragment comes without any indication of time or place; in view of the sparsity of *grammateis* in Galilee, it may be out of place, belonging perhaps in the later phase of Jesus' ministry when he was in Judea.

What is significant here is that a teacher of the law is so attracted by Jesus—presumably by his teaching—that he offers to become a disciple. Jesus' teaching, then, did not deter teachers of the law, most of whom were Pharisees. France significantly points out that "His scribal training leads him to take it for granted that it is for him to follow Jesus, as did the disciples of rabbis, rather than for Jesus to call him as he has done in [Matt] 4:19, 22; c.f. 9:9."[12] Jesus, however, did not reject this man outright on the basis that "It is *I* who choose my disciples," but instead pointed out the lack of security and home comforts which discipleship would entail. Matthew does not say what happened next, but if the enquirer had persisted, claiming that he was willing to endure these hardships in order to follow Jesus, surely he would have recorded as much. That he has not leaves us to infer that the man went away disillusioned, as did another in Matt 19:22. Perhaps Jesus often used the saying about foxes and birds to weed out unsuitable candidates; that this particular enquirer was a *grammateus* may be the reason that this incident was remembered and committed to writing.

---

12. France, *Matthew*, 325f.

Healing of the paralyzed man

> At this, some of the teachers of the law [*grammateōn*] said to themselves, "This fellow is blaspheming!" (Matt 9:3)
>
> Now some teachers of the law [*grammateōn*] were sitting there, thinking to themselves, "Why does this fellow talk like that? He's blaspheming! Who can forgive sins but God alone?" (Mark 2:6f)
>
> One day as he was teaching, Pharisees and teachers of the law [*nomodidaskaloi*], who had come from every village of Galilee and from Judea and Jerusalem, were sitting there. And the power of the Lord was present for him to heal the sick. Some men came carrying a paralytic on a mat and tried to take him into the house to lay him before Jesus. When they could not find a way to do this because of the crowd, they went up on the roof and lowered him on his mat through the tiles into the middle of the crowd, right in front of Jesus. When Jesus saw their faith, he said, "Friend, your sins are forgiven."
>
> The Pharisees and the teachers of the law [*grammateis*] began thinking to themselves, "Who is this fellow who speaks blasphemy? Who can forgive sins but God alone?" (Luke 5:17–21)

It is interesting that Mark and Matthew mention the presence only of teachers of the law (*grammateis*) and only towards the end of the account. Luke, in contrast, mentions Pharisees and teachers of the law (*nomodidaskaloi*) at the start of his account and at the later point corresponding to the mention in Mark and Matthew refers to them again although they have now become *grammateis*. Here then is an example of the gospel writers using these terms interchangeably; that they could do so is evidence that most if not all teachers of the law were Pharisees.

Luke alone mentions that these Pharisees and teachers of the law had traveled some distance, some indeed from Jerusalem. Although John Nolland describes them as "evaluators" who will subject Jesus "to the most searching scrutiny,"[13] he dismisses Luke's claim that they had come from "every village of Galilee and Judea and from Jerusalem" as "hardly to be taken literally."[14] Consequently he fails to recognize the significance of this visitation: it was almost certainly an official deputation from the Sanhedrin

---

13. Nolland, *Luke*, 1:232f. Nolland implies that Luke's interest in the Pharisees is in comparing Pharisaism with Christianity; there are affinities between them, but they are essentially alternatives.

14. Ibid., 1:234.

to investigate Jesus, supported by officials who were more locally based. A similar delegation had visited the Baptist (see *Pharisees and Sadducees visit John the Baptist,* p. 14). Presumably, local community leaders had sent a report about Jesus to the Sanhedrin in Jerusalem where it must have caused some concern. Later the gospels contain other mentions of Pharisees from Jerusalem observing Jesus[15] and other references to Jesus being under surveillance, although not necessarily by officials from Jerusalem (Mark 3:2; Luke 14:1). There are also accounts of tests and trick questions being put to Jesus in the hope that his answer might contain grounds for his arrest (Matt 22:15; Luke 6:7). The officials' principal concern would have been to discover whether or not Jesus' ministry complied with the Torah tradition (see the comments on the visit to John the Baptist). That there are so many such references suggests that Jesus was kept under some form of continuous surveillance from then on—not surprisingly, the evangelists considered this an important aspect of his ministry.

Not only is this Jesus' first recorded encounter with such officialdom,[16] which probably visited despised Galilee only rarely (for further see *Numbers and distribution,* p. 141), but also it is the first occasion on which he encountered opposition from Pharisees and/or teachers of the law. Ostensibly the reason for their opposition was his declaration of the paralyzed man's sins as forgiven; because they regarded such forgiveness as the prerogative of God alone, this amounted to a claim to be God, which they considered blasphemous. The following demonstration of his power to effect physical healing which might have led them to further investigate the nature of Jesus' authority seems to have been conveniently overlooked.

Dining with tax collectors and "sinners"

> While Jesus was having dinner at Matthew's house, many tax collectors and "sinners" came and ate with him and his disciples. When the Pharisees saw this, they asked his disciples, "Why does your teacher eat with tax collectors and 'sinners'?"
> On hearing this, Jesus said, "It is not the healthy who need a doctor, but the sick. But go and learn what this means: 'I desire mercy, not sacrifice.' For I have not come to call the righteous, but sinners." (Matt 9:10–13)

15. Mark 3:22; Matt 15:1f/Mark 7:1–5.
16. With the possible exception of the *grammateus* in Matt 8:19f (see above).

When the teachers of the law who were Pharisees [*hoi grammateis tōn Pharisaiōn*] saw him eating with the "sinners" and tax collectors, they asked his disciples: "Why does he eat with tax collectors and 'sinners'?"

On hearing this, Jesus said to them, "It is not the healthy who need a doctor, but the sick. I have not come to call the righteous, but sinners." (Mark 2:16f)

But the Pharisees and the teachers of the law who belonged to their sect [*kai hoi grammateis autōn*] complained to his disciples, "Why do you eat and drink with tax collectors and 'sinners'?"

Jesus answered them, "It is not the healthy who need a doctor, but the sick. I have not come to call the righteous, but sinners to repentance." (Luke 5:30–32)

Matthew mentions only Pharisees, while Mark and Luke also involve *grammateis*, Mark's *hoi grammateis tōn Pharisaiōn* being rendered by the NIV as "the teachers of the law who were Pharisees," while the NIV interpolates Luke's parallel even further, rendering *kai hoi grammateis autōn* as "and the teachers of the law who belonged to their sect." The implication that there were other *grammateis* who were not Pharisees finds support later in the gospels where *grammateis* appears frequently in conjunction with the chief priests; those *grammateis*, like them, were probably Sadducees; probably they were the priests' administrative assistants or legal advisors.

Although Nolland claims that "The presence of the Pharisees is unexplained,"[17] perhaps the evangelists expected readers to recognize them as the same officials who had made their appearance at the healing of the paralyzed man (see above); the delegation sent by the Sanhedrin to investigate Jesus was dutifully continuing its observation. In all three synoptics this episode follows immediately after that one. Only Luke gives any indication of how much time had passed since that healing and his "After this" (*Kai meta tauta*) could mean "immediately afterwards" or "some time afterwards." That none of the evangelists attempts to insert any material between them may be evidence that this episode followed shortly after the previous.

Jesus had recently called as a disciple the tax collector named as Matthew in Matthew and Levi in Mark and Luke. In first-century Palestinian Jewish society tax collectors were *odium humani generis*. Wright gives the reason for this as follows:

---

17. Nolland, *Luke*, 1:245.

Hypocrites or Heroes?

> It is commonly said that they were hated as collaborators with Rome; this needs nuancing somewhat, since in the Galilee of Jesus' day monies would be collected not for Rome but for Herod. This may not make too much of a difference, since Herod was scarcely a popular monarch: kept in power by Rome as a client king, his Jewish orthodoxy was widely suspect. Even if, as seems to be the case with Zacchaeus in Luke 19:1–10, the real problem was simply that tax- or toll-collectors were widely regarded as dishonest and rapacious, that does not lessen the point that they had a reputation not just as "people of the land" but as sinners, regarded not just by Pharisees but by other "people of the land" as a class apart, almost as the moral equivalent of lepers.[18]

Perhaps, in these circumstances it is not surprising that there is evidence in the gospels that many tax collectors were repenting and seeking to be readmitted to the Jewish community.[19] It was probably for this reason, then, that it was not so much Jesus' *calling* of the tax collector as its sequel that attracted the criticism of the Pharisees. Eager for his friends in the underclass to meet this teacher who so unusually was willing to consort with even their kind, the tax collector held a dinner to which Jesus and his disciples were invited, along with other tax collectors and "sinners." Inevitably the delegation of officials heard about this: Matthew and Mark both use the verb *idontes*, "seeing," a literal reading of which conjures visions of the Pharisees gathered around the tax collector's house staring in through the windows at the festivities proceeding inside. The reality was that large Palestinian houses were generally constructed around a central courtyard and had no windows on to the outside world, so that outsiders could not have seen what was happening inside. Perhaps the Pharisees witnessed Jesus and his disciples together with tax collectors and "sinners" arriving at Matthew/Levi's house at the customary hour for dinner and drew the obvious conclusion. Alternatively they may have heard subsequent reports of the dinner. The verb has a broad range of meaning, including "hear about." Their approach to Jesus' disciples probably took place after the event.

This is a significant episode for four reasons. Firstly, it shows that the Pharisees and teachers of the law would not have entered that house

---

18. Wright, *Jesus*, 266f.

19. For example, Matt 21:32; Luke 3:12f; 7:29. Furthermore Jesus' Parable of the Pharisee and the Tax Collector (Luke 18:10–14), which depends for its impact upon the accuracy of its portrayal of the two contrasting types, depicts the tax collector as a repentant sinner.

themselves. To enter the home of a "sinner," especially a tax collector, was unacceptable behavior for them; respectable people did not consort with the likes of these and certainly did not share meals with them. The Torah, however, did not forbid entering a "sinner's" house and doing so did not render one ritually unclean, as some scholars have mistakenly claimed. The most likely reason for the Pharisees' abhorrence of dining with "sinners" was fear that food consumed in their homes might not conform to Pharisaic food purity laws. So this prohibition was either an oral law or a convention that did not have the status of a law at all.

Secondly, this is the first of several encounters in the synoptics in which Pharisees expect Jesus and his disciples to behave as they themselves would. It might be argued that the Pharisees expected *everyone* to conduct themselves as they did, but surely this would not have extended to tax collectors and sinners themselves who were beyond the pale. The most likely explanation for this expectation is that they regarded Jesus and his disciples as Pharisees themselves; moreover, they may have been afraid that such unconventional behavior from a teacher with an enviable reputation might bring the Pharisee movement into disrepute. For a more detailed discussion of Jesus' status as a Pharisee see *Was Jesus a Pharisee?*, p. 164.

Thirdly, Jesus' reply with its parable of the doctor not needed by the healthy hints at his own understanding of his agenda: the tax collectors and "sinners" needed his attention, while the Pharisees did not—and indeed had shown themselves unwilling to receive it. In the circumstances his implication that the Pharisees are "healthy" and "righteous" is probably ironical.

Fourthly, Jesus pronounces what sounds like a mission statement in the saying, "I have not come to call the righteous, but sinners." That Matthew and Luke have reproduced the Marcan original *verbatim* suggests that the early Christian communities regarded this as a significant pronouncement. Previously Jesus had associated primarily with other pious Jews/Pharisees, but now he had begun a new phase of his ministry which targeted the "sinners" whom the Pharisees shunned. Moreover, the evangelists' treatment of "the righteous" and "sinners" as antonyms ("not . . . the righteous, but sinners") may be the key to the vexed question concerning their understanding of the "sinners." If, as implied here, "the righteous" refers to the Pharisees, then the "sinners" can only be those (especially Jews) who were outside the Pharisee movement, such as the people with whom Jesus was now so controversially socializing. This leaves as the unknown variable

Hypocrites or Heroes?

in the equation the breadth of the Pharisee movement. If, as Deines[20] and Maccoby[21] advocate, Pharisaism was the normative Judaism to which ordinary Jews belonged by default, the "sinners" must have constituted a special category comprising those Jews whose actions or lifestyle disqualified them from the main body of the movement. Although there appears to have been no formal admission procedure to Pharisaism, there is evidence of an official process for excluding or excommunicating those individuals whose conduct was deemed unsatisfactory—see *Those "put out of the synagogue"—the "sinners,"* p. 155—and presumably these folk constitute the "sinners" who now form the primary target of Jesus' ministry.

The question about fasting

> Then John's disciples came and asked him, "How is it that we and the Pharisees fast, but your disciples do not fast?" (Matt 9:14)
>
> Now John's disciples and the Pharisees were fasting. Some people came and asked Jesus, "How is it that John's disciples and the disciples of the Pharisees are fasting, but yours are not?" (Mark 2:18)
>
> They said to him, "John's disciples often fast and pray, and so do the disciples of the Pharisees, but yours go on eating and drinking." (Luke 5:33)

Notwithstanding the minor differences between the three accounts, the synoptists clearly believed that the Pharisees, like the members of John the Baptist's movement, fasted frequently. The minor differences between the accounts of this incident concern mainly the identity of the questioners. Both Matthew and Luke seem dissatisfied with Mark's non-committal "Some people," Matthew attributing the question to "John's disciples," while Luke appends this pericope to the previous, making it a continuation of the conversation with the Pharisees and teachers of the law in the deputation of observers. Luke's interpolation might seem the most probable inasmuch as only those who had been observing Jesus' disciples over a period of time could have detected that they were not fasting—and continuous observation was, of course, the very purpose for which the Sanhedrin had dispatched this deputation (see *Healing of the paralyzed man*, p. 19). If this is correct, the incident provides another instance of confrontation between

---

20. Deines, *Pharisees*, 503.
21. Maccoby, *Jesus*, 74.

Jesus and the officials keeping him under surveillance. But it is also possible that some of John's disciples had attached themselves to Jesus and become aware of his disciples' failure to fast.

There are two separate issues here. One is that there were differences between the Pharisees and Jesus and his disciples—in this instance concerning the frequency of fasting. The Day of Atonement was the only obligatory fast in Judaism; all others were optional. If the fictitious Pharisee in the Parable of the Tax Collector and the Pharisee (Luke 18:10–14) is typical of the genre, some Pharisees fasted voluntarily twice per week. If this was common practice for Pharisees at that time and especially if, as suggested by Jesus in Matt 6:16, some even "disfigured their faces" to make their fasting and therefore their piety more conspicuous, it is not surprising that the failure of Jesus and his disciples to do the same was noticed. The other issue, as in the previously considered episode, is that people were surprised by what they perceived as a discrepancy: the public expected Jesus and his disciples to behave as the Pharisees (and John's followers) did. This might be because Jesus and his disciples were popularly regarded as Pharisees themselves or it might be because such regular fasting was regarded as the hallmark of piety for Jews of all persuasions.

Exorcism using demonic power

> But the Pharisees said, "It is by the prince of demons that he drives out demons." (Matt 9:34)

The Pharisees said this after Jesus had successfully exorcized a man rendered dumb by demon-possession, thrilling the crowds. The Pharisees—presumably members of the deputation of officials sent by the Sanhedrin to observe Jesus—must have been amongst the crowd. Apparently they were less impressed, attributing Jesus' authority over the spirit world to assistance from the demonic realm. The implication is that Jesus was either in league with this "prince of demons" or possessed by him. One might query why a group sent to observe Jesus was apparently now actively seeking to undermine his authority. Presumably they rejected the alternative explanation—that Jesus exorcized using divine authority—because they regarded as Jesus as standing outside Torah tradition, which necessarily made him an enemy of God. Clearly these Pharisees did not regard Jesus as one of their own number—this happened after Jesus' change of agenda (see *"Reading between the lines" in the gospels*, p. 162).

A similar incident is recorded later in Matt 12:24, paralleled in Mark 3:22 (see *Exorcism using Beelzebub*, p. 31). In that episode Jesus responds to the accusation that he uses demonic power by the use of simple logic.

Breaking the Sabbath

> When the Pharisees saw this, they said to him, "Look! Your disciples are doing what is unlawful on the Sabbath." (Matt 12:2)
> The Pharisees said to him, "Look, why are they doing what is unlawful on the Sabbath?" (Mark 2:24)
> Some of the Pharisees asked, "Why are you doing what is unlawful on the Sabbath?" (Luke 6:2)

We are not told why Jesus and his disciples were walking through a cornfield on the Sabbath; the most likely reason is that they were on their way to the synagogue. Because his disciples were hungry, they began plucking and eating the ripe corn heads. Only Matthew records that the Pharisees, who as in the previously described episode, would have formed part of the delegation sent by the Sanhedrin to investigate Jesus, *saw (idontes)* this. In Mark and Luke the Pharisees appear unannounced in the narrative as though it were common knowledge that they were also in the cornfield that Sabbath keeping a watchful eye on Jesus and his disciples. It is most improbable that Pharisees would be found in a cornfield on a Sabbath, especially in Galilee. It is more likely that, as with Matthew/Levi's feast, they approached Jesus later, after some witness—perhaps the farmer or the owner of the cornfield—reported the disciples' supposedly illegal action to them. *idontes* can have the meaning "when they heard about."

It was not illegal to pluck individual heads of corn in someone else's field; only the unauthorized use of a sickle on a crop constituted theft (Deut 23:25). Indeed Torah encouraged farmers to leave some grain unharvested so that the needy might avail themselves of it (Deut 24:19). The Pharisees' objection was that even the plucking of individual corn heads constituted work and it had taken place on the Sabbath when all work was illegal unless essential to save endangered life. The accusation was leveled at Jesus himself rather than the disciples because a teacher or rabbi was considered to be morally responsible for the actions of his students or disciples.

A literal understanding of this episode presents the Pharisees as zealous defenders of the Sabbath laws who clearly expected Jesus' disciples to observe them as rigorously as they themselves did. This interpretation has been questioned on the grounds that the Pharisees worked to *relax* the Sabbath laws. It is likely that the delegation observing Jesus included Sadducees as well as Pharisees; Maccoby's theory that the argument about Sabbath breaking was between Jesus and those Sadducees rather than Pharisees is discussed later under *Sabbath breaking*.

The plot against Jesus

> But the Pharisees went out and plotted how they might kill Jesus. (Matt 12:14)
>
> Then the Pharisees went out and began to plot with the Herodians how they might kill Jesus. (Mark 3:6)
>
> The Pharisees and the teachers of the law [*grammateis*] were looking for a reason to accuse Jesus, so they watched him closely to see if he would heal on the Sabbath. (Luke 6:7)

The context is Jesus' healing in a synagogue on the Sabbath of a man with a shriveled hand. All three synoptics mention early in the pericope that "Some of them were looking for a reason to accuse Jesus, so they watched him closely to see if he would heal him on the Sabbath" (Mark 3:2, paralleled in Matt 12:10 and Luke 6:7). Luke specifies that the "they" who were a seeking grounds for Jesus' accusation are Pharisees and teachers of the law, presumably the same deputation from the Sanhedrin, which probably also included Sadducees, that had been keeping Jesus under observation since the healing of the paralyzed man (see *Healing of the paralyzed man,* p. 19).

It is significant that in these verses the plot is not to kill Jesus (so the NIV of Matt 12:14 and Mark 3:6), but to find grounds to arrest him, which is inherently more likely. The presence in the synagogue of a man who had a shriveled hand is itself suspicious, because a person suffering such a condition would not normally be welcome there; the situation had been contrived by the plotters to test Jesus. Moreover, if the healing took place, a whole congregation of observant Jews would be available as witnesses in any subsequent court hearing. Only Mark mentions that the Pharisees subsequently allied themselves with the Herodians, a political group that supported the pro-Rome Herod dynasty and whose interests were in general diametrically opposed to their own. Maccoby argues that the plotters were Sadducees, not Pharisees, Sadducees being more likely than Pharisees to collaborate with Herodians.[22]

The healing itself is also unusual in that Jesus departs from his normal practice: he elicits no statement of faith from the sufferer and gives no command to the condition to leave the victim; he merely asks the sufferer to stretch out the affected hand which then is discovered to be healthy. The most likely reason for Jesus' "low key" approach on this occasion is to deter those present in the synagogue from appearing as witnesses in any future trial for breach of the Sabbath. Could any of them honestly affirm that they had seen Jesus perform the healing? The affected hand might have undergone a spontaneous recovery, albeit an unusually rapid one.

This passage portrays the Pharisees in a poor light. Firstly, they deliberately set a trap in order to tempt Jesus to perform what they allegedly regard as an illegal act so that they may have grounds on which to bring charges against him. Secondly, they plot his downfall; although they might justify this on the grounds that Jesus was a persistent lawbreaker and perhaps therefore a danger to the public. For a more detailed discussion of this episode, including whether the plot was to kill him (so the NIV of Matt 12:14 and Mark 3:6) or to get rid of him by destroying his reputation, see *The plots against Jesus,* p. 148. Thirdly, according to Mark, they consort in this scheme with their sworn enemies the Herodians who also had an interest in getting rid of him.

The Pharisees reject God's way

> (All the people, even the tax collectors, when they heard Jesus' words, acknowledged that God's way was right, because they had been baptized by John. But the Pharisees and experts in the law [*nomikoi*] rejected God's purpose for themselves, because they had not been baptized by John.) (Luke 7:29f)

In this parenthetical comment Luke links the contrasting responses of the two groups of people to Jesus' ministry with their reception of John the Baptist's ministry, as though the latter determines the former. It is inherently more likely that the responses of both groups to first John and then Jesus were conditioned by their circumstances, most notably their openness to God and willingness to obey the call to repentance that was central

---

22. Ibid., 125.

to both ministries. It was easier for a tax collector, ostracized by society, to believe himself in need of repentance and restoration than for a Pharisee or teacher of the law, revered as a model Jew and pillar of society, to believe that he needed to repent. There is a partial parallel in Matt 21:32 where Jesus contrasts the response to John of the tax collectors and prostitutes with that of the delegation from the Sanhedrin.

Surely Luke is using hyperbole here: not everyone who heard Jesus responded positively to him and not all Pharisees rejected him, but this was probably the general trend.

Jesus dines in a Pharisee's home

> Now one of the Pharisees invited Jesus to have dinner with him, so he went to the Pharisee's house and reclined at the table. When a woman who had lived a sinful life in that town learned that Jesus was eating at the Pharisee's house, she brought an alabaster jar of perfume, and as she stood behind him at his feet weeping, she began to wet his feet with her tears. Then she wiped them with her hair, kissed them and poured perfume on them. When the Pharisee who had invited him saw this, he said to himself, "If this man were a prophet, he would know who is touching him and what kind of woman she is—that she is a sinner."
>
> Jesus answered him, "Simon, I have something to tell you."
>
> "Tell me, teacher," he said.
>
> "Two men owed money to a certain money-lender. One owed him five hundred denarii, and the other fifty. Neither of them had the money to pay him back, so he cancelled the debts of both. Now which of them will love him more?"
>
> Simon replied, "I suppose the one who had the bigger debt cancelled."
>
> "You have judged correctly," Jesus said. Then he turned towards the woman and said to Simon, "Do you see this woman? I came into your house. You did not give me any water for my feet, but she wet my feet with her tears and wiped them with her hair. You did not give me a kiss, but this woman, from the time I entered, has not stopped kissing my feet. You did not put oil on my head, but she has poured perfume on my feet. Therefore, I tell you, her many sins have been forgiven—for she loved much. But he who has been forgiven little loves little." Then Jesus said to her, "Your sins are forgiven."

> The other guests began to say among themselves, "Who is this who even forgives sins?"
>
> Jesus said to the woman, "Your faith has saved you; go in peace." (Luke 7:36–50)

This is the first of three occasions unique to Luke on which Jesus accepts dinner invitations from Pharisees, the others being Luke 11:37–54 and 14:1–6. The other three gospels also contain accounts of Jesus being anointed by a woman,[23] but only Luke sets the anointing early in his ministry (rather than during its last week) and locates it in the home of a Pharisee; Mark and Matthew, however, agree that the host's name was Simon. Perhaps two such anointings took place and the details have become confused.

The context suggests that this incident took place in Galilee. So did Simon the Pharisee live in Galilee? Although not impossible, this is unlikely—see *Numbers and distribution,* p. 141. Simon and the "other guests" of verse 49 were probably members of the deputation keeping surveillance on Jesus (Luke 5:17). Although the text refers to "the Pharisee's house" (verse 36), this may be a shorthand way of indicating the house where Simon was lodging rather than the one he owned.

The woman is described as a "sinner" (*hamartōlos*) in verses 37 and 38. If this term has the technical meaning of a person excluded from the Jewish/Pharisee community as the penalty for a serious offense (see *Those "put out of the synagogue"—the "sinners,"* p. 155), she was probably a prostitute and as such Pharisees would have regarded her as beyond hope of restoration. Her presence in the Pharisee's house—even if he did not own it—is distinctly suspicious: such a person would not normally be admitted into any self-respecting Pharisee's home. Although the public were sometimes invited to such dinners as observers, not participants, a "sinner" would not have been welcome. The most likely explanation is that this dinner (like the other two recorded by Luke) formed part of the official surveillance of Jesus and the woman's presence had been deliberately arranged in order to test Jesus' reaction to her.[24] Evidence to support this is the presence of the "other guests" mentioned in verse 49; these other members of the

---

23. Mark 14:3–9; Matt 26:6–13; John 12:1–8.

24. Confronting Jesus with "challenging" persons seems to have been a favorite technique of the Pharisees investigating Jesus: compare the presence of the man suffering from dropsy in another Pharisee's house in Luke 14:1f, when Jesus was definitely "being carefully watched," the man with the shriveled hand in the synagogue (Luke 6:6f), and the woman caught in the act of adultery (John 8:2–11).

The Pharisees in the New Testament

deputation would be available as corroborating witnesses if Jesus uttered any heresy or committed any illegal action. Although on this occasion they do not charge Jesus with any offense, they are clearly concerned by his claim to forgive sins. In this respect the incident resembles the healing of the paralyzed man.

Although the surveillance and Jesus' kindly disposition towards the sinful woman place this incident in the later (pro-sinner) phase of Jesus' ministry (see *"Reading between the lines" in the gospels,* p. 162), the friendly—if somewhat formal—interactions between Jesus and Simon suggest a setting early in that second phase, before Jesus was expelled from the Jewish/Pharisee community (see *Jesus' expulsion from Pharisaism,* p. 181). Simon would surely not have invited Jesus into his home after that.

That Simon used the woman to test Jesus need not in any way detract from the sincerity of her repentance. She might have been chosen for this test precisely because she had expressed her admiration for Jesus and her desire to anoint him. According to Matt 21:32 large numbers of tax collectors and prostitutes had responded to John the Baptist's ministry. Jesus' acceptance of her sacrificial action as evidence of sincere repentance led him to pronounce her sins forgiven (verse 48) and herself as saved (verse 50). This indicates that he valued her, in stark contrast with the attitude of the Pharisees who dismissed such "sinners" as under God's curse.

Exorcism using Beelzebub

> But when the Pharisees heard this, they said, "It is only by Beelzebub, the prince of demons, that this fellow drives out demons." (Matt 12:24)
>
> And the teachers of the law [*grammateis*] who came down from Jerusalem said, "He is possessed by Beelzebub! By the prince of demons he is driving out demons." (Mark 3:22)

That Matthew has changed Mark's *grammateis* to "Pharisees" suggests that he considered the terms synonymous. Mark's mention that these teachers of the law "came down from Jerusalem" confirms that this is yet another encounter with the deputation sent by the Sanhedrin to investigate Jesus, but after describing several previous such exchanges why does Mark leave it until now to inform his readers that it had come from Jerusalem? It is of course possible that it was not until Mark had reached this point in writing his gospel that he realized that he had not previously mentioned the deputation's origin (unlike Luke who mentioned it at its first appearance in Luke 5:17) and he wished to ensure that his readers did not assume that these *grammateis* were locally based officials. Another possibility is that a change of surveillance team had just taken place and Mark is recording his observation that these *grammateis* were strangers, newly arrived from Jerusalem. There is evidence of another such changeover in Matt 15:1f/Mark 7:1–5 when both evangelists refer to Pharisees and teachers who had come from Jerusalem.

There is a parallel to this incident in Luke 11:14f, but there the same accusation is attributed to unidentified onlookers who proceed to ask Jesus for a sign from heaven. Perhaps Luke had Pharisees in mind but chose not to name them. There is another parallel in Matt 9:34 (see above); Matthew's two similar accounts may be doublets.

The incident shows that the Pharisees believed in a hierarchy of evil spirits. Jesus' reply in Mark 3:23–27/Matt 12:25–29 indicates that he too believed in it, but also demonstrates the logical absurdity of this suggestion; Beelzebub is hardly likely to undermine his own kingdom. Presumably the Pharisees attributed Jesus' exorcisms to collaboration with Beelzebub,[25] the prince of demons, because—in view of his alleged breaches of the Sabbath and of the oral law—they considered Jesus an enemy of God. For this reason his supernatural powers could not be divine in origin.

The request for a miraculous sign

> Then some of the Pharisees and teachers of the law [*grammateōn*] said to him, "Teacher, we want to see a miraculous sign from you." (Matt 12:38)

There is a parallel in Luke 11:16, but there the persons demanding the sign are not identified. The incident follows a diatribe from Jesus in response to the accusation that he was in league with Beelzebub (see above on Matt 12:24). It demonstrates that Pharisees believed in miracles and implies that the performance on demand of "a miraculous sign" would

---

25. Beelzebub is a somewhat corrupted form of the Hebrew for "Lord of the dwelling," which occurs in 2 Kgs 1:2, where it is the name of the pagan god of Ekron. Nowhere in Jewish literature is this name identified with Satan and the evangelist's placing of "chief of demons" in apposition to Beelzebub makes it most likely that in popular Jewish piety this was the name or nickname of a supposed arch-demon, one of the captains in Satan's army of demons.

have been accepted as proof that the performer had special authority and was therefore, perhaps, a prophet or even the Messiah. On the other hand, failure to perform one could be taken as evidence of the absence of such powers and therefore that the claimant was a charlatan.

Presumably these Pharisees were the same as the *grammateis* who according to Mark 3:22 had come from Jerusalem. That this was the investigative deputation sent by the Sanhedrin makes the request for a miraculous sign more understandable; they needed to give their sender a definitive answer to the question of who and what Jesus was. See also on Matt 16:1/ Mark 8:1 below. The two Matthean accounts may be doublets.

Teachers of the law instructed about the kingdom

> He said to them, "Therefore every teacher of the law [*grammateus*] who has been instructed about the kingdom of heaven is like the owner of a house who brings out of his storeroom new treasures as well as old." (Matt 13:52)

This little parable, peculiar to Matthew, forms the conclusion to a teaching session (Matt 13:10–51) which consisted of a series of parables. Its setting at the close of the session is the key to its meaning. Those being taught are Jesus' disciples (13:10). Although they had found some parables difficult (13:36), now they claim to understand them all (13:51). Since *mathēteuein* means to "make disciples," the teachers of the law who had been instructed (*mathēteutheis*) about the kingdom are Jesus' disciples themselves. They are to be the new *grammateis*, who understand the kingdom—by which Jesus often means God's governance of the world—in implicit contrast with the Pharisaic *grammateis* who (mostly) do not. There is thus a similarity in meaning with Matthew's three polemical parables (Matt 21:28–22:10), all of which predict the replacement of Israel's present incompetent leadership by a God-serving people whom they despise.

The *homoios estin*, "is like," found in many parable introductions, marks the beginning of the parable proper. A householder would be expected to have a store from which he could produce any item that the residents and guests in the house might reasonably need. By analogy a teacher needs a store of material to aid his or her teaching. Jesus probably intended that on their preaching missions the disciples should re-use the parables he had just told them. So the *new treasures as well as old* probably refers to parables. The *old* might be those that they had heard from Jesus and the *new* those that they had composed themselves. Alternatively, the *old* might be traditional parables[26] and the *new* those created by themselves or Jesus.

Breaking the tradition of the elders

> Then some Pharisees and teachers of the law [*grammateis*] came to Jesus from Jerusalem and asked, "Why do your disciples break the tradition of the elders? They don't wash their hands before they eat!"
>
> Jesus replied, "And why do you break the command of God for the sake of your tradition? For God said, 'Honor your father and mother' and 'Anyone who curses his father or mother must be put to death.' But you say that if a man says to his father or mother, 'Whatever help you might otherwise have received from me is a gift devoted to God,' he is not to 'honor his father' with it. Thus you nullify the word of God for the sake of your tradition. (Matt 15:1–6)
>
> The Pharisees and some of the teachers of the law [*grammateōn*] who had come from Jerusalem gathered round Jesus and saw some of his disciples eating food with hands that were "unclean," that is, unwashed. (The Pharisees and all the Jews do not eat unless they give their hands a ceremonial washing, holding to the tradition of the elders. When they come from the marketplace they do not eat unless they wash. And they observe many other traditions, such as the washing of cups, pitchers and kettles.) So the Pharisees and teachers of the law [*grammateis*] asked Jesus, "Why don't your disciples live according to the tradition of the elders instead of eating their food with 'unclean' hands?"
>
> He replied, "Isaiah was right when he prophesied about you hypocrites; as it is written: 'These people honor me with their lips, but their hearts are far from me. They worship me in vain; their teachings are but rules taught by men.' You have let go of the commands of God and are holding on to the traditions of men."
>
> And he said to them: "You have a fine way of setting aside the commands of God in order to observe your own traditions! For Moses said, 'Honor your father and your mother,' and, 'Anyone

---

26. Maccoby claims that parables were used by the Rabbis before the time of Jesus—they had been used by Hillel and Rabbi Johanan was an expert on them (Maccoby, *Jesus*, 93). Archetypal material for oral transmission, they were probably in widespread circulation when Jesus instructed his disciples.

who curses his father or mother must be put to death.' But you say that if a man says to his father or mother: 'Whatever help you might otherwise have received from me is Corban' (that is, a gift devoted to God), then you no longer let him do anything for his father or mother. Thus you nullify the word of God by your tradition that you have handed down. And you do many things like that." (Mark 7:1–13)

As in Luke 5:17—see on *Healing of the paralyzed man*, p. 19—and Mark 3:22—see on *Exorcism using Beelzebub*, p. 31—the evangelists mention that the Pharisees and *grammateis* had come from Jerusalem and so are either *the* or *an* official surveillance team; this detail is now mentioned by Matthew as well as Mark and so must have been considered significant. That they *gathered around* Jesus suggests a special interest in him. It is possible that they were a fresh team sent by the Sanhedrin to relieve the previous one that had been observing Jesus.

In this encounter their question, "Why don't your disciples live according to the tradition [*paradosin*] of the elders?" was prompted by the observation that Jesus' disciples ate without first cleansing their hands. Although the question concerned his disciples, it was addressed to Jesus because, as their teacher, he was considered responsible for their actions, as in Matt 12:2.

In fact there is no requirement in the Torah that hands be washed before eating and the deputation does not accuse Jesus or his disciples of infringing Torah. Nor had any statute of the Pharisees' oral law been broken; although the Pharisees did introduce such an oral law, this was not enacted until 30 years after Jesus' death and so no law of any kind had been broken.[27] Rather, what they had infringed was *the tradition of the elders*, an informal code of good practice. So, although these Pharisees asked why the disciples broke with convention—and there may be implicit criticism in the question—there were no grounds for any formal charge. The incident shows that the Pharisees were so eager to find fault in Jesus and his disciples that even small departures from what was considered normal behavior were noted.

Jesus does not respond at once to the question; instead, for the first time, he levels a counter-accusation at the Pharisees, charging them with allowing their own traditions to subvert Torah. The specific example that he cites concerns care for parents. Without a formal social security system,

---

27. Maccoby, *Jesus*, 28.

Jewish society regarded all Jews as having a responsibility to care for their parents, especially when through age or infirmity they could no longer support themselves. When, as often in Jewish families, there were many siblings, this burden was widely spread and therefore not necessarily onerous. There was no specific commandment concerning this, but Jesus probably regarded it as implicit in the Fifth Commandment of the Decalogue (Exod 20:12, Deut 5:16).

The Pharisees, however, had devised a legal loophole that freed people from the burden of providing for parents: by declaring that *Whatever help you might otherwise have received from me is Corban (that is, a gift devoted to God)*, the declarant was released from his obligation to his parents. The scheme sounds pious—it would be hard to gainsay the argument that God is more important than the elderly. However, even if the offering were given to God's service, the scheme would still have been indefensible, because it threatened the destitution of the vulnerable and undeserving for whom the Torah made special provision. In practice, however, the "offering" was often not made at all; the primary purpose of this "tradition" was to provide an escape clause for those who preferred not to accept the financial liability of caring for their elderly dependents. It is the existence of this legal loophole that Jesus condemns as an example of a human tradition overruling God's law.

This incident shows the Pharisees in a particularly bad light. Not only were they apparently going to great lengths to make trouble for Jesus, but also, according to Jesus, they had devised cunning legal loopholes to free themselves from family obligations that were not unreasonable.

The Pharisees take offense

> Then the disciples came to him and asked, "Do you know that the Pharisees were offended when they heard this?" (Matt 15:12)
> One of the experts in the law [*nomikōn*] answered him, "Teacher, when you say these things, you insult us also." (Luke 11:45)

These similar Matthean and Lucan passages occur in different contexts and may be unrelated. The Lucan version occurs during the long speech in which Jesus repeatedly denounces the Pharisees and teachers of the law as hypocrites; it is perfectly understandable that this should elicit the response in the Lucan version. But in the Matthean version it is impossible to ascertain precisely what upset the Pharisees. It could be Jesus' denouncement of their tradition that overruled the commandment to honor one's parents (see above). But since then Jesus had returned to the matter of hand-washing and stated that, "What goes into a man's mouth does not make him 'unclean', but what comes out of his mouth, that is what makes him 'unclean.'" (Matt 15:11). According to Maccoby, Jesus "was following the opinion of a highly respected section of the Pharisee movement, the *Chasidim*, who rejected the majority Pharisee regulations on hygienic matters as showing lack of faith in the protective power of God."[28] To this Jesus added a moral lesson: although one cannot be made unclean by what goes *into* one's mouth, one can be made unclean by what comes *out* of it, meaning presumably lies, malicious gossip, the plotting of evil and blasphemy. Perhaps what Jesus had in mind was the Pharisees' plot against him.

Pharisees (and Sadducees) ask for a sign

> The Pharisees and Sadducees came to Jesus and tested him by asking him to show them a sign from heaven. (Matt 16:1)
> The Pharisees came and began to question Jesus. To test him, they asked him for a sign from heaven. (Mark 8:11)

See on the similar incident in Matt 12:38 above. Only Matthew records the presence of Sadducees; rarely do Pharisees and Sadducees act in concert as each group regarded the other as heretical; the unexpectedness of such collaboration supports the truth of the report. These Pharisees (and Sadducees) were part of the deputation sent by the Sanhedrin to investigate Jesus (see on Luke 5:17 in *Healing of the paralyzed man*, p. 19, Mark 3:22 in *Exorcism using Beelzebub*, p. 31, and Matt 15:1–6 and parallels in *Breaking the tradition of the elders*, p. 34). The earlier similar deputation sent to investigate John the Baptist also consisted of Pharisees and Sadducees, reflecting the representation of both groups in the Sanhedrin—see *Pharisees and Sadducees visit John the Baptist*, p. 14.

Matthew and Mark both state that the purpose of the request for "a sign from heaven," presumably some kind of miracle, was to test Jesus. The aim was to determine whether Jesus was a genuine prophet or a charlatan.

---

28. Ibid., 30.

Hypocrites or Heroes?

Popular Jewish piety maintained that a true prophet had the power to perform miracles as the archetypal prophets Moses and Elijah had done.

The yeast of the Pharisees (and Sadducees)

> "Be careful," Jesus said to them. "Be on your guard against the yeast of the Pharisees and Sadducees." (Matt 16:6)
> "Be careful," Jesus warned them. "Watch out for the yeast of the Pharisees and that of Herod." (Mark 8:15)
> Meanwhile, when a crowd of many thousands had gathered, so that they were trampling on one another, Jesus began to speak first to his disciples, saying: "Be on your guard against the yeast of the Pharisees, which is hypocrisy." (Luke 12:1)

This is a sequel to the previously considered passage (see above). Despite its wholly beneficial use in the making of bread, in Jewish culture yeast (or "leaven" as some EVV render it) was regarded as a symbol of sin, the symbolism perhaps being suggested by the ability of a little yeast to permeate a large lump of dough. In the Lucan version the yeast is specifically identified with hypocrisy (*hupocrisis*). For a detailed discussion of the meaning of this term see under *Hypocrisy*, p. 146. This is the first time that Jesus accuses the Pharisees of hypocrisy. The reference to Sadducees in the Matthean version reflects the mention of them in verse 1 (see above).

Interpretation of the yeast of the Pharisees (and Sadducees)

> "How is it you don't understand that I was not talking to you about bread? But be on your guard against the yeast of the Pharisees and Sadducees." Then they understood that he was not telling them to guard against the yeast used in bread, but against the teaching of the Pharisees and Sadducees. (Matt 16:11f)

Not long previously the disciples had professed to understand Jesus' parables (Matt 13:36), but they failed to recognize the parabolic nature of the saying about yeast (Matt 16:6) and assumed that he was speaking literally about bread. It may be significant that apparently they understood the phrase "the yeast of the Pharisees and Sadducees" as designating a particular kind of yeast. Was this actually so? If the Pharisees were a larger group than is widely believed, there might conceivably have been a "yeast of the

Pharisees," which perhaps was certified as conforming to their food purity laws. Matthew explains that the yeast represented "the teaching of the Pharisees and Sadducees," while Luke 12:1 identified it with hypocrisy (see above)—the two are not necessarily incompatible. Only here and in Matt 16:6 does Jesus bracket the Pharisees and Sadducees in a saying: they were so different that they did not naturally belong together. Presumably what Jesus means is that there is error in the teaching of both groups and that his disciples must be ready to question and to test the claims made by both.

Jesus' first passion prediction

> From that time on Jesus began to explain to his disciples that he must go to Jerusalem and suffer many things at the hands of the elders, chief priests and teachers of the law [*grammateōn*], and that he must be killed and on the third day be raised to life. (Matt 16:21)
>
> He then began to teach them that the Son of Man must suffer many things and be rejected by the elders, chief priests and teachers of the law, [*grammateōn*] and that he must be killed and after three days rise again. (Mark 8:31)
>
> And he said, "The Son of Man must suffer many things and be rejected by the elders, chief priests and teachers of the law [*grammateōn*], and he must be killed and on the third day be raised to life." (Luke 9:22)

All three synoptics testify to Jesus' prediction of his suffering and death at the hands of the elders, chief priests, and *grammateōn*. Jesus was referring to the Sanhedrin, which consisted of representatives from those three groups; as France observes, "The fact that it [the Messiah's suffering] comes from those who made up the Sanhedrin indicates the official and judicial rejection of Jesus by those who had formal responsibility for the life of Israel as the people of God, and so presents us with the paradox of the rejection of Israel's Messiah by the official leadership of Israel."[29] The teachers of the law on the Sanhedrin were probably drawn from both the Pharisee and the Sadducee communities, but it may be significant that the Pharisees are not mentioned explicitly in any of the three versions.

---

29. France, *Matthew*, 632.

Hypocrites or Heroes?

The question about Elijah

> The disciples asked him, "Why then do the teachers of the law [*grammateis*] say that Elijah must come first?"
>
> Jesus replied, "To be sure, Elijah comes and will restore all things. But I tell you, Elijah has already come, and they did not recognize him, but have done to him everything they wished. In the same way the Son of Man is going to suffer at their hands."
>
> Then the disciples understood that he was talking to them about John the Baptist. (Matt 17:10–13)
>
> And they asked him, "Why do the teachers of the law [*grammateis*] say that Elijah must come first?"
>
> Jesus replied, "To be sure, Elijah does come first, and restores all things. Why then is it written that the Son of Man must suffer much and be rejected? But I tell you, Elijah has come, and they have done to him everything they wished, just as it is written about him."
>
> When they came to the other disciples, they saw a large crowd around them and the teachers of the law [*grammateis*] arguing with them. (Mark 9:11–14)

Two events prompted the disciples' question. The more recent was the appearance of Elijah at the Transfiguration, concerning which Jesus subsequently instructed the disciples who had witnessed it to tell no-one else (Matt 17:3, 9). The earlier was Jesus' commendation of Peter for recognizing him as Messiah (Matt 16:16f). Presumably during the intervening six days news of Jesus' messianic claim had spread. It had, however, met with opposition from the teachers of the law on grounds which Robert Gundry explains as follows: "The teachers of the law could argue against Jesus' Messiahship that according to scripture Elijah had to come before the Messiah, yet he had not."[30]

The passage to which the teachers of the law were allegedly referring is Mal 4:5: "See, I will send you the prophet Elijah before that great and dreadful day of the Lord comes." This passage had led to the widespread belief at the time of Jesus that in the end times Elijah would return to herald Messiah's advent.[31] Jesus apparently believed this himself and he countered

---

30. Gundry, *Matthew*, 347.

31. The significance of Elijah's return to earth is that in the Old Testament Elijah did not die, but was taken to heaven in "a chariot of fire" (2 Kgs 2:11). He was therefore regarded as still alive and available at God's bidding to return to earth to herald the Messiah.

the objection by claiming that Elijah had already come but had not been recognized. Only Matthew explicitly identifies the returned Elijah with the Baptist at this point[32] and he does so tentatively, hedging his bets by insisting that this was the disciples' understanding of Jesus' statement, the implication being that they might have been mistaken.

Matthew omits Mark's mention of the teachers of the law arguing with the other disciples. The argument probably concerned exorcism, the disciples having proved unable to heal a boy who was supposedly troubled by an evil spirit. Pharisees believed in evil spirits as well as benign ones and they too practiced exorcism.

The question about divorce

> Some Pharisees came to him to test him. They asked, "Is it lawful for a man to divorce his wife for any and every reason?" (Matt 19:3)
>
> Some Pharisees came and tested him by asking, "Is it lawful for a man to divorce his wife?" (Mark 10:2)

Matthew and Mark agree that this approach was made by Pharisees and that its purpose was to "test" Jesus. Presumably as Jesus was still in Galilee these Pharisees were members of the delegation sent to observe him. This question was a test of his orthodoxy, which they hoped might lead him to make a statement sufficiently heretical to provide grounds for his arrest. They had chosen their subject well, divorce being the subject of hot debate in Pharisee communities, which Maccoby describes as follows:

> We find that the House of Hillel and the House of Shammai have, as one of their disagreements, the question of divorce. On this matter, the House of Hillel is far more lenient than the House of Shammai, for it permits divorce on mere grounds of incompatibility, whereas the House of Shammai says that a husband may divorce his wife only if he finds that she has betrayed him sexually in some way (the disagreement obviously turns on the interpretation of . . . Deut 24:1, the House of Hillel putting the stress on the first clause "finds no favor in his eyes", while the House of Shammai

---

32. Matthew had previously identified the Baptist with Elijah twice (Matt 11:14, 12:10–13).

Hypocrites or Heroes?

> puts the stress on the second clause "because he hath found some uncleanness in her").[33]

There is a subtle difference between Mark's and Matthew's versions of the question, Matthew having added *kata pasan aitian*, literally "according to all reason," the spirit of which is admirably conserved in the NIV's rendering "for any and every reason." In both gospels Jesus' reply is more stringent than Hillel's: in Mark he outlaws divorce altogether, while in Matthew he reluctantly permits it only on grounds of "marital unfaithfulness," as does Shammai.

Jesus' third passion prediction

> We are going up to Jerusalem, and the Son of Man will be betrayed to the chief priests and the teachers of the law [*grammateusin*]. They will condemn him to death (Matt 20:18)
> "We are going up to Jerusalem," he said, "and the Son of Man will be betrayed to the chief priests and teachers of the law [*grammateusin*]. They will condemn him to death and will hand him over to the Gentiles" (Mark 10:33)

See on *Jesus' first passion prediction,* p. 39. On this occasion the elders, one of the constituent bodies of the Sanhedrin, are not mentioned, so that Jesus' death is attributed to the chief priests and *grammateis*, who may be their administrative assistants or legal advisors. Significantly the Pharisees are again not mentioned by name.

Pharisees ask Jesus to rebuke his disciples

> Some of the Pharisees in the crowd said to Jesus, "Teacher, rebuke your disciples!"
> "I tell you," he replied, "if they keep quiet, the stones will cry out." (Luke 19:39f)

This incident, during Jesus' triumphal entry into Jerusalem, is peculiar to Luke. Crowds of disciples, who might be lining the roadside or accompanying Jesus in the procession, begin singing words inspired by Ps 118:26, "Blessed is he who comes in the name of the Lord." The "Pharisees in the

---

33. Maccoby, *Jesus,* 193.

crowd" could still be the delegation sent to observe him, but as this is Jerusalem they could equally be other local Pharisees. Considering the song inappropriate, their instruction addressing Jesus as "Teacher" implies that it is his responsibility to keep his pupils in order. To this Jesus replies, "if they keep quiet, the stones will cry out."

There are undercurrents here. Ps 118:26 is ambiguous, many scholars believing that it was originally a pilgrimage song, whose lines were chanted either by pilgrims on the ascent to the Temple for a festival or by a choir within the Temple itself to greet arriving pilgrims. The original meaning was "Blessed in the name of the LORD is the coming one," referring to the pilgrim who was an ordinary worshipper. Popular usage, however, reassociated the words "in the name of the LORD" with "the coming one" so that this was no longer an ordinary worshipper, but a divine representative whose coming was expected, such as the Messiah himself. Luke confirms this understanding by adding "the king" to the line. Although this is absent from both the Marcan and Matthean parallels, both allude to David, from whom the Messiah was descended. Luke may have changed "David" to "king" as his Gentile readers may not have heard of David.

The Pharisees, then, are depicted as objecting to the Messianic implications of the singing, presumably because they do not believe that Jesus is the Messiah. Jesus' reply, "if they keep quiet, the stones will cry out," suggests that he believed that the occasion was auspicious. It is significant that the Pharisees address Jesus as "Teacher"; it is unlikely that they would have used this title had he not been a Pharisee himself. This suggests that some aspect of his person—his dress perhaps?—still identified him as a Pharisee.

The chief priests and teachers of the law are indignant at Jesus' reception

> But when the chief priests and the teachers of the law [*grammateis*] saw the wonderful things he did and the children shouting in the temple area, "Hosanna to the Son of David," they were indignant. (Matt 21:15)

This happened in the Temple courts shortly after Jesus' triumphal entry to Jerusalem. Presumably the chief priests and the teachers of the law were indignant primarily because of the Messianic implications of the appellation "Son of David." It is understandable that the chief priests were concerned. It was widely believed that the Messiah would lead an uprising against the Roman occupation; the chief priests were not only pro-Roman but effectively appointed by the Romans, so a Messianic claimant was potentially a threat to their livelihood. The *grammateis* in the temple may have been Sadducees themselves or possibly the administrative or legal staff of the chief priests, who would have shared their interests; this stands in contrast with most teachers of the law who were Pharisees and anti-Rome, so would be expected to support Messianic claimants.

The chief priests and the teachers of the law plot to kill Jesus

> The chief priests and the teachers of the law [*grammateis*] heard this and began looking for a way to kill him, for they feared him, because the whole crowd was amazed at his teaching. (Mark 11:18)
>
> Every day he was teaching at the temple. But the chief priests, the teachers of the law [*grammateis*] and the leaders among the people were trying to kill him. (Luke 19:47)

Jesus' cleansing of the Temple was a provocative action, committed with the express intention of forcing a confrontation with the authorities. It is not altogether surprising, then, that following it the religious authorities were moved to action. Those authorities are described as the "chief priests and teachers of the law [*grammateis*]" as in the previously considered passage and this probably refers to the same individuals. The indignation described there has escalated so that Mark and Luke inform us that they now began seeking how they might kill (*apolesōsin*) him. An earlier plot against Jesus allegedly by Pharisees but possibly by Sadducees and described in Mark 3:6 and Matt 12:14 similarly considered how they could rid themselves of the threat that Jesus posed. The two principal difficulties are that the verb *apollumi* has a broad range of meanings and does not necessarily mean "kill"—for more details see *The plots against Jesus,* p. 148—and that the Sadducees (which included the chief priests), despite their reputation for rudeness to all and sundry, respected Torah making it unlikely that they would contemplate murder. It is far more likely that they would seek grounds on which to arrest Jesus and thereby deprive him of his influence, so that "ruin"—another possible meaning of *apollumi*—would be a possible alternative rendering. Of course, in the end, the Sadducees persuaded the Roman Governor to execute Jesus for insurrection; they no doubt justifying their action on the grounds that Jesus had committed blasphemy.

The Pharisees in the New Testament

A delegation from the Sanhedrin questions Jesus' authority

> They arrived again in Jerusalem, and while Jesus was walking in the temple courts, the chief priests, the teachers of the law [*grammateis*] and the elders came to him. (Mark 11:27)
>
> One day as he was teaching the people in the temple courts and preaching the gospel, the chief priests and the teachers of the law [*grammateis*], together with the elders, came up to him. (Luke 20:1)

There are also parallels in Matthew (Matt 21:23) and John (John 2:18), but these do not mention the teachers of the law;[34] John, however, mentions "the Jews"—see on *A deputation from the Sanhedrin,* p. 94. As this deputation contains representatives of the chief priests, the teachers of the law, and the elders, it appears to be from the Sanhedrin. A response to Jesus' cleansing of the temple, its purpose was to challenge Jesus' authority. Jesus had deliberately sought such a confrontation with the nation's religious leadership. This encounter is considered in more detail later—see *Building a new community from the "sinners,"* p. 185.

The Pharisees understand the Parable of the Wicked Tenants

> When the chief priests and the Pharisees heard Jesus' parables, they knew he was talking about them. They looked for a way to arrest him, but they were afraid of the crowd because the people held that he was a prophet. (Matt 21:45f)
>
> The teachers of the law [*grammateis*] and the chief priests looked for a way to arrest him immediately, because they knew he had spoken this parable against them. But they were afraid of the people. (Luke 20:19)

The parallel in Mark (Mark 12:12) mentions neither Pharisees nor teachers of the law.

This verse follows Jesus' telling the Parable of the Wicked Tenants (in Matthew preceded by the Two Sons and followed by the Wedding Feast) in reply to the challenge concerning his authority by the deputation from the

---

34. Matthew later mentions Pharisees hearing the Parable of the Wicked Tenants which was told on this same occasion (Matt 21:45—see below) and John describes the deputation as "the Jews," which is one of his favorite appellations for Pharisees and other Jewish authority figures—see the next chapter.

Hypocrites or Heroes?

Sanhedrin following his cleansing of the temple. The content of the three parables will be considered later—see *The Pharisees in the parables of Jesus*, p. 188.

The vivid detail in the Wicked Tenants makes this a particularly easy parable to understand and all three synoptists record that Jesus' hearers, who included Pharisees according to Matthew and teachers of the law according to Luke, recognized themselves as the people it condemned. It is not surprising then that they "looked for a way to arrest him," although it is hard to see on what grounds; his arrest at that time would serve only to underline the painful truth of the story. In practice fear of the people, many of whom considered Jesus to be a prophet, led them to postpone that particular course of action.

Pharisees (and Herodians) lay a trap

> Then the Pharisees went out and laid plans to trap him in his words. (Matt 22:15)
> Later they sent some of the Pharisees and Herodians to Jesus to catch him in his words. (Mark 12:13)
> When Jesus left there, the Pharisees and the teachers of the law [*grammateis*] began to oppose him fiercely and to besiege him with questions, waiting to catch him in something he might say. (Luke 11:53f)
> The teachers of the law [*grammateis*] and the chief priests looked for a way to arrest him immediately, because they knew he had spoken this parable against them. But they were afraid of the people. Keeping a close watch on him, they sent spies, who pretended to be honest. They hoped to catch Jesus in something he said so that they might hand him over to the power and authority of the governor. (Luke 20:19f)

Apart from Luke 11:53f, which appears in a different context and may be a doublet of Luke 20:19f, these sayings are the sequel to the Wicked Tenants (and in Matthew the other two polemical parables), showing the action that the teachers of the law, Pharisees, and chief priests (Sadducees) took. This takes the form of a sequence of trick questions addressed to Jesus in the hope that his answers might incriminate him. The first of these concerned the propriety of paying taxes to Caesar.

Again, this shows the Pharisees and teachers of the law forming alliances with parties such as the Sadducees and Herodians with whom normally relationships were strained and using underhand methods to find a reason to arrest Jesus.

The Sadducees' question

> Some of the teachers of the law [*grammateōn*] responded, "Well said, teacher!" (Luke 20:39)

An approach to Jesus by the Sadducees involved a question intended to ridicule the concept of resurrection, in which they did not believe. Jesus' answer apparently proved the resurrection from the Pentateuch, the only scriptures which the Sadducees accepted as authoritative. The teachers of the law in Luke 20:39 were presumably Pharisees, who would have welcomed Jesus siding with them and demonstrating scriptural support for resurrection from the Pentateuch which Sadducees ought to accept. In this round of sectarian rivalry Jesus is clearly on the of the side Pharisees.

The greatest commandment

> Hearing that Jesus had silenced the Sadducees, the Pharisees got together. One of them, an expert in the law [*nomikos*], tested him with this question: "Teacher, which is the greatest commandment in the Law?" (Matt 22:34f)
>
> One of the teachers of the law [*grammateōn*] came and heard them debating. Noticing that Jesus had given them a good answer, he asked him, "Of all the commandments, which is the most important?"
>
> "The most important one," answered Jesus, "is this: 'Hear, O Israel, the Lord our God, the Lord is one. Love the Lord your God with all your heart and with all your soul and with all your mind and with all your strength.' The second is this: 'Love your neighbor as yourself.' There is no commandment greater than these."
>
> "Well said, teacher," the man [*grammateus*] replied. "You are right in saying that God is one and there is no other but him." (Mark 12:28-32)
>
> On one occasion an expert in the law [*nomikos*] stood up to test Jesus. "Teacher," he asked, "what must I do to inherit eternal life?" (Luke 10:25)

Hypocrites or Heroes?

This question comes from Pharisees according to Matthew and a teacher of the law (*grammateōn*) in Mark. The Lucan passage concerning an expert in the law (*nomikos*) occurs in a different context, but all are likely to be Pharisees, taking their turn in trying to trip Jesus up. The question about the great commandment is typical of Pharisaic debate and Mark alone records that Jesus' reply pleased the questioner.

Maccoby claims that Matthew's removal of the friendliness evident in the Marcan account of the dialogue provides an example of a later anti-Pharisee editor toning down earlier pro-Pharisee material, but it may represent no more than Matthew's habitual abridgment of Marcan passages. Maccoby also points out that "Jesus' singling out of these two verses of the Hebrew Bible (one from Deuteronomy and the other from Leviticus) as the greatest of the commandments was not an original idea of his own, but an established part of Pharisee thinking."[35]

Jesus challenges the Pharisees

> While the Pharisees were gathered together, Jesus asked them, "What do you think about the Christ? Whose son is he?"
> "The son of David," they replied.
> He said to them, "How is it then that David, speaking by the Spirit, calls him 'Lord'? For he says, 'The Lord said to my Lord: "Sit at my right hand until I put your enemies under your feet."' If then David calls him 'Lord,' how can he be his son?"
> No-one could say a word in reply, and from that day on no-one dared to ask him any more questions. (Matt 22:41–46)
> While Jesus was teaching in the temple courts, he asked, "How is it that the teachers of the law [*grammateis*] say that the Christ is the son of David?" (Mark 12:35)

Matthew makes this snatch of theological debate the sequel to the previous approach by the Pharisees, while Mark simply identifies it as taking place during a teaching session in the Temple. Jesus challenges the Pharisees' teaching that the Messiah, as a descendant of David, is inferior to him by arguing that in Ps 110 even David acknowledges him as Lord. This makes the Messiah superior, not to mention pre-existent, to David. Apparently this teaching silenced the Pharisees.

---

35. Maccoby, *Jesus*, 121.

This passage offers an interesting insight into first-century Jewish theological debate. Jesus is happy to attribute Ps 110 to David, although the Old Testament does not credit an author, and to assert that David was "speaking by the Spirit" when he composed this Psalm. Evidently Jesus had a well-defined belief in the inspiration of scripture and, since the Pharisees do not challenge it, this presumably was their understanding too. Jesus and the Pharisees usually agree on the fundamentals of their faith.

Jesus acknowledges the Pharisees as arbiters of the law

> The teachers of the law [*grammateis*] and the Pharisees sit in Moses' seat. So you must obey them and do everything they tell you. But do not do what they do, for they do not practice what they preach. They tie up heavy loads and put them on men's shoulders, but they themselves are not willing to lift a finger to move them. (Matt 23:2–4)
>
> Jesus replied, "And you experts in the law [*nomikoi*], woe to you, because you load people down with burdens they can hardly carry, and you yourselves will not lift one finger to help them." (Luke 11:46)

The Matthean version marks the beginning of Jesus' long address denouncing the Pharisees and teachers of the law; Matthew has skillfully woven this speech together from various sources. Other sections of it will be considered below. Verses 2 and 3 are peculiar to Matthew. Luke's parallel to verse 4 (Luke 11:46) falls in the middle of his version of the same long address.

The teachers of the law and the Pharisees occupy Moses' seat inasmuch as they are the successors of Moses, fulfilling in contemporary society the same rôle that Moses did in his. Moses was revered as the founder of Judaism, since it was through him that Yahweh delivered the law that was its basis. To obey Moses is to obey the law and, in Jewish thought, that is the same as pleasing God. The Pharisees and especially the teachers of the law see their principal task as the interpretation of that law as it applies in specific circumstances.

An alternative meaning for this passage has been suggested by T. W. Manson: "Moses' seat . . . has hitherto been explained as a figure of speech . . . Recent archaeological work in Israel shows that the 'seat of Moses' was no mere figure of speech, but a part of the furniture of the

Hypocrites or Heroes?

synagogue."[36] He proceeds to quote E. L. Sukenik who describes two such seats found at Hammath-by-Tiberias and Chorazin.[37] These faced the congregation and were clearly reserved either for distinguished worshippers, which is perhaps what the teachers of the law and Pharisees considered themselves, or for the person giving instruction in the law: these are "the most important seats in the synagogue"[38] (see below). These seats, then, may have been known as "Moses' seat" and were occupied by those whose function was to interpret and teach the Torah.

Thus the teachers of the law and Pharisees regarded themselves as the guardians of an unbroken tradition handed down since Moses and Jesus does not deny this. On the contrary, he enjoins the people to obey them. This saying is altogether typical of Matthew's theology with its high view of the law: his Jesus always upholds the sanctity of the law and the necessity for humanity to obey it. Maccoby is surely correct in his observation that, "Since Jesus is here recommending his listeners to follow the teachings of the Pharisees in every detail, we can safely conclude that he did this himself and that he was therefore a practising member of the Pharisee movement."[39]

The "But" that follows (in "But do not do what they do") is a heavy load for the mildly disjunctive *de*; while Jesus commands obedience to the legal dictats of the teachers of the law and Pharisees, he claims that their lifestyle is not worthy of emulation. Craig Keener describes their failure to conduct their lives according to the standards they demand of others as "a dichotomy known to exist among many religious professionals and other religious people today."[40] Later sections of the discourse provide examples. The Greek which literally means, "for they say and they do not do," may reflect an Aramaic proverb.

Jesus' complaint in Matt 23:4 and Luke 11:46 is that while the Pharisees and teachers of the law are over-zealous in their interpretation of the law, they have failed to take into account human weakness. They have developed such a welter of written and oral laws concerning every area of life that a Jew can hardly move a muscle without infringing one law or another. This leaves ordinary Jews disillusioned, believing themselves cut off from a God whom it is impossible to please. The graphic imagery of the "heavy

36. Manson, *Sayings*, 228.
37. Sukenik, *Synagogues*, 58f.
38. As mentioned in Matt 23:6; Mark 12:39; Luke 11:43; Luke 20:46.
39. Maccoby, *Jesus*, 155.
40. Keener, *Matthew*, 540.

loads . . . on men's shoulders" recalls that of Matt 11:28–30, in which Jesus addresses this situation and promises that he himself will provide relief.

A warning about the teachers of the law

> "Everything they do is done for men to see: They make their phylacteries wide and the tassels on their garments long; they love the place of honor at banquets and the most important seats in the synagogues; they love to be greeted in the market-places and to have men call them 'Rabbi.'" (Matt 23:5–7)
>
> As he taught, Jesus said, "Watch out for the teachers of the law [*grammateōn*]. They like to walk around in flowing robes and be greeted in the market-places, and have the most important seats in the synagogues and the places of honor at banquets. They devour widows' houses and for a show make lengthy prayers. Such men will be punished most severely." (Mark 12:38–40)
>
> "Woe to you Pharisees, because you love the most important seats in the synagogues and greetings in the market-places." (Luke 11:43)
>
> "Beware of the teachers of the law [*grammateōn*]. They like to walk around in flowing robes and love to be greeted in the market-places and have the most important seats in the synagogues and the places of honor at banquets. They devour widows' houses and for a show make lengthy prayers. Such men will be punished most severely." (Luke 20:46f)

While Mark and Luke 20 identify the persons being denounced as *grammateōn*, the Matthean parallel continues the speech which began in Matt 23:2 where the subject is stated to be "the teachers of the law and the Pharisees" and Luke 11 is addressed to "you Pharisees."

Matthew omits the most serious of the accusations made in the otherwise nearly identical Marcan and Lucan versions: that "they devour widows' houses."[41] Precisely what this saying means is uncertain. It may be an example of oriental hyperbole: perhaps the Pharisees so frequently abuse the generous hospitality extended to them by pious wealthy widows that those widows are now in danger of being "eaten out of house and home." An alternative interpretation is that they persuade those widows to bequeath their estates to them. Either action constitutes a serious abuse

---

41. Most scholars dismiss the parallel in Matt 23:14 as a gloss, absent from the most reliable MSS.

of trust, exploitation of the vulnerable; the Torah makes extensive provision for widows and orphans and attaches corresponding gravity to crimes which victimize them.[42]

The other accusations are arguably less serious inasmuch as the only harm done to people is that of deception: they are well summarized by Matthew's opening statement, "Everything they do is done for men to see." The offenses are those of ostentation: flowing robes, wide phylacteries, long tassels, public greetings, the places of honor, the most important seats in the synagogue (for further on which see on the previous item), and lengthy prayers. Jesus devoted a section of the Sermon on the Mount (Matt 6:1–18) to this kind of sin, although in that passage he did not identify the perpetrators.

Woe to the (teachers of the law and) Pharisees

To ease comparison the two versions of this speech have been divided into sections, following the Matthean order rather than the Lucan.

> "Woe to you, teachers of the law [*grammateis*] and Pharisees, you hypocrites! You shut the kingdom of heaven in men's faces. You yourselves do not enter, nor will you let those enter who are trying to.
>
> "Woe to you, teachers of the law [*grammateis*] and Pharisees, you hypocrites! You travel over land and sea to win a single convert, and when he becomes one, you make him twice as much a son of hell as you are. (Matt 23:13–15)
>
> Woe to you experts in the law [*nomikoi*], because you have taken away the key to knowledge. You yourselves have not entered, and you have hindered those who were entering. (Luke 11:52)

This first denunciation is the most serious of Jesus' accusations against the teachers of the law and the Pharisees. In Matt 23:2 he acknowledged that they "occupy Moses' seat," meaning that they have inherited the administration of God's law. In Pharisee thought observance of the law determined admission to the Kingdom of Heaven, itself a characteristically Pharisaic concept. Maccoby states that, "in Pharisaic thinking, the kingdom of God had two meanings: it meant the present kingdom or reign of God, or it could mean the future reign of God over the whole world in the Messianic

---

42. Exod 22:22; Deut 10:18; 24:17–21.

Age. It is possible to discern in Jesus' frequent use of the same expression the same twofold meaning . . ."[43] The prime responsibility of the Pharisees and teachers of the law was therefore to *help* people to understand and observe that law and thereby enter the Kingdom. Jesus' accusation is that they were doing the very opposite. Donald Hagner ably summarizes the accusation as follows: "their teaching and practice were false and thus misled others . . . their teaching of Torah should have been the key . . . that opened the door for others to enjoy the rule of God."[44] Keener amusingly compares them with "a porter abusing authority to keep welcome guests out."[45] Certainly "You shut" (*kleiete*) implies the use of a key and it is probably no coincidence that the somewhat different Lucan parallel, "you have taken away the *key* to knowledge," (thus preventing ordinary people from understanding the truth of God's word) also uses this *motif*. In view of the symbolic importance of gates in Matt 16:18f, it is reasonable to assume that the picture in Jesus' mind is of the figurative gates at the entrance of the Kingdom, whose keys he entrusted to Peter as a representative disciple (Matt 16:19). The Pharisees are now locking those gates to keep out the very people whom they are supposed to be assisting into the Kingdom. To add insult to injury, the verse implies that this locking is performed in the sight of those seeking to gain access (*emprosthen tōn anthrōpōn*).

So who are the unfortunates who wish to enter the Kingdom but are being hindered by the Pharisees? There are two possibilities. There was a section of the Jewish population that had become disenfranchised through the excessive demands of Pharisaic Judaism, for example, in regard to Sabbath observance; the teachers of the law have made the law too difficult for ordinary Jews to observe. These are the same victims that Jesus mentioned in Matt 23:4/Luke 11:46: "They tie up heavy loads and put them on men's shoulders, but they themselves are not willing to lift a finger to move them." But there was also a huge underclass of people, the "sinners," who had been excommunicated from Jewish society as a penalty for various crimes—see *Those "put out of the synagogue"—the "sinners,* p. 155." Although the ministries of John the Baptist and Jesus sparked a revival amongst these people who repented in large numbers, demonstrating their sincerity by submitting to baptism (Matt 21:32; Luke 7:29), institutional Judaism remained

---

43. Maccoby, *Jesus*, 121.
44. Hagner, *Matthew*, 2:668.
45. Keener, *Matthew*, 547.

suspicious of them, because it failed to recognize John and Jesus as having divine authority (Matt 21:23–27).

Moreover, Jesus considers that, as a consequence of their actions, the teachers of the law and the Pharisees have effectively locked *themselves* out of the Kingdom also: "you yourselves do not enter/have not entered . . .". In Matt 12:22–37 Jesus told the Pharisees that they were in danger of committing "blasphemy against the Holy Spirit," for which there was no forgiveness and which would therefore result in their exclusion from the kingdom. Moreover, the Wicked Tenants (indeed Matthew's sequence of three polemical parables[46]) carried the message that, on account of their incompetence, the present guardians of Judaism would forfeit their rôle and incur God's judgment, leaving others to inherit their office and its privileges.

In a saying peculiar to Matthew (Matt 23:15) Jesus makes a further observation about the Pharisees' attitude to the acquisition of new adherents. This saying seems almost to contradict the previous accusation. Despite their reluctance to accept John's and Jesus' converts, they nevertheless put considerable effort into missionary work: "You travel over land and sea to win a single convert (*poiēsai hena prosēluton*)." Keener reports that there is convincing evidence of such Jewish proselytism:

> Although Judaism had no central sending agency and hence no "missionaries" in the formal sense . . . plenty of evidence, especially in Diaspora Jewish apologetics . . . and Gentile criticisms of Jewish conversions . . . testifies to many Jewish people seeking Gentile converts in the course of their work . . .
>
> The Pharisees were probably no less interested in this process than others, especially if we may judge from the favorable light in which their successors viewed stories of Hillel's openness to converts; one cannot therefore use the lack of ancient Jewish "missionaries" to regard the saying as inauthentic.[47]

What Jesus is condemning is not missionary zeal *per se* (*c.f.* Matt 28:19f in which he sends his followers out to "make disciples of all nations"), but that the Pharisees' efforts are counter-productive inasmuch as the teaching that they give to their converts and the lifestyle that they promote contain the same fatal flaws that the previous saying declared would keep them out of the Kingdom. Perhaps in their enthusiasm these converts

---

46. Matt 21:28–22:10.
47. Keener, *Matthew*, 548f.

sometimes exaggerated these errors and thereby merited the hyperbolic description "twice as much a son of hell as you are." The phrase *son of hell* (*huion geennēs*) is a Semitism, meaning simply, "one destined for hell."

> "Woe to you, teachers of the law [*grammateis*] and Pharisees, you hypocrites! You give a tenth of your spices—mint, dill, and cummin. But you have neglected the more important matters of the law—justice, mercy, and faithfulness. You should have practiced the latter, without neglecting the former. You blind guides! You strain out a gnat but swallow a camel. (Matt 23:23f)
>
> "Woe to you Pharisees, because you give God a tenth of your mint, rue, and all other kinds of garden herbs, but you neglect justice and the love of God. You should have practiced the latter without leaving the former undone. (Luke 11:42)

Here Jesus addresses what he regards as errors in the Pharisaic teaching regarding tithing. It is true that the Torah specified that "seed from the ground or fruit from the tree" and "herd and flock" (Lev 27:30–32) should be tithed and the tithes given to the Levites "in return for the services that they perform" (Num 18:21). In the Torah this tithing applied only to agricultural crops, herbs in kitchen gardens being exempt. By New Testament times the tithing of such herbs was the subject of Rabbinic debate, some herbs (such as dill and cummin) being reckoned tithable while others (such as mint) were not. According to Jesus, the teachers of the law and Pharisees now tithed not only the dill and cummin that Rabbinic teaching required, but also the mint that it did not. Keener's explanation, "In their eagerness to avoid violating any portion of the law, the ultrastrict Pharisees Jesus addresses here . . . tithe even the most disputable of substances,"[48] sounds eminently reasonable.

Jesus does not condemn the tithing of these herbs; on the contrary, he commends it, as "without neglecting the former/without leaving the former undone" clearly indicates. What he criticizes is the inconsistency in the lifestyles of those regarded as arbiters of the law. Despite their apparent zeal to observe even the *minutiae* of the law, they were guilty of transgressing "the more important matters of the law." These Jesus summarizes as "justice, mercy, and faithfulness," this trio paralleling the earlier trio of herbs.

Matthew appends a piece of delightful oriental hyperbole. Jesus' depiction of a man meticulously filtering his wine after a gnat has fallen into it (to obviate the risk of swallowing unclean matter) and then proceeding

---

48. Ibid., 551.

to swallow a camel is capable of provoking laughter even among those unaware that in the original Aramaic the saying involved a play on words, "gnat" and "camel" being the similar sounding *qalma* and *qamla* respectively. Both gnats and camels were unclean in Judaism and therefore could not be eaten. The gnat was one of the smallest and the camel the largest animal known to the Jews, the contrast in size providing the comic element in the saying. As with the tithing of herbs, Jesus' message is that the Pharisees manage correctly that which is insignificant, while they bungle the genuinely important.

> "Woe to you, teachers of the law [*grammateis*] and Pharisees, you hypocrites! You clean the outside of the cup and dish, but inside they are full of greed and self-indulgence. Blind Pharisee! First clean the inside of the cup and dish, and then the outside also will be clean. (Matt 23:25f)
>
> When Jesus had finished speaking, a Pharisee invited him to eat with him; so he went in and reclined at the table. But the Pharisee, noticing that Jesus did not first wash before the meal, was surprised. Then the Lord said to him, "Now then, you Pharisees clean the outside of the cup and dish, but inside you are full of greed and wickedness. You foolish people! Did not the one who made the outside make the inside also? But give what is inside [the dish] to the poor, and everything will be clean for you. (Luke 11:37–41)

The Matthean version falls towards the end of the speech; whereas the Lucan forms its beginning, following immediately after the incident that supposedly provoked it (Luke 11:37–41). Luke depicts Jesus as accepting an invitation to a meal in the home of an unnamed Pharisee. This probably formed part of the official surveillance of Jesus, the host scrutinizing Jesus for breaches of the Pharisaic code of conduct. Indeed it is this that leads him to express surprise when Jesus fails to wash before the meal. Instead of justifying this omission with an explanation like that in Mark 7:14–23 which he used in similar circumstances, Jesus launches into his diatribe about the faults of the Pharisees, beginning with the only words on which Matthew and Luke agree: "You clean the outside of the cup and dish, but inside . . ." The saying seems inappropriate in its Lucan context: the Pharisee has accused Jesus of not washing himself, to which Jesus' reply about Pharisees inadequately washing cups and dishes is hardly relevant. It is as though Luke had received the saying without any indication of context and, needing a suitable occasion to present it, re-used the dinner invitation to the Pharisee's home in Luke 7:36 as a close-enough match. But is it likely that Jesus would so blatantly transgress the conventions of Jewish hospitality by haranguing the host who has generously welcomed him into his own home? The saying surely belongs in a public teaching session about the faults of the Pharisees, as indeed Matthew has placed it. Nolland offers a detailed discussion of the origin of the Lucan parallel.[49]

The saying central to this passage, "You clean the outside of the cup and dish, but inside . . ." is clearly figurative. Jesus is not talking about literal cups and dishes but human lifestyles. Indeed, the interpretation of the following saying in Matthew's version, which cloaks the same message in different imagery, expresses its meaning succinctly: "In the same way, on the outside you appear to people as righteous but on the inside you are full of hypocrisy and wickedness" (Matt 23:28). It is the familiar accusation of play-acting, the Pharisees' outward appearance being a mere façade quite unlike their inner character, which Jesus declares to be full of "greed and self-indulgence" in Matthew and "greed and wickedness" in Luke.

The Matthean and Lucan accounts of the remedy are differently worded, although both arguably reach the same conclusion. Matthew appeals simply for inward purity, which will inevitably be reflected in a new outward lifestyle: "First clean the inside of the cup and dish, and then the outside also will be clean." Luke is more thoughtful, arguing first for the unity of inner and outer selves: "Did not the one who made the outside make the inside also?" Evidence of inner purity will be reflected by such outward actions as charitable deeds: "But give what is inside [the dish] to the poor, and everything will be clean for you." This is echoed in Jesus' reply to the wealthy ruler (Luke 18:22 and parallels): "Sell everything you have and give to the poor, and you will have treasure in heaven. Then come, follow me."

> "Woe to you, teachers of the law [*grammateis*] and Pharisees, you hypocrites! You are like whitewashed tombs, which look beautiful on the outside but on the inside are full of dead men's bones and everything unclean.
> "In the same way, on the outside you appear to people as righteous but on the inside you are full of hypocrisy and wickedness. (Matt 23:27f)
> "Woe to you, because you are like unmarked graves, which men walk over without knowing it." (Luke 11:44)

---

49. Nolland, *Luke*, 2:551f.

Hypocrites or Heroes?

As noted above, there are close parallels between these sayings and the previous; only the metaphor is changed. From cups and dishes that were clean on the outside, but rancid on the inside, the illustration changes to "whitewashed tombs, which look beautiful on the outside but on the inside are full of dead men's bones and everything unclean" (Matthew) and "you are like unmarked graves, which men walk over without knowing it" (Luke). To walk over a grave rendered a Jew ritually unclean. For this reason it was standard practice before the Passover to carefully mark out all graves with fresh chalk to minimize the risk of people unintentionally walking on them and thereby becoming unfit to participate in the Passover. Some scholars believe that the Matthean version refers to this practice. But although the message of the two versions is similar, the way in which the imagery is used is different. The Matthean version refers to newly whitewashing a tomb, paving the way for the next illustration (Matt 23:29–32). Only the wealthy and distinguished had tombs capable of being whitewashed; others had the minimal dignity of a grave. In the Matthean version the message lies in the contrast between the "beautiful" exterior and its unclean contents, like the cup and dish that were clean on the outside only representing the Pharisees as outwardly respectable, but inwardly corrupt (Matt 23:28). The Lucan version is more subtle; why are the Pharisees like unmarked graves that people walk over unawares? Because the ordinary Jews trust them to lead them in the ways of Torah that will bring them into the kingdom, unaware that their teaching is false and indeed is having the opposite effect, estranging them from God; there is a parallel with the message of Luke 11:52/Matt 23:13.

The ending of the denunciation of the Pharisees

> "Woe to you, teachers of the law (*grammateis*) and Pharisees, you hypocrites! You build tombs for the prophets and decorate the graves of the righteous. And you say, 'If we had lived in the days of our forefathers, we would not have taken part with them in shedding the blood of the prophets.' So you testify against yourselves that you are the descendants of those who murdered the prophets. Fill up, then, the measure of the sin of your forefathers!
>
> "You snakes! You brood of vipers! How will you escape being condemned to hell? Therefore I am sending you prophets and wise men and teachers (*grammateis*). Some of them you will kill and crucify; others you will flog in your synagogues and pursue from

town to town. And so upon you will come all the righteous blood that has been shed on earth, from the blood of righteous Abel to the blood of Zechariah son of Barakiah, whom you murdered between the temple and the altar. I tell you the truth, all this will come upon this generation. (Matt 23:29–36)

"Woe to you, because you build tombs for the prophets, and it was your forefathers who killed them. So you testify that you approve of what your forefathers did; they killed the prophets, and you build their tombs. Because of this, God in his wisdom said, 'I will send them prophets and apostles, some of whom they will kill and others they will persecute.' Therefore this generation will be held responsible for the blood of all the prophets that has been shed since the beginning of the world, from the blood of Abel to the blood of Zechariah, who was killed between the altar and the sanctuary. Yes, I tell you, this generation will be held responsible for it all. (Luke 11:47–51)

This passage forms a dramatic conclusion to Jesus' speech denouncing the Pharisees and teachers of the law, although Luke appends a further verse, Luke 11:52, considered earlier as parallel to Matt 23:13.

Its opening continues the imagery of the previous Matthean saying (Matt 23:27f). The Jews as a whole venerated the prophets and righteous men of the past; this was fashionable in the first century, as Herod's lavish shrine to David bears witness. Ironically, however, many of the saints whose tombs they built and ritually adorned had been persecuted and even killed for their faith (Heb 11:32–38) by the religious leaders of their day; in fact, the veneration of their memorials was regarded as an act of reparation for their murder. Jesus does not condemn such veneration, but the hypocritical assertion of the teachers of the law and Pharisees is that if they had been alive at the time of those heroes, which they describe significantly as "the days of our forefathers," they would have had the nous to recognize their worth and so would not have participated in their persecution.

Jesus interprets this assertion as meaning: (i) that the present generation of Pharisees admits to being the descendants of the murderers of the prophets; and (ii) that the guilt of those crimes persists and could still be imputed to the present generation.[50] In Jewish thought guilt was often

---

50. In Old Testament theology the guilt of sins persisted and Yahweh reserved the right to punish descendants for the sins of their forefathers (Exod 20:5; Jer 32:18; Lam 5:7; Ezek 18:2). Indeed, for some Old Testament prophets one of the characteristics of the coming Messianic age was the ending of the system of inherited guilt: "all shall die for their own sins" (Jer 31:30, *c.f.* Ezek 18:4).

regarded as corporate rather than individual, as this saying exemplifies. To the Jews the very word "son" indicated close resemblance rather than genetic descent; thus a "son of man" usually meant a mortal man, a "human being"; a "son of God" meant a god-like person; and a "son of thunder" was a tempestuous person. Although the Pharisees' intention had been to protest their innocence, to Jewish ears their admission that they were the sons (*huioi*, rendered "descendants" in the NIV) of those who had persecuted and murdered the prophets implied that they had inherited not only a share in the guilt for those crimes, but also a similar genetic disposition to persecution and murder.

The next saying, "Fill up, then, the measure of the sin of your forefathers!" (peculiar to Matt 23:32) is ironical. Jesus has spoken of the guilt persisting upon the teachers of the law and Pharisees as a consequence of their forefathers' persecution of the prophets. In this verse he regards that persecution as a task that those forefathers had left unfinished, so he appeals to their successors, the current generation, to finish it. It is as though he were saying, "Go on then! Finish off the job your forefathers started! Persecute another prophet!" The victim that he has in mind is, of course, himself. He appreciates that the cross is inevitable; moreover, it will be the ultimate proof that the current leaders of Judaism are true sons of their forefathers.

The inevitability of the cross in no way exonerates the current generation of Jewish leaders; God's judgment upon them is inescapable. Matt 23:33 (no Lucan parallel) is a reiteration of the warning of the Wicked Tenants and the other polemical parables. Jesus addresses his hearers, assumed to be the Pharisees and teachers of the law, as "snakes" probably because of their cunning, their venom and, especially, their uncanny ability to sense impending danger and escape from it. His further term of abuse, "vipers' brood," echoes Matt 3:7 where John the Baptist used it of the investigative deputation of Pharisees and Sadducees that he thought was presenting itself for baptism. Jesus' rhetorical question, "How will you escape being condemned to hell?" echoes that of the Baptist on that earlier occasion.

The *dia touto* at the start of Matt 23:34 ("Therefore") and Luke 11:49 ("Because of this") looks back to what has been said previously. It was because of the certainty of the coming judgment that Jesus in Matthew or God in his wisdom (rendering *hē sofia tou theou*) in Luke sent (the historic present tense is used for dramatic effect) "prophets and wise men and teachers" (the latter rendering, ironically, *grammateis*) in Matthew and "prophets and apostles" in Luke to warn people of the necessity of repentance. But even the persecution of God's servants is amazingly within the providence of God.

Matthew's version makes Jesus the sender, while in Luke it is "God in his wisdom." In Matthew Jesus is not claiming pre-existence, but rather stating his solidarity with the Old Testament prophets; he and they are part of one and the same *heilsgeschichte*. The same emphatic wording, *idou egō apostellō*, occurs in 10:16 where Jesus tells his disciples that he is sending them on a preaching mission as sheep in the midst of wolves.

The fate of these messengers of God's word recalls that of the servants who represented them in the Wicked Tenants and Matthew's version of the Marriage Feast. Matthew's use of the second person, "you will kill and crucify; others you will flog in your synagogues and pursue from town to town," reflects the inherited guilt of the present generation of leaders on account of their forefathers' crimes (see on Matt 23:31). Although it is unlikely that many prophets were literally crucified before Jesus, Matthew might well feel justified in ascribing crucifixion to the martyrs of the Old Testament because of their solidarity with Jesus (see above).

Although Matthew and Luke disagree about the extent of the crime (Matthew has "all the righteous blood" and Luke "the blood of all the prophets that has been shed") with which the present generation is to be charged (Matt 23:35f/Luke 11:51f), they agree that this generation is to bear a unique quantity of guilt. This is because they regard this period, culminating in the crucifixion of Jesus, as the climax and centerpiece of cosmic history. God who visits the iniquity of the fathers on the children of succeeding generations (Matt 23:31) has stored up his wrath concerning the blood of the Old Testament saints from "Abel" to "Zechariah" for this generation. To reject a prophet is to reject the one who sent him (Matt 10:33, Luke 10:16) and the sender is Jesus himself (Matt 23:34); therefore those who killed the prophets were in effect guilty of crucifying Jesus *in advance*. Moreover, the sin of this generation is greater than that of previous generations, because those had rejected Jesus only by proxy, while this generation is in the process of rejecting Jesus in person. This generation has had the greatest opportunity to repent and yet has not done so. If to reject a prophet is to reject the one who sent him, to reject the sender is also to reject those whom he has sent. So those who reject Jesus are also guilty of rejecting all the prophets and messengers whom he has sent throughout history. Thus the generation that rejects Jesus will also have "all innocent blood" taken into consideration.

Friendly Pharisees advise Jesus to flee from Herod

> At that time some Pharisees came to Jesus and said to him, "Leave this place and go somewhere else. Herod wants to kill you." (Luke 13:31)

The gospels do not always present incidents in strict chronological order. It is possible, therefore, that this episode happened before Jesus' tirade against the Pharisees in Luke 11/Matt 23. If it took place after that, as its Lucan setting suggests, it may seem remarkable that anyone in the Pharisee movement was still sufficiently well disposed towards Jesus to wish to help him.

As in previously discussed passages, these Pharisees were probably members of the deputation keeping Jesus under surveillance. Although the deputation often seems hostile to Jesus, it must not be forgotten that on three occasions members invited Jesus to dinner and they would certainly have been more hostile towards Herod Antipas than to Jesus. Perhaps, therefore, it was not so much a desire to protect Jesus as to frustrate Antipas whom they loathed that led them to risk their own safety by warning Jesus in this way. The Pharisee movement was vehemently anti-Rome and would have regarded Antipas, a puppet ruler kept in power by Rome, as a traitor. Moreover, his Jewish orthodoxy was suspect and the licentiousness of the whole Herod dynasty, especially in its tortuous marriages, made it a prime target of Pharisaic zeal for the Torah. Anyone whom Antipas wanted to kill would have been deemed worthy of Pharisaic support. Nolland's suggestion that these Pharisees wanted Jesus "out of their hair"[51] therefore seems unlikely.

Luke gives no hint of the reason for Antipas' murderous intentions. Presumably Antipas regarded Jesus as posing some kind of threat. He had heard the widespread rumors that Jesus was John the Baptist, whom he had had beheaded, returned from the dead (Luke 9:7). According to some sources he dismissed this suggestion (Luke 9:9), while others claim that he believed it (Matt 14:2). Perhaps Antipas feared that Jesus, whose supernatural powers were delighting the crowds, would seek him out and exact

---

51. Nolland, *Luke*, 2:740.

terrible revenge on behalf of John. To forestall this he decided to have him eliminated first.

Jesus challenges Pharisees about the Sabbath

> One Sabbath, when Jesus went to eat in the house of a prominent Pharisee, he was being carefully watched. There in front of him was a man suffering from dropsy. Jesus asked the Pharisees and experts in the law [*nomikois*], "Is it lawful to heal on the Sabbath or not?"
> But they remained silent. So taking hold of the man, he healed him and sent him away. Then he asked them, "If one of you has a son or an ox that falls into a well on the Sabbath day, will you not immediately pull him out?"
> And they had nothing to say. (Luke 14:1–6)

This third occasion[52] on which Luke records Jesus as dining in the home of a Pharisee has many parallels with the first. Luke's insistence that Jesus "was being carefully watched" suggests that not only did this occasion form part of the official surveillance, but also that the surveillance had now intensified, as though Jesus had now been identified as constituting a greater threat than was formerly believed. Luke's description of the host as "a prominent Pharisee" (*tinos tōn archontōn Pharisaiōn*) may imply that he was a member of the Sanhedrin. Since the setting is Galilee, however, the host and the several "Pharisees and experts in the law" mentioned in verse 3 were probably members of the delegation from the Sanhedrin observing Jesus and the house therefore temporarily occupied by the host rather than forming his permanent home. The other officials among the guests would serve as witnesses if Jesus committed any offense.

As in the first such dinner, the delegation chose to confront Jesus with a "challenging" individual to see how he would react. It is hard to imagine that a man suffering from edema had just wandered in off the street or that he was an invited guest at the dinner. Surely this was a trap; the Pharisees had admitted the sick man to the house especially to discover whether Jesus would heal him on the Sabbath. According to Luke, Jesus challenged the officials present concerning the legality of such healing and, as they remained silent, he proceeded to perform it. It is possible that the *nomikoi*, or some of them, were Sadducees; there is evidence that it was Sadducees rather

---

52. The others are Luke 7:36 and 11:37.

Hypocrites or Heroes?

than Pharisees with whom Jesus debated the legality of healing on the Sabbath—see *Sabbath breaking*, p. 197.

Pharisees and teachers of the law complain about Jesus befriending sinners

> Now the tax collectors and "sinners" were all gathering round to hear him. But the Pharisees and the teachers of the law [*grammateis*] muttered, "This man welcomes sinners, and eats with them." (Luke 15:1f)

Presumably these Pharisees are the delegation observing Jesus. They noticed that his teaching attracted tax collectors and "sinners." Indeed, these constituted Jesus' primary target in this later phase of his ministry. There is a partial parallel in the people's reaction, "The Son of Man came eating and drinking, and they say, 'Here is a glutton and a drunkard, a friend of tax collectors and "sinners".'"[53] Perhaps a closer parallel is the Pharisees' criticism of Jesus attendance at Matthew's feast (Matt 9:10–13 and parallels)—see *Dining with tax collectors and "sinners"*, p. 20. for a discussion of the issues raised here.

If Luke 15:1f serves as an introduction to the following sequence of three parables about the lost—the Lost Sheep (Luke 15:3–7), the Lost Coin (Luke 15:8–10), and the Lost (Prodigal) Son (Luke 15:11–32)—the "lost" (parts of the verb *apollumi* are used throughout) may be a technical term for the "sinners." Although the Pharisees are not mentioned explicitly in any of those three parables, they are certainly the reason for their telling. All depict God's joy when an errant sinner returns to the fold. Moreover, the Prodigal Son contrasts this with the elder son's displeasure at his brother's homecoming, clearly representing the self-righteousness of the Pharisees (Luke 15:28f). For a more detailed consideration of the Prodigal Son see *The Pharisees in the parables of Jesus*, p. 188.

Pharisees sneer at Jesus

> The Pharisees, who loved money, heard all this and were sneering at Jesus. (Luke 16:14)

---

53. Matt 11:19; Luke 7:34, Luke 15:2.

This incident follows Jesus' saying "You cannot serve both God and Money" (Luke 16:13). To say that Pharisees "loved money" sounds like a sweeping generalization. Although there was a popular belief among first-century Jews that wealth was evidence of God's blessing while poverty indicated divine disfavor, it is unthinkable that the Pharisees promoted such a belief. Not all Pharisees were rich: some of their greatest teachers earned their living with their hands, Hillel being a carpenter and Shammai a tree feller. Nolland explains this saying as influenced by the circumstances of Luke's own community: "we should not caricature the Pharisees . . . as more inclined to be lovers of money than any other group who benefit from some existing status quo. The Pharisees are chosen only because of Luke's need to explain ongoing Pharisaic hostility to the Christian movement in his own context of concern."[54] Another possibility is that this passage originally read "Sadducees" and this has been amended to "Pharisees"—see *Sabbath breaking*, p. 197 for further on this. The Sadducees were mostly wealthy and "sneering" is certainly more typical of the boorish attitude attributed to them.

Pharisees ask about the kingdom of God

> Once, having been asked by the Pharisees when the kingdom of God would come, Jesus replied, "The kingdom of God does not come with your careful observation, nor will people say, 'Here it is,' or 'There it is,' because the kingdom of God is within you." (Luke 17:21f)

There are partial parallels in Jesus' apocalyptic discourse in Matt 24:23 and Mark 13:19, although these mention neither the kingdom nor the Pharisees; the subject there is the *parousia* of Jesus.

The kingdom of God, as noted earlier when considering Matt 23:13, is a concept of considerable importance in Pharisaic thought, referring either to the future reign of God when he will judge the world and abolish all evil or to God's present reign within his servants. The form of the Pharisees' question suggests that they were using the term in the former eschatological sense. Although Jesus appears to dismiss the question as meaningless and suggest that the kingdom should be understood only in the latter sense, that is probably not how Luke intends us to interpret Jesus' reply. After

---

54. Nolland, *Luke*, 2:810.

all, elsewhere in Luke Jesus uses "the kingdom" in what is unmistakably its eschatological sense, for example, Luke 13:28f. Surely Jesus' reply is to be understood in the context of his saying "No-one knows about that day or hour, not even the angels in heaven, nor the Son, but only the Father" (Mark 13:32 and parallels). What Jesus is saying in Luke 17:21f may be paraphrased, "Don't try to work out when it will come, because you will never succeed. Instead, concentrate upon bringing about God's kingdom on earth through faithfully doing God's will, which is the same as having God's kingdom inside you."

The Parable of the Pharisee and the tax collector

> "Two men went up to the temple to pray, one a Pharisee and the other a tax collector. The Pharisee stood up and prayed about himself: 'God, I thank you that I am not like other men—robbers, evildoers, adulterers—or even like this tax collector. I fast twice a week and give a tenth of all I get.' But the tax collector stood at a distance. He would not even look up to heaven, but beat his breast and said, 'God, have mercy on me, a sinner.' I tell you that this man, rather than the other, went home justified before God. For everyone who exalts himself will be humbled, and he who humbles himself will be exalted." (Luke 18:10-14)

This pronouncement parable explaining the memorable saying in verse 14 is peculiar to Luke. Jesus told it to "some who were confident of their own righteousness and looked down on everybody else," presumably meaning the Pharisees themselves. Its purpose is to highlight the contrast between the archetypal Pharisee as a person whom first-century Jewish culture considered worthy of emulation and the archetypal tax collector. Tax collectors, as explained in connection with Matthew/Levi's feast—see *Dining with tax collectors and "sinners"*, p. 20—were pariahs, regarded as traitors because they worked ultimately for either Herod or the Romans. They were also considered thieves because the vague and scarcely enforced rules concerning tolls and taxes encouraged them to line their pockets by overtaxing the public.

This parable would have shocked its hearers through its reversal of the fortunes of these two archetypes: it presents the Pharisee as obsessed with himself and his exemplary piety and the tax collector as a penitent, aware of his faults, and seeking God's forgiveness and restoration to the community.

Of the two, only the tax collector "went home justified before God." The Greek word rendered "justified" is *dedikaiōmenos*, which literally means "having been made righteous." Contrary to popular belief, it was he and not the Pharisee who was "right with God."

Although the Pharisee in the story is a fictitious character, the parable would not have delivered its intended impact unless he were typical of the *genre*; he needed to be a credible type that hearers would instantly recognize. On this basis, then, we may confidently conclude that Pharisees were typically law-abiding (not robbers, evildoers or adulterers), they fasted twice per week (although in the Torah the annual Day of Atonement is the only obligatory fast) and gave a tenth of their income to charity. This is one of the most complete and trustworthy descriptions of Pharisee behavior in the documentation of the period. Of course, this conduct *per se* is exemplary and Jesus is not condemning it. What he condemns is self-congratulation ("I am not like other men . . . or even like this tax collector") and the belief that through good conduct alone it is possible to please God.

What Jesus commends, by implication, is complete self-effacement, ultimately the recognition that *nothing* humanity can do will please God and therefore the only appropriate approach to God is that of the tax collector in the parable: "God, have mercy on me, a sinner." Ironically, this remains true even when one's conduct is outwardly as respectable as that of the Pharisee in the parable. As the parable concludes, "he who humbles himself will be exalted."

Of course, not every Pharisee was as self-righteous as the one in the Parable, nor was every tax collector a penitent. But these must have been a familiar trend in order for the parable to be credible.

The chief priests and the teachers of the law plot to arrest and kill Jesus

> Now the Passover and the Feast of Unleavened Bread were only two days away, and the chief priests and the teachers of the law [*grammateis*] were looking for some sly way to arrest Jesus and kill him. (Mark 14:1)
>
> Every day he was teaching at the temple. But the chief priests, the teachers of the law [*grammateis*] and the leaders among the people were trying to kill him. (Luke 19:47)

> and the chief priests and the teachers of the law [*grammateis*] were looking for some way to get rid of Jesus, for they were afraid of the people. (Luke 22:2)

There are also parallels in Matt 26:3f and John 11:53, but these do not mention Pharisees or teachers of the law. Only Mark uses the verb *apokteinō* which definitely means "kill"; in both Lucan passages the verb is *apollumi*, which can mean "kill," but also has less drastic meanings. It is significant that the conspirators are consistently described as "the chief priests and the teachers of the law [*grammateis*]," although the additional mention of "the leaders among the people" in Luke 19:47 makes that a possible reference to the Sanhedrin. The absence of any clear reference to the Pharisees suggests that this was a priestly initiative, in which Pharisees were not involved, the *grammateis* being the priests' administrative assistants or legal advisers. For further see *The plots against Jesus,* p. 148.

Clearly Jesus was perceived as constituting such a threat to the Jewish leaders as to leave them with no alternative but to get rid of him. They probably considered Jesus to be a political figure who might motivate his considerable following to rise in revolt against Rome. The ensuing political upheaval would almost certainly remove Israel's leaders from office since they depended upon Roman patronage; they were seeking to defend a precarious *status quo*. In view of Jesus' popularity, however, public arrest was not an option, for this itself might incite the crowds into the rebellion that they so feared. So the arrest must be in what Mark calls some "some sly way" (*dolō*). Accordingly they decided to arrest Jesus when he was alone or nearly so and to hand him over to the Roman authorities as a known insurgent against Rome; insurrection carried a mandatory death penalty.

Judas brings a crowd to arrest Jesus in Gethsemane

> Just as he was speaking, Judas, one of the Twelve, appeared. With him was a crowd armed with swords and clubs, sent from the chief priests, the teachers of the law [*grammateōn*], and the elders. (Mark 14:43)
> So Judas came to the grove, guiding a detachment of soldiers and some officials from the chief priests and Pharisees. They were carrying torches, lanterns, and weapons. (John 18:3)

The Pharisees in the New Testament

This is part of the account of Jesus' arrest in Gethsemane. Only Mark mentions that *grammateis* were involved in the sending of the armed band to arrest him (see the previous section) and only John mentions Pharisees, but both are probably references to the Sanhedrin. There is no suggestion that Pharisees or Pharisaic teachers of the law took part in the arrest itself. The previous passage suggested that the initiative was priestly rather than involving the whole Sanhedrin and the next passage in which Jesus is taken to the high priest's house confirms this.

Jesus is brought to the Sanhedrin

> Those who had arrested Jesus took him to Caiaphas, the high priest, where the teachers of the law [*grammateis*] and the elders had assembled. (Matt 26:57)
> They took Jesus to the high priest, and all the chief priests, elders, and teachers of the law [*grammateis*] came together. (Mark 14:53)
> At daybreak the council of the elders of the people, both the chief priests and teachers of the law [*grammateis*], met together, and Jesus was led before them. (Luke 22:66)

It is significant that none of these three parallels mentions the Sanhedrin by name, although Mark refers to its three constituent bodies: the chief priests, elders, and teachers of the law, while Matthew and Luke each name a different pair of those constituents. Indeed Matthew and Mark later mention "the whole Sanhedrin" (Matt 26:59; Mark 14:55), thereby giving the impression that this was an assembly of the full Sanhedrin in the high priest's house. Its purpose was not only to interview Jesus, but also to devise a story that would guarantee Roman co-operation.

There is, however, considerable evidence that this was not a meeting of the full Sanhedrin; if it was, in several respects it was sitting illegally. It is more likely to have been a less formal pre-hearing procedure. That this meeting took place in Caiaphas' house instead of a regular courtroom supports this view. The Sanhedrin was normally dominated by Pharisees, but in this setting those present were probably priests and a few other officials; the *grammateis* may not have been the regular teachers of the law who were mostly Pharisees, but administrative or legal assistants to the priests. There is further evidence (see *Jesus' trial and passion: the unexpected twist in the tale,* p. 193) that the Pharisees withdrew their support from the plot

Hypocrites or Heroes?

to have Jesus executed and were not involved in any of the preceding legal proceedings.

Jesus is handed over to Pilate

> Very early in the morning, the chief priests, with the elders, the teachers of the law [*grammateōn*] and the whole Sanhedrin, reached a decision. They bound Jesus, led him away, and turned him over to Pilate. (Mark 15:1)

The parallels in Matt 27:1 and Luke 23:1 do not mention teachers of the law, although they are mentioned in Luke 23:10, see below. Mark makes it sound as though the Sanhedrin was unanimous in its decision, but (see on the above passage) almost certainly this was a preliminary hearing rather than a meeting of the full Sanhedrin. It is difficult to believe that Nicodemus or Joseph of Arimathea would have supported this course of action.

The trial before Pilate

> The chief priests and the teachers of the law [*grammateis*] were standing there, vehemently accusing him. (Luke 23:10)

There is a parallel in Matt 27:12, but this does not mention the teachers of the law. In the Matthean and Marcan accounts of this trial the chief priests are the Jewish protagonists most frequently mentioned. Probably the *grammateis* mentioned here were not regular (Pharisaic) teachers of the law, but administrative or legal assistants to the chief priests.

On the cross Jesus is mocked

> In the same way the chief priests, the teachers of the law [*grammateōn*], and the elders mocked him. (Matt 27:41)
>
> In the same way the chief priests and the teachers of the law [*grammateōn*] mocked him among themselves. "He saved others," they said, "but he can't save himself!" (Mark 15:31)

The crucifixion took place beside a busy main road, as was the custom, the intention being that these macabre executions should deter would-be criminals. Members of the public, therefore, had an opportunity to mock victims of crucifixion and this was probably encouraged, as it added to the victims' discomfort. As the *grammateōn* mentioned here were with the chief priests they were probably their assistants (see above), who either happened to be passing that way or whose duties required their attendance on such occasions.

The Pharisees and chief priests approach Pilate

> The next day, the one after Preparation Day, the chief priests and the Pharisees went to Pilate. (Matt 27:62)

This detail, peculiar to Matthew, is unusual in showing the Pharisees acting in concert with the chief priests who were Sadducees. Their mutual concern is that Jesus' disciples might steal his body from the tomb and hide it, then claiming that he had risen from the dead on the third day as he had predicted. Accordingly they request a guard for the tomb, which Pilate grants. It is possible that "the chief priests and the Pharisees" means a deputation from the Sanhedrin and that Pharisees were not involved, as throughout the arrest, interrogation and crucifixion of Jesus.

JOHN

Nicodemus visits Jesus

> Now there was a man of the Pharisees named Nicodemus, a member of the Jewish ruling council. He came to Jesus at night and said, "Rabbi, we know you are a teacher who has come from God. For no-one could perform the miraculous signs you are doing if God were not with him." (John 3:1f)

John describes Nicodemus as a Pharisee and a "member of the Jewish ruling council," by which presumably he means the Sanhedrin. Later Jesus addresses him as "Israel's teacher" (John 3:10). He is also mentioned in John 7:50 as participating in a meeting of Pharisees (the Sanhedrin?) and in John 19:39 where he and Joseph of Arimathea anoint the body of Jesus.

Hypocrites or Heroes?

John gives no indication of where this meeting took place; Nicodemus' status makes it more likely to be in Jerusalem than in Galilee.

Clearly Nicodemus was an important personage. That he made his visit to Jesus "at night" was presumably to minimize the risk that he, a respected teacher of Israel, be seen to consult Jesus, the upstart preacher from despised Galilee. The incident tells us little about the Pharisees apart from the fact that there was at least one who was sympathetic towards Jesus and sufficiently open-minded to meet with him for a serious discussion, although even he took precautions to protect his reputation. The two later references to him in John confirm this view.

The Pharisees hear about Jesus' ministry overtaking that of the Baptist

> The Pharisees heard that Jesus was gaining and baptizing more disciples than John, although in fact it was not Jesus who baptized, but his disciples. When the Lord learned of this, he left Judea and went back once more to Galilee. (John 4:1–3)

Taken out of context, the first part of verse 1 seems to serve no purpose: why does John tell us that "The Pharisees heard that..." when he does not mention Pharisees by name again until 7:32? G. R. Beasley-Murray is surely right in claiming[55] that the intention is to explain verse 3: it was fear that opposition from the Pharisees would put a premature end to his ministry that led Jesus to leave Judea and return to Galilee.

From this seemingly insignificant passage three intriguing facts emerge. Firstly, here is confirmation that the Pharisees were taking a keen interest in Jesus, as they had in John the Baptist—see *Pharisees and Sadducees visit John the Baptist*, p. 14. As John mentions their interest in Jesus several times;[56] he must have regarded this as an important aspect of Jesus' ministry, as the synoptists had done. It is no exaggeration to state that they had Jesus under surveillance. Saldarini describes the Pharisees as having a "supervisory role" in Jewish society,[57] which would require them to keep abreast of social and religious developments.

---

55. Beasley-Murray, *John*, 59.
56. For example, in John 4:1; 7:32; 9:13; 11:46, and 12:19.
57. Saldarini, *Pharisees*, 189.

Secondly, it is surely significant that Jesus, who had spent most of his life in Galilee and therefore must have been familiar with its religious *milieu*, expected to escape the attention of the Pharisees by returning there. Clearly he assumed that there would be fewer Pharisees there than in Judea, and perhaps none at all. This is why it seems likely that Jesus' many encounters with Pharisees in Galilee recorded in the synoptic gospels[58] were mostly if not exclusively with members of the delegation sent from Jerusalem by the Sanhedrin especially to monitor his activities.

Thirdly, this is the first of several passages[59] in John's Gospel which reveal "inside knowledge" of the proceedings of an influential committee of Pharisees. In this passage he reports what the Pharisees had heard about Jesus. Moreover, these are not details that came to light long after the events concerned. Jesus "learned" (John 4:3) about the Pharisees' intentions soon enough to take evasive action, perhaps within an hour of their formulation; the evangelist's source may even have rushed from the meeting to Jesus in order to warn him. That Jesus at once returned to Galilee suggests that whatever action against him the Pharisees intended must have been dire: arrest, perhaps, although it is hard to see on what grounds.

Although John never identifies the body whose meetings he reports, there is compelling evidence in some of the accounts—especially that in John 9—that it was the Sanhedrin itself rather than some other committee. It was probably easier to "eavesdrop" on the Sanhedrin than a closed committee. The only source of the proceedings of a committee that met behind locked doors would be one of the committee members, whereas the Sanhedrin met in one of several courtrooms. It is likely, then, that the Sanhedrin's proceedings were open to the public.

So there is no need for John's Sanhedrin informant to be Nicodemus or some other sympathetic high-ranking Pharisee. Any of Jesus' regular disciples might have attended those meetings as a spectator, although it remains possible that the informant was indeed a member of the Sanhedrin. One possible candidate is the "disciple . . . known to the high priest" mentioned in John 18:15 who had sufficient influence to secure Peter's admission to Jesus' hearing. If this disciple were also the evangelist, this would explain the gospel's vivid, eyewitness-style accounts of these council meetings in which we seem to hear the actual words spoken. It would also explain one of the striking differences between John's Gospel and the

---

58. For example, Luke 5:17–21; Mark 3:22; Matt 15:1f/Mark 7:1–5.
59. For example, in John 4:1–3; 7:32, 45–53; 9:13–34, and 11:46–51.

Hypocrites or Heroes?

Synoptics, namely, the proportion of his ministry that Jesus spends in Jerusalem: the synoptics record only one visit to Jerusalem which lasted about a week and culminated in the crucifixion, while John records at least three such visits, the final one lasting six months.[60] This greater concentration on Jerusalem is to be expected of a Jerusalem-based evangelist. Attempts to identify this Jerusalem-based disciple who had access to the Sanhedrin and the high priest have failed. Of course, it is difficult to reconcile such an evangelist with the tradition that the Fourth Gospel was written by John, son of Zebedee, the fisherman from Capernaum.

The chief priests and Pharisees attempt to arrest Jesus

> The Pharisees heard the crowd whispering such things about him. Then the chief priests and the Pharisees sent temple guards to arrest him. . . .
>
> Finally the temple guards went back to the chief priests and Pharisees, who asked them, "Why didn't you bring him in?"
>
> "No-one ever spoke the way this man does," the guards declared.
>
> "You mean he has deceived you also?" the Pharisees retorted. "Has any of the rulers or of the Pharisees believed in him? No! But this mob that knows nothing of the law—there is a curse on them."
>
> Nicodemus, who had gone to Jesus earlier and who was one of their own number, asked, "Does our law condemn a man without first hearing him to find out what he is doing?"
>
> They replied, "Are you from Galilee, too? Look into it, and you will find that a prophet does not come out of Galilee." Then each went to his own home. (John 7:32, 45–53)

The reference to the chief priests and the Pharisees in verses 32 and 45 suggests that this was a meeting of the Sanhedrin, as elsewhere the two groups tended to avoid contact with each other. This, then, is another example of the evangelist's "inside knowledge" of the proceedings of the Sanhedrin (see on John 4:1–3).

This incident is curious for several reasons. According to verse 31, "Still, many in the crowd put their faith in him. They said, 'When the Christ comes, will he do more miraculous signs than this man?'" Whatever the crowd believed Jesus to be, apparently it was not Messiah; verse 52 suggests

---

60. Kummel, *Introduction*, 142.

that it regarded him as a prophet. When this came to the attention of the Pharisees, the Sanhedrin decided to arrest Jesus. But on what grounds? It was not a crime to be a prophet nor, for that matter, Messiah. Even if it were, Jesus himself, so far as we are told, had made no claim to be either; it was the crowd's perception of him that sparked the threatened arrest.[61]

There are two possible explanations. Firstly, the chief priests are named first as the instigators of the attempted arrest and the deployment of the temple guard also suggests a priestly rather than a Pharisaic initiative. The chief priests were fiercely pro-Roman and had a vested interest in maintaining the *status quo*. Messianic expectations were running high; it was widely believed that the Messiah would lead a successful insurrection against the Roman occupation.[62] In these circumstances the chief priests may have considered even the crowds' acclamation of Jesus as a prophet sufficient reason for a pre-emptive strike. They, like Pontius Pilate himself, were concerned to quell even mild unrest among the Jewish populace, for fear that it might escalate into full-blown insurrection. Precisely what they would have done with Jesus had the arrest succeeded is uncertain, but the chief priests may have regarded the removal of the "irritant" that was agitating the people as justifiable in the tense circumstances.

Secondly, there may have been an element of jealousy on the part of both chief priests and Pharisees. Jesus' preaching was critical of the religious authorities; that he was attracting more attention than those authorities may have been perceived as a threat to national security. There is delightful irony in the temple guards' empty-handed return, having apparently fallen under Jesus' spell themselves.

Since it seems that the action against Jesus in this passage was instigated by the Sadducee chief priests rather than the Pharisees, the latter can be largely exonerated. Even the attitude to the uneducated crowd which

---

61. According to John's Gospel some pious Jews were expecting the advent of a person described as the Prophet (John 1:21, 25; 6:14; 7:40). From John 1:19-26 it seems that this Prophet was distinct from both the Messiah and Elijah whose return was expected to herald the Messiah. Perhaps in popular piety the Prophet and the Messiah were sometimes confused, so that confession of Jesus as the Prophet (or even *a* prophet) was regarded as equivalent to confessing him as Messiah. Since legislation was in force to excommunicate any Jew who confessed Jesus as Messiah (John 9:22; 12:42f), almost any confession concerning Jesus might incur dire consequences and it is only to be expected that severe confusion sometimes resulted from the actions and sayings of a religiously excited crowd.

62. This is reflected, for example, in the disciples' question in Acts 1:6: "Lord, are you at this time going to restore the kingdom to Israel?"

Hypocrites or Heroes?

this passage attributes to Pharisees, "there is a curse on them," is untypical of Pharisaism which saw itself in an educative role; indeed it is more typical of the Sadducees whose boorish attitude to all and sundry is attested in Josephus.[63] Indeed, this passage could provide evidence of editing that changed "Sadducees" or "the chief priests" in several places to "Pharisees." There is a textual variant in verse 32 that changes the first instance of "The Pharisees" to "The Chief Priests" and omits the second. For further see *Sabbath breaking*, p. 197. If Nicodemus is typical of the Pharisees, his insistence that no-one should be condemned without a fair trial is reassuring.

The woman caught in the act of adultery

> At dawn he appeared again in the temple courts, where all the people gathered round him, and he sat down to teach them. The teachers of the law [*grammateis*] and the Pharisees brought in a woman caught in adultery. They made her stand before the group and said to Jesus, "Teacher, this woman was caught in the act of adultery. In the Law Moses commanded us to stone such women. Now what do you say?"
>
> They were using this question as a trap, in order to have a basis for accusing him. But Jesus bent down and started to write on the ground with his finger. When they kept on questioning him, he straightened up and said to them, "If any one of you is without sin, let him be the first to throw a stone at her." Again he stooped down and wrote on the ground.
>
> At this, those who heard began to go away one at a time, the older ones first, until only Jesus was left, with the woman still standing there. Jesus straightened up and asked her, "Woman, where are they? Has no-one condemned you?"
>
> "No-one, sir," she said.
>
> "Then neither do I condemn you," Jesus declared. "Go now and leave your life of sin." (John 8:2–11)

This passage's place in John's Gospel has long been questioned. So closely does it resemble the accounts in the synoptic gospels of the challenges put to Jesus in the temple by various religious groups during the final week of his ministry that it surely belongs amongst them. On this occasion the approach is by the "teachers of the law [*grammateis*] and the Pharisees."

---

63. Josephus, *War*, 2:8:14.

That this is the only occurrence in John's Gospel of *grammateus* is further evidence that the pericope is out of place.

The author acknowledges in verse 6 that the question put to Jesus is a trap. In fact, in its cunning it resembles that concerning taxes to Caesar (Mark 12:13-17 and parallels). The Mosaic law did indeed prescribe the death penalty for adulterers (Lev 20:10). So, if Jesus advocated sparing the woman, the religious authorities could accuse him of teaching contrary to Torah. But, as the Romans had abolished Jewish death penalties, if Jesus approved her execution he could be reported to them for incitement to break their law. Thus to answer the question either way would lay Jesus open to accusation, which presumably is why he gave no reply at first and then made a statement that was calculated to silence his questioners.

That statement, "If any one of you is without sin, let him be the first to throw a stone at her," is subtle. The one-by-one departure of the accusers (as their consciences pricked them, according to some manuscripts) need not mean that they had committed similar offenses, but that they had been reminded of their own failure to correctly apply the law in which they were supposed to be experts. The Mosaic law concerning adultery reads, "If a man commits adultery with another man's wife—with the wife of his neighbor—*both the adulterer and the adulteress must be put to death*" (Lev 20:10). Are these words—or perhaps just the italicized ones—what Jesus so enigmatically wrote on the ground in order to shame the woman's accusers? According to their own testimony in verse 4, the woman had been "caught in the act of adultery." If so, the adulterer must have been present too; why then had he not been apprehended and brought before Jesus as well? Standard practice, when not suspended by the Romans, was to stone both guilty parties to death at the same time. But the Pharisees and teachers of the law had effectively absolved the man, leaving the woman to face the charge alone. Presumably it was the realization on the part of the supposed experts in the law that they had committed this miscarriage of justice that pricked their consciences, leading them to steal away as discreetly as possible.

Another possibility is that no adultery had been committed at all: the accusation was a ruse, the woman simply acting out a role. After all, it is surely too remarkable a coincidence that a couple should be caught *in flagrante delicto* nearby at the precise moment that the Pharisees had concocted this trick question for Jesus, to which in theory any answer would provide grounds for arrest. Jesus' reply showed that he had seen through the façade and was aware that the accusation was untrue and the situation a trap. It was the custom for the witnesses to adultery to throw the first stones; if there had been no crime, there could be no witnesses and therefore no one qualified to cast a stone. Jesus' final admonition to the woman, "leave your life of sin," need not imply that she had committed adultery; even if she had been acting a role, she was still guilty of attempted deception.

Either interpretation shows the Pharisees in a poor light. Here they are acting almost as *agents provocateurs* in their effort to find grounds for a charge against Jesus. Or might this be another passage where "Sadducees" has been amended to "Pharisees" (see on the previous item). The setting in the Temple makes the presence of Sadducees likely.

Pharisees challenge the validity of Jesus' testimony

> The Pharisees challenged him, "Here you are, appearing as your own witness; your testimony is not valid." (John 8:13)

The setting is not specified. The last-mentioned location is the temple courts in verse 2, but as that falls in the disputed pericope concerning the woman caught in adultery (see above), it would be unsafe to conclude that this debate also took place there. Nevertheless, it was a place where Jesus was able to address the people (verse 12) and where Pharisees could challenge him, so it could have been in the temple courts. Jesus had just proclaimed, "I am the light of the world. Whoever follows me will never walk in darkness, but will have the light of life." This claim to enhance life by providing guidance was not in itself controversial.

The point at issue is typical of Pharisaic debate. Jewish law stated that a single witness' testimony was admissible only if corroborated by at least one other witness (Num 35:30; Deut 19:15). Originally this ruling was intended to prevent execution on the evidence of a single witness, but the principle had subsequently been extended to all criminal cases, where it was arguably sensible, and even to theological debate, where its suitability was questionable. In Jewish society there was, of course, no distinction between sacred and secular; all aspects of life were subject to one and the same law and therefore the Pharisees were making what they considered to be a valid challenge inasmuch as Jesus had no corroborating witness to support his testimony.

The man blind from birth

> They brought to the Pharisees the man who had been blind. Now the day on which Jesus had made the mud and opened the man's eyes was a Sabbath. Therefore the Pharisees also asked him how he had received his sight. "He put mud on my eyes," the man replied, "and I washed, and now I see."
> Some of the Pharisees said, "This man is not from God, for he does not keep the Sabbath."
> But others asked, "How can a sinner do such miraculous signs?" So they were divided. . . .
> Some Pharisees who were with him heard him say this and asked, "What? Are we blind too?" (John 9:13-16, 40)

The story of the man blind from birth occupies the whole of John 9 and is a key episode in John's Gospel, dramatically contrasting Jesus' compassion for the needy—represented by his healing of the man blind from birth—with the Pharisees' misplaced priorities—demonstrated in their insistence that any worth in the healing was abrogated by its performance on the Sabbath. John includes in this narrative (in verses 13–34) another vivid account of the proceedings of the Sanhedrin (see above on John 4:1–3), which usefully demonstrates that he sometimes uses the term "the Pharisees" to denote the Sanhedrin, perhaps because he considered that the Pharisees dominated it. Incidentally, "the Jews" in verses 18 and 22 clearly refers to the Pharisees mentioned in verses 15 and 16, showing that John sometimes uses this term as a synonym for "the Pharisees."

An interesting point is that in verses 16 and 24 Pharisees describe Jesus as a "sinner" (*hamartōlos*) because his healing of the blind man profaned the Sabbath; for this reason, they conclude, he cannot be from God. As will be seen—in *Those "put out of the synagogue"—the "sinners,"* p. 155—there is evidence that "sinner" was used as a technical designation for a Jew who had been excommunicated as the penalty for some crime. Is verse 16 therefore a pronouncement that Jesus has been excommunicated? We shall return to that possibility shortly.

The term "threw out" (*exebalon . . . exō*) in verses 34 and 35 is ambiguous. Does John intend this term literally, meaning that the Pharisees violently ejected the man from their presence? Or is this figurative language, meaning that they excommunicated him from the synagogue? Although the presence of *exō* might favor the former, John has recently mentioned excommunication; verse 22 states that "the Jews had decided that anyone who acknowledged that Jesus was the Christ would be put out of the synagogue (*aposunagōgos genētai*)." (This legislation is attributed to the Pharisees in John 12:42, but by "Pharisees" John may mean the Sanhedrin—see on John 11:45–47 below.) Although, so far as we know, this man had confessed Jesus only as a prophet (verse 17), that may have been sufficient grounds for legal action, as it appears to have been when the Sanhedrin regarded the crowd's acclamation of Jesus as a prophet as sufficient reason for Jesus' arrest—see *The chief priests and Pharisees attempt to arrest Jesus*, p. 74. Moreover, the Pharisees' words in verse 34 sound more like an execration than a regular dismissal.

A further point arises from this: since the Pharisees had made confession of Jesus as Messiah grounds for excommunication from the synagogue, they could hardly allow Jesus himself to remain a Jew in good standing. Presumably, then, Jesus himself had been "put out of the synagogue"—for further details see *Jesus' expulsion from Pharisaism*, p. 181. This may explain the Pharisees' declaration in verse 24, "We know this man is a sinner"; it was the announcement that Jesus was now officially excluded from their Jewish/Pharisee community.

Stephen Motyer makes an interesting observation concerning the Pharisees mentioned in verse 40:

> These Pharisees do not understand 9:39 to refer to literal sight (as undoubtedly they would, if they were total unbelievers); and suddenly we realise, that, from a narrative perspective, they have accompanied Jesus while he has searched out a man just expelled from the synagogue, and have watched without murmur while the man has worshipped him. *These Pharisees are the 'others' of 9:16b*, who are open to the possibility that Jesus may not be a sinner, and are now 'with him'—a phrase which elsewhere denotes at least uinterested association, and usually discipleship . . .[64]

The text of 9:40 clearly states that these Pharisees were in Jesus' company at the time and it is certainly possible that they had accompanied him on his search for the man born blind. But to read "with him" as implying discipleship is perhaps a little optimistic, especially in the light of Jesus' somewhat harsh reply in 9:41.

---

64. Motyer, *Your Father*, 132f.

The Pharisees in the New Testament

The Sanhedrin decides to arrest and kill Jesus

> Therefore many of the Jews who had come to visit Mary, and had seen what Jesus did, put their faith in him. But some of them went to the Pharisees and told them what Jesus had done. Then the chief priests and the Pharisees called a meeting of the Sanhedrin. "What are we accomplishing?" they asked. "Here is this man performing many miraculous signs." . . .
>
> So from that day on they plotted to take his life. . . .
>
> But the chief priests and Pharisees had given orders that if anyone found out where Jesus was, he should report it so that they might arrest him. (John 11:45–47, 53, 57)

This is the sequel to the raising of Lazarus. We are told that "many Jews" had visited Mary, presumably to offer their condolences regarding Lazarus, and that some who witnessed his raising believed in Jesus, while others "went to the Pharisees and told them what Jesus had done." Although there is a distinction here between "Jews" and "the Pharisees," on careful examination it seems most likely that by "Jews" John means "Pharisees," while "the Pharisees" to whom these unbelieving Jews (who were themselves Pharisees) went were, in fact, the Sanhedrin (see above). In support of this, as soon as the Pharisees (meaning the Sanhedrin) had been told (verse 46), "the chief priests and the Pharisees called a meeting of the Sanhedrin" (verse 47). In verses 47–50 we eavesdrop on this meeting (see on John 4:1–3).

In verse 53 we learn for the first time in John about the Sanhedrin plotting to kill Jesus (*ebouleusanto hina apokteinōsin auton*). Since, however, the verse follows a speech by the high priest Caiaphas about the expediency of one man dying for the nation, it is possible that "they" in verse 53 refers only to the chief priests or Sadducees. For a more detailed consideration see *The plots against Jesus*, p. 148. In verse 57 "the chief priests and Pharisees" refers to the Sanhedrin, which had the authority to make the kind of order described. Presumably the grounds on which they proposed to arrest Jesus were idolatry or blasphemy (for example, John 10:33).

Hypocrites or Heroes?

Pharisees reflect on Jesus' success

> So the Pharisees said to one another, "See, this is getting us nowhere. Look how the whole world has gone after him!" (John 12:19)

This is just after Jesus' triumphal entry into Jerusalem. That we learn what the Pharisees were saying to one another in committee suggests that this was the Sanhedrin—John's "spy" has been active again (see on John 4:1–3). If it seems remarkable that the Pharisees were unable to arrest Jesus when he was the center of attention, perhaps the explanation is that such was his popularity that the Sanhedrin was afraid that his public arrest would spark a riot, which it was eager to avoid.

Pharisees threaten to excommunicate believers in Jesus

> Yet at the same time many even among the leaders believed in him. But because of the Pharisees they would not confess their faith for fear they would be put out of the synagogue; for they loved praise from men more than praise from God. (John 12:42f)

John has commented on the general reluctance of people to believe in Jesus (for example, 7:48; 11:46), even after witnessing his miraculous acts. Now, in contrast, he admits that "many even among the leaders" did believe in him. Presumably, by "the leaders" he means members of the Sanhedrin and he may have in mind Nicodemus and possibly the unidentified individual who is his informant concerning the Sanhedrin's proceedings. It was fear of the Pharisees' decree (attributed to "the Jews" in John 9:22) that "anyone who acknowledged that Jesus was the Christ would be put out of the synagogue" that forced these believers to keep their faith in Jesus secret. Being excommunicated would, of course, have cost them far more than their seats in the Sanhedrin—they would have become outcasts, as described later in *Those "put out of the synagogue"—the "sinners,"* p. 155. John comments that "they loved praise (*doxan*) from men more than praise (*doxan*) from God." *doxa* here might be more aptly rendered "respect" or "approval." Jesus makes a similar accusation in Matt 23:5–7.

ACTS

A meeting of the Sanhedrin

> The next day the rulers, elders and teachers of the law [*grammateis*] met in Jerusalem. (Acts 4:5)

This appears to be a meeting of the Sanhedrin, although "the rulers" seems to have replaced "the chief priests." The next verse, however, confirms the presence of Caiaphas (the chief priest), Annas and "other men of the high priest's family."

Gamaliel speaks out for Peter and the apostles

> But a Pharisee named Gamaliel, a teacher of the law [*nomodidaskalos*], who was honored by all the people, stood up in the Sanhedrin and ordered that the men be put outside for a little while. (Acts 5:34)

Maccoby devotes much of chapter 1 of *Jesus the Pharisee* to this incident,[65] and with good reason: it ably illustrates the paradoxical nature of the New Testament's portrayal of the Pharisees. Not long previously, according to the gospels, the Pharisees had been plotting Jesus' downfall.[66] Now it seems as though the author of Acts is loath to mention that this Gamaliel who persuades the Sanhedrin to release the apostles charged with preaching in the name of Jesus was in fact the leader of the whole Pharisee movement; he must have been aware of this. While there appears to be an anti-Pharisee bias in the gospels, especially John, Luke mentions a number of incidents not recorded elsewhere in which Pharisees seem kindly disposed towards Jesus.[67] Since Acts 5:36–39 purports to record Gamaliel's address to the Sanhedrin, presumably the author of Acts was present or someone else who was present later told him the content of Gamaliel's speech. For a possible reason for the Sanhedrin's change of attitude regarding Jesus and his apostles, see later under *Jesus' trial and passion: the unexpected twist in the tale*, p. 193.

---

65. Maccoby, *Jesus*, 1.
66. For example, Matt 12:14; Mark 3:6; John 8:40.
67. For example, Luke 7:36; 11:37; 13:31; 14:1.

Hypocrites or Heroes?

Synagogue leaders incite hatred against the apostles

> So they stirred up the people and the elders and the teachers of the law [*grammateis*]. They seized Stephen and brought him before the Sanhedrin. (Acts 6:12)

The Twelve had appointed seven gifted disciples to take responsibility for their food distribution program; one of these was Stephen who "did great wonders and miraculous signs among the people" (verse 8). This led to opposition from the Synagogue of the Freedmen, which persuaded people to claim that Stephen had committed blasphemy (verse 11). These false witnesses convinced "the elders and the teachers of the law," probably meaning the two non-priestly constituents of the Sanhedrin, to arrest Stephen for trial by the Sanhedrin. Stephen's speech of defense and his death by stoning, which in the light of the Roman ban on Jewish death sentences must have been an illegal lynching, occupies the whole of Acts 7. The marked contrast with the experience of Peter and the other apostles in Acts 5 leads the reader to wonder why Gamaliel did not intervene on this occasion. Perhaps at this time the attitude of the Jewish hierarchy to the Christian movement was in a constant state of flux.

Pharisee Christians demand the circumcision of Gentile converts

> Then some of the believers who belonged to the party of the Pharisees [*tines tōn apo tēs haireseōs tōn Pharisaiōn pepisteukotes*] stood up and said, "The Gentiles must be circumcised and required to obey the law of Moses."
> The apostles and elders met to consider this question. After much discussion, Peter got up and addressed them: "Brothers, you know that some time ago God made a choice among you that the Gentiles might hear from my lips the message of the gospel and believe. God, who knows the heart, showed that he accepted them by giving the Holy Spirit to them, just as he did to us. He made no distinction between us and them, for he purified their hearts by faith. Now then, why do you try to test God by putting on the necks of the disciples a yoke that neither we nor our fathers have been able to bear?" (Acts 15:5–10)

After hearing in John's Gospel about Pharisees like Nicodemus who were sympathetic to Jesus, it is not altogether surprising to learn here about

Pharisees who, having become Christian believers, were now active in the Jerusalem church. The wording, especially "who belonged to the party of the Pharisees," implies that these believers were still recognized as members of the Pharisee movement despite the legislation that excommunicated Christian believers (John 9:22; 12:42). Presumably that legislation had now been rescinded; it would be unthinkable for Pharisees to flout legislation that remained on the statute book.

Peter's response in verse 10 is illuminating, as it confirms that the Christian movement had been founded as an alternative to Pharisaic Judaism: surely it is the multiplicity of commands in the *paradosis* which Peter describes as the "yoke that neither we nor our fathers have been able to bear." Compare Jesus' teaching in Matt 11:28–30[68] and Matt 23:4/Luke 11:46.

It is understandable, however, that the Pharisee Christians' adherence to their Jewish traditions caused problems with Gentile Christian converts. This incident provoked the conference of church leaders that decided that the only requirements for Gentile converts were that they "abstain from food polluted by idols, from sexual immorality, from the meat of strangled animals and from blood" (verse 20).

At Ephesus

> The city clerk [*grammateus*] quietened the crowd and said: "Men of Ephesus, doesn't all the world know that the city of Ephesus is the guardian of the temple of the great Artemis and of her image, which fell from heaven? (Acts 19:35)

This is a secular use of *grammateus* relating to a pagan Gentile and therefore outside the scope of this study.

---

68. Perhaps the striking contrast in the symbolism of *zugos*, "yoke," in Acts 15:10 and Matt 11:29 owes its origin to a popular theme in the preaching of Jesus and the apostles. The use of a yoke to allow two oxen to co-operate in drawing a heavy load would have been familiar throughout the ancient Near East. It is easy to imagine a preacher offering his hearers the choice between the intolerable yoke of Pharisaic legalism and the easy yoke that Jesus offered.

Hypocrites or Heroes?

Paul forces a dispute between the Pharisees and the Sadducees

> Then Paul, knowing that some of them were Sadducees and the others Pharisees, called out in the Sanhedrin, "My brothers, I am a Pharisee, the son of a Pharisee. I stand on trial because of my hope in the resurrection of the dead."
>
> When he said this, a dispute broke out between the Pharisees and the Sadducees, and the assembly was divided. (The Sadducees say that there is no resurrection, and that there are neither angels nor spirits, but the Pharisees acknowledge them all.) There was a great uproar, and some of the teachers of the law [*grammateōn*] who were Pharisees stood up and argued vigorously. "We find nothing wrong with this man," they said. "What if a spirit or an angel has spoken to him?" (Acts 23:6–9)

Paul is the only person in the whole of Jewish literature who claimed that he himself was a Pharisee (see also below on Acts 26:5 and Phil 3:5); Pharisees normally referred to themselves simply as "Jews" and others identified them as "Pharisees" only when referring to officials enforcing the twofold law and when necessary to distinguish them from other groups such as the Sadducees or Essenes. Here Paul was on trial before the Sanhedrin. As a Pharisee himself, familiar with the doctrinal differences between the Pharisees and the Sadducees, he used these to cause such violent disorder amongst the Sanhedrin members that he had to be removed to the Roman barracks for his own protection. It is here that the New Testament gives its clearest description of the doctrinal differences between the two groups.

Paul testifies to his Pharisee origins

> They have known me for a long time and can testify, if they are willing, that according to the strictest sect of our religion, I lived as a Pharisee. (Acts 26:5)

This is part of Paul's defense before Herod Agrippa. He also claims to have been a Pharisee in Phil 3:5 (see below) and to have studied under Gamaliel in Acts 22:3, this presumably being the Gamaliel mentioned in Acts 5, who according to Maccoby[69] was then the leader of the Pharisee

---

69. Maccoby, *Jesus*, 5f.

movement. What is germane to this study is Paul's reference to Pharisaism as "the strictest sect (*hairesin*) of our religion." *hairesis* occurs nine times in the New Testament (six of them in Acts), which in the NIV are all rendered either "sect" or "heresy" depending upon context. The noun is derived from a verb (*haireō*) whose middle voice means "take for oneself, choose" and strictly refers to the matter so chosen. This can be a lifestyle or set of beliefs separate from the norm, hence its application to Pharisaism. Paul's reference to Pharisaism as the *strictest* sect may imply not only the most demanding in terms of observances, but also, in his opinion, the most authentic Judaism, the one which most closely recaptures the intentions of its founder Moses.

1 CORINTHIANS
The folly of wisdom

> Where is the wise man? Where is the scholar [*grammateus*]? Where is the philosopher of this age? Has not God made foolish the wisdom of the world? (1 Cor 1:20)

The NIV's rendering "scholar" is reasonable in this context, but as a Pharisee Paul may well have had the teachers of the law in mind when he wrote this. His point is that all kinds of earthly wisdom are irrelevant in the light of God's self-revelation to humanity in Jesus.

PHILIPPIANS
Reasons for confidence in the flesh

> If anyone else thinks he has reasons to put confidence in the flesh, I have more: circumcised on the eighth day, of the people of Israel, of the tribe of Benjamin, a Hebrew of Hebrews; in regard to the law, a Pharisee; as for zeal, persecuting the church; as for legalistic righteousness, faultless. But whatever was to my profit I now consider loss for the sake of Christ. (Phil 3:4b–7)

Paul is contrasting his former life, now abandoned, with his present life as a follower of Jesus. He claims that by the standards of Jewish culture he "had it all"—born a Jew, a member of the favored tribe of Benjamin, and so far as the law is concerned, a Pharisee and even a persecutor of the Christian community. The passage demonstrates that "in regard to the law" the Pharisees were the acknowledged masters; to be a Pharisee was the highest possible accolade in law-keeping. Paul also claims to have been a Pharisee in his defense before the Sanhedrin (Acts 23:6–9) and Herod Agrippa (Acts 26:5).

As this study will seek to show, Pharisaism was normative Judaism, the branch of Judaism to which ordinary Jews belonged by default. This contrasted with the Essenes and Sadducees, membership of which entailed special initiation procedures. On this basis, Paul's claim to be a Pharisee would have meant little beyond that he was a Jew, but not a Sadducee or Essene. Since clearly he regards his claim to have been a Pharisee as proof of his scrupulous observance of the law—and his zealous persecution of the church may be linked to this—for the New Testament writers the word "Pharisee" has a particular nuance. While Pharisaism was normative Judaism, the term "Pharisee" in the New Testament never denotes an ordinary Jew, but usually an official exercising a special function in regard to the observation of the twofold law. Surely it was in his capacity as a law-enforcement official, indeed one of high rank, that Paul had pursued his persecution of the Christian community which was regarded as in breach of Torah in a several respects.

1 TIMOTHY

Would-be teachers of the law

> They want to be teachers of the law [*nomodidaskaloi*], but they do not know what they are talking about or what they so confidently affirm. (1 Tim 1:7)

Paul is writing about certain members of the Christian community in Ephesus who have deserted the essentials of the Christian faith and turned to "meaningless talk" (verse 6). They claimed that they wanted to become *nomodidaskaloi*, but how they understood this term is open to speculation. If they were Jews they would presumably be familiar with the role of "teachers of the law." If they were Gentiles (and Ephesus was in Gentile territory), this is less likely and they may have wanted to become teachers of the Christian faith as they (inadequately) understood it.

TITUS

Legal matters

> But avoid foolish controversies and genealogies and arguments and quarrels about the law [*machas nomikas*], because these are unprofitable and useless. ... Do everything you can to help Zenas the lawyer [*nomikon*] and Apollos on their way and see that they have everything they need. (Titus 3:9, 13)

Two contrasting occurrences of *nomikos*. The first is adjectival, qualifying *machas*, "arguments," and so is not relevant to this investigation. The second describes Zenas, a companion of Apollos on one of his missionary journeys. Nothing else is known about Zenas. As a *nomikos* he may have been a former teacher of the law.

3

"The Jews" in John's Gospel

JOHN'S GOSPEL HAS SOMETIMES been accused of anti-Semitism.[1] Undoubtedly one reason for this is its frequent use of the phrase "the Jews" (*hoi Ioudaioi*), often with apparent connotations of hostility. The phrase occurs no fewer than 67 times in John and to these could be added other passages which refer to "Jews" (without the article) or where "the Jews" are implied as the subject.[2] For the purposes of this study, however, we shall confine our attention to the 67 occurrences of *hoi Ioudaioi* in the Greek text.

Even a cursory examination of these occurrences reveals that John is not consistent in his usage of the phrase. Sometimes the meaning is generic, denoting the Jewish people as a whole, as in such phrases as "feast of the Jews" and "king of the Jews." But more often he uses it in a technical sense, to denote Jews of a particular kind. For example, five times in John 11:19–45 (the raising of Lazarus) John refers to "the Jews" who had come out to Bethany from nearby Jerusalem to mourn with Mary, Lazarus' sister. Living in such close proximity to Jerusalem, surely one's neighbors and acquaintances are most likely to be Jews? If John had referred instead

---

1. S. Motyer (in *Your Father*, 1f) cites the Jewish scholar Lillian Freudman who described John the Evangelist as "the father of anti-Semitism" and Roy Eckhardt who stated that John 8:44–47 can be called "the road to Auschwitz."

2. For example, in John 18:28 NIV there are two occurrences of "the Jews," but in the Greek text the first instance is implied and the second renders the pronoun *autoi*.

"The Jews" in John's Gospel

to "people" or "friends" coming out from Jerusalem, readers would still assume that these were Jews. So, by consistently referring to them as "the Jews" John is drawing special attention to their Jewishness; surely the implication is that these were extra-ordinary Jews, Jews of some importance. In John 11:45 we read that "many of the Jews who had come to visit Mary, and had seen what Jesus did, put their faith in him." It is as though this were not what one would expect of this kind of Jew—and indeed verse 46 tells of others who did not believe and who reported to the Pharisees (almost certainly meaning the Sanhedrin, *c.f.* verse 47) what Jesus had done. Surely what John is implying is that "the Jews" in this passage are Pharisees, probably teachers of the law closely associated with the temple in Jerusalem, and possibly members of the Sanhedrin.

Indeed, it is the contention of this study that most instances of "the Jews" in John refer to the Pharisees. In some occurrences this is demanded by the context. One example is John 9:18 where "The Jews" clearly refers back to the Pharisees mentioned earlier in verses 13, 15 and 16; similarly, the same legislation attributed to "the Jews" in John 9:22 is attributed to the Pharisees in John 12:42. In these examples, then, there is no doubt that "the Jews" and "the Pharisees" are used synonymously.

The following analysis of the 67 occurrences of *hoi Ioudaioi* classifies them according to the degree of hostility shown by "the Jews" to Jesus or his followers. Each occurrence in turn is examined and assigned to one of four categories. In increasing order of hostility these categories are: (i) *neutral or generic*—"the Jews" refers to the Jewish people as a whole and no hostility towards Jesus is involved—these instances include such phrases as "a feast of the Jews" and "king of the Jews"; (ii) *authority*—"the Jews" represent some kind of Jewish officialdom, which may carry connotations of cold hostility; (iii) *hostile*—these are similar to (ii), but "the Jews" are mentioned explicitly as the cause of persecution or fear, as in the phrase "for fear of the Jews"; (iv) *violent*—these are similar to (iii), but "the Jews" are explicitly the perpetrators of violence or murder or the threats of these, directed towards Jesus or his followers. Inevitably the borders between these categories, especially between (ii) and (iii), are tenuous so that the choice of category in some instances is somewhat arbitrary.

Because the neutral or generic occurrences (category i) are hardly relevant to our study, these are listed separately at the beginning, comments being appended only where some feature holds special interest.

Hypocrites or Heroes?

THE 21 NEUTRAL OR GENERIC OCCURRENCES OF "THE JEWS"

> Nearby stood six stone water jars, the kind used by the Jews for ceremonial washing, each holding from twenty to thirty gallons. (John 2:6)
>
> When it was almost time for the Jewish Passover [*to pascha tōn Ioudaiōn*], Jesus went up to Jerusalem. (John 2:13)
>
> Now there was a man of the Pharisees named Nicodemus, a member of the Jewish ruling council [*archōn tōn Ioudaiōn*]. (John 3:1)
>
> You Samaritans worship what you do not know; we worship what we do know, for salvation is from the Jews. (John 4:22)

This is part of Jesus' conversation with the Samaritan woman by the well outside Sychar. As in John 2:6 (see above), the reference is to the Jewish people as a whole and is the only instance of "the Jews" in John's Gospel to have positive connotations: the *Heilsgeschichte* is intimately associated with the Jewish people. Thus this is a category (i) generic instance.

> Some time later, Jesus went up to Jerusalem for a feast of the Jews. (John 5:1)
>
> The Jewish Passover Feast [*hē heortē tōn Ioudaiōn*] was near. (John 6:4)
>
> But when the Jewish Feast [*hē heortē tōn Ioudaiōn*] of Tabernacles was near, (John 7:2)
>
> At these words the Jews were again divided. (John 10:19)

This is the aftermath of Jesus' "Good Shepherd" speech. John does not tell us where this speech took place so the identity of these "Jews" is unknown. On this basis the only safe course is to assign this occurrence in category (i), neutral.

> When it was almost time for the Jewish Passover [*to pascha tōn Ioudaiōn*], many went up from the country to Jerusalem for their ceremonial cleansing before the Passover. (John 11:55)
>
> "I have spoken openly to the world," Jesus replied. "I always taught in synagogues or at the temple, where all the Jews come together. I said nothing in secret." (John 18:20)

This is part of Jesus' defense before the high priest. The point that Jesus was making was that his teaching had been conducted openly, in the hearing of all interested parties; no one could accuse him of making clandestine plots or teaching different truths to different groups. The significance of the temple was that it was the spiritual heart of the nation, the symbolic dwelling place of God, "where all the Jews come together," although its outermost court was also open to Gentiles. The reference to *all* the Jews demands that this be classified as a category (i), generic, instance of "the Jews."

> Pilate then went back inside the palace, summoned Jesus and asked him, "Are you the king of the Jews?" (John 18:33)
> But it is your custom for me to release to you one prisoner at the time of the Passover. Do you want me to release 'the king of the Jews'? (John 18:39)
> The soldiers twisted together a crown of thorns and put it on his head. They clothed him in a purple robe and went up to him again and again, saying, "Hail, king of the Jews!" And they struck him in the face. (John 19:2f)
> Pilate had a notice prepared and fastened to the cross. It read: JESUS OF NAZARETH, THE KING OF THE JEWS. Many of the Jews read this sign, for the place where Jesus was crucified was near the city, and the sign was written in Aramaic, Latin, and Greek. The chief priests of the Jews protested to Pilate, "Do not write 'The King of the Jews,' but that this man claimed to be king of the Jews." (John 19:19–21)

All five instances of "the Jews" in this passage are generic, three of them forming part of the phrase "the king of the Jews." The reference to "Many of the Jews" reading the sign which was in a public place would include Jews of all kinds and the phrase "The chief priests of the Jews" really means "The Jewish chief priests."

> Taking Jesus' body, the two of them wrapped it, with the spices, in strips of linen. This was in accordance with Jewish burial customs [*kathōs ethos estin tois Ioudaiois entafiazein*]. (John 19:40)
> Because it was the Jewish day of Preparation [*tēn paraskeuēn tōn Ioudaiōn*] and since the tomb was near by, they laid Jesus there. (John 19:42)

Hypocrites or Heroes?

THE 46 NON-NEUTRAL OCCURRENCES OF "THE JEWS"

The Jews send a deputation

> Now this was John's testimony when the Jews of Jerusalem sent priests and Levites to ask him who he was ... (John 1:19)

These "Jews" were not only based in Jerusalem but plainly had the authority to send a deputation of priests and Levites; verse 24 refers to "some Pharisees who had been sent" presumably in the same deputation. This deputation may be the one also mentioned in Matt 3:7. Probably, then, "the Jews" here denotes the Sanhedrin, placing this in category (ii), authority. For further see *Pharisees and Sadducees visit John the Baptist*, p. 14.

A deputation from the Sanhedrin

> Then the Jews demanded of him, "What miraculous sign can you show us to prove your authority to do all this?"
> Jesus answered them, "Destroy this temple, and I will raise it again in three days."
> The Jews replied, "It has taken forty-six years to build this temple, and you are going to raise it in three days?" (John 2:18–20)

This is John's version of the question about authority following Jesus' cleansing of the temple. John offers no clues as to the identity of "the Jews" in this passage, but in the synoptics it is posed by a deputation from the Sanhedrin—see *A delegation from the Sanhedrin questions Jesus' authority*, p. 45. Even if there were no parallels, the nature of the interrogation indicates that the questioners were officials. So this is classified in category (ii) authority.

A healing on the Sabbath

> At once the man was cured; he picked up his mat and walked. The day on which this took place was a Sabbath, and so the Jews said to the man who had been healed, "It is the Sabbath; the law forbids you to carry your mat."
> ... The man went away and told the Jews that it was Jesus who had made him well. So, because Jesus was doing these things on

"The Jews" in John's Gospel

> the Sabbath, the Jews persecuted him. Jesus said to them, "My Father is always at his work to this very day, and I, too, am working."
>
> For this reason the Jews tried all the harder to kill him; not only was he breaking the Sabbath, but he was even calling God his own Father, making himself equal with God. (John 5:9f, 15–18)

This is the healing of the crippled man at Bethesda. Of the four occurrences of "the Jews" in this passage all represent Jewish individuals having authority, but as the last two also mention their persecution of Jesus and their plotting to kill him, those belong in category (iii) and (iv) respectively and the earlier two in category (ii). It is possible that "the Jews" who sought to kill Jesus were in fact Sadducees—see *The plots against Jesus*, p. 148.

A debate with "the Jews"

> At this the Jews began to grumble about him because he said, "I am the bread that came down from heaven."
>
> ... Then the Jews began to argue sharply among themselves, "How can this man give us his flesh to eat?" (John 6:41, 52)

These are two of the Jews' responses in one of their debates with Jesus. This took place in Galilee and began with Jesus teaching a "crowd" (verse 24). "The Jews" appear to be certain individuals within the crowd, perhaps more accustomed to theological debate than the rest. Probably, then, they are members of the delegation sent by the Sanhedrin to observe Jesus in the hope of finding grounds to arrest him: see *Healing of the paralyzed man*, p. 19. They may have been Pharisees or Sadducees, either representing officialdom. Because of their negative attitude to Jesus these instances have been allocated to category (iii), hostile.

The Jewish Feast of Tabernacles

> After this, Jesus went around in Galilee, purposely staying away from Judea because the Jews there were waiting to take his life. (John 7:1)

Presumably "the Jews" in Judea "were waiting to take his life" as a consequence of the healing at Bethesda (John 5:18). These Jews must have been officials holding authority, probably members of the Sanhedrin. Because

95

Hypocrites or Heroes?

they were plotting to take his life, this counts as a category (iv) violent instance.

At the Feast of Tabernacles

> Now at the Feast the Jews were watching for him and asking, "Where is that man?"
>
> Among the crowds there was widespread whispering about him. Some said, "He is a good man." Others replied, "No, he deceives the people." But no-one would say anything publicly about him for fear of the Jews. Not until halfway through the Feast did Jesus go up to the temple courts and begin to teach. The Jews were amazed and asked, "How did this man get such learning without having studied?"
>
> ... The Jews said to one another, "Where does this man intend to go that we cannot find him? Will he go where our people live scattered among the Greeks, and teach the Greeks?" (John 7:11–15, 35)

There is an element of contradiction in this set of four examples. In verse 13, a typical category (iii) hostile example, we read "no-one would say anything publicly about him for fear of the Jews." This is hardly surprising as in verse 1 we learned that the Jews were waiting to take Jesus' life. It is understandable, then, that in verse 11 "the Jews were watching for him"; presumably these were Jewish officials, probably Pharisees, making this a category (ii) authority example. Who, then, were "the Jews" in verses 15 and 35? John must be using the term in a different way here, since, far from arresting him or attempting to kill him, these seem amazed at his teaching and freely discuss its meaning. In verse 15 their interest in learning suggests that they were teachers of the law, and, if the setting is the temple, that is very likely. Verse 35 is the response to a saying of Jesus in verses 33f, immediately preceding in which there is a reference to the Pharisees monitoring what the crowds were saying about Jesus. "The Jews" in verse 35 may refer back to those Pharisees. Since these last two examples are not hostile, they have been placed in category (ii), authority.

Jesus is going away

> This made the Jews ask, "Will he kill himself? Is that why he says, 'Where I go, you cannot come'?" (John 8:22)

This incident is similar to that in 7:34 (see above). While teaching in the temple Jesus announced, "I am going away, and you will look for me, and you will die in your sin. Where I go, you cannot come." That provoked this question from "the Jews." This audience had been described as Pharisees in verse 13. For that reason this as another authority, category (ii), instance.

Jews believe in Jesus

> To the Jews who had believed him, Jesus said, "If you hold to my teaching, you are really my disciples." (John 8:31)

This continues the teaching session in the temple (see on verse 22 above). Clearly some of those present believed Jesus and this is addressed to them. Although, as in verse 22, it is impossible to be specific about the identity of these people, the context makes it likely that they were Pharisees, probably teachers of the law, and so this passage is placed in category (ii), authority.

Jews accuse Jesus of being demon-possessed

> The Jews answered him, "Aren't we right in saying that you are a Samaritan and demon-possessed?"
> ... At this the Jews exclaimed, "Now we know that you are demon-possessed! Abraham died and so did the prophets, yet you say that if anyone keeps your word, he will never taste death.
> ..."You are not yet fifty years old," the Jews said to him, "and you have seen Abraham!" (John 8:48, 52, 57)

This is still the same teaching session in the temple as in 8:22 and 31 (see above). The language has become heated, Jesus calling this group of adversaries "children of the devil" (verse 44), because they were plotting to kill him (verse 37), while they accuse him of being demon-possessed, *c.f.*

the Beelzebub controversy in the synoptics (Mark 3:22 and parallels). L. T. Johnson points out that, although such language may sound unacceptable by 21st-century standards, the polemic in John's Gospel is typical of its day and age. He compares the debates between Apollonius and Euphrates:

> Apollonius of Tyana and Euphrates were two first-century philosophers who hated and plotted against each other. Their polemic became intensely personal. They tossed the terms *goēs* (charlatan) and *magos* (magician) back and forth, each accusing the other of operating out of love for money and love for glory. Since people who were supposed to be self-controlled and passionless were, in such fights, obviously out of control, they tended to bring philosophy itself into disrepute.[3]

Since the setting is the temple and these opponents seem familiar with the conventions of rhetoric, it is most likely that they were teachers of the law. In view of the hostility of the language, these three instances are classified in category (iii), hostile.

The man blind from birth

> The Jews still did not believe that he had been blind and had received his sight until they sent for the man's parents.
> . . . His parents said this because they were afraid of the Jews, for already the Jews had decided that anyone who acknowledged that Jesus was the Christ would be put out of the synagogue. (John 9:18, 22)

In verse 18 "The Jews" clearly refers to the Pharisees mentioned in verses 13, 15 and 16. This is one of the clearest examples of John using "the Jews" as a synonym for "the Pharisees." As these Pharisees are acting in an official capacity, this example is classified in category (ii), authority. The two examples in verse 22 are both in category (iii), hostile, since both refer to the fear aroused by "the Jews."

---

3. Johnson, "Ancient Polemic," 432.

"The Jews" in John's Gospel

At the Feast of Dedication

> The Jews gathered round him, saying, "How long will you keep us in suspense? If you are the Christ, tell us plainly."
> ... Again the Jews picked up stones to stone him,
> ... "We are not stoning you for any of these," replied the Jews, "but for blasphemy, because you, a mere man, claim to be God."
> (John 10:24, 31, 33)

This exchange took place at the Feast of Dedication, when Jesus was walking in the part of temple known as Solomon's Colonnade (verses 22f). Verse 24 is borderline; taken out of context it is a straight question put to Jesus without any connotations of hostility. It could be argued in the light of the developments in verses 31 and 33 that there must have been some hostility, but because this was the temple area and the Jews are discussing theological matters, they were probably teachers of the law and the safest classification of this occurrence is category (ii), authority. Both verses 31 and 33 refer to their intention to stone Jesus and so these belong in category (iv), violent.

Jesus proposes to return to Judea

> "But Rabbi," they said, "a short while ago the Jews tried to stone you, and yet you are going back there?" (John 11:8)

Because of the hostility of Jewish officialdom Jesus had retreated across the Jordan, where he must have considered himself safer (John 10:39f). Now, on learning that Lazarus was sick in Bethany, Jesus suggested to his disciples that they return to Judea and this was their response. Since this is a reference to the attempted stoning of Jesus, this, like 10:31 and 33, belongs in category (iv), violent.

The raising of Lazarus

> and many Jews had come to Martha and Mary to comfort them in the loss of their brother.
> ...When the Jews who had been with Mary in the house, comforting her, noticed how quickly she got up and went out, they followed her, supposing she was going to the tomb to mourn there.

Hypocrites or Heroes?

> ... When Jesus saw her weeping, and the Jews who had come along with her also weeping, he was deeply moved in spirit and troubled.
> ... Then the Jews said, "See how he loved him!"
> ... Therefore many of the Jews who had come to visit Mary, and had seen what Jesus did, put their faith in him. (John 11:19, 31, 33, 36, 45)

These five verses all concern "the Jews" who had come to visit Mary, to mourn with her the death of her brother Lazarus. Verses 18f imply that they had come from Jerusalem, which was within walking distance. That John refers to them repeatedly as "the Jews" rather than "friends" or "people" suggests that they were Jews of some importance, perhaps temple officials, teachers of the law or members of the Sanhedrin. For this reason they are assigned to category (ii), authority. See also on *The Sanhedrin decides to arrest and kill Jesus*, p. 81.

After the raising of Lazarus

> Therefore Jesus no longer moved about publicly among the Jews. Instead he withdrew to a region near the desert, to a village called Ephraim, where he stayed with his disciples. (John 11:54)

Some of "the Jews" who had witnessed Jesus' raising of Lazarus reported the matter to "the Pharisees" (verse 46), by which John almost certainly means the Sanhedrin (verse 47). Out of fear that Jesus' miracles would destabilize the tense political situation, the Sanhedrin began plotting Jesus' death (verse 53). Although neither fear nor violence is mentioned in verse 54, it was nevertheless what John elsewhere describes as "fear of the Jews" that now prevented Jesus traveling freely in public and so this occurrence of "the Jews" belongs in category (iii), hostile.

Many of "the Jews" follow Jesus after the raising of Lazarus

> Meanwhile a large crowd of Jews [*ochlos polus ek tōn Ioudaiōn*] found out that Jesus was there and came, not only because of him but also to see Lazarus, whom he had raised from the dead. So the chief priests made plans to kill Lazarus as well, for on account of

him many of the Jews [*polloi . . . tōn Ioudaiōn*] were going over to
Jesus and putting their faith in him. (John 12:9–11)

It was six days before the Passover (verse 1) and Jesus had returned to Bethany for a dinner given in his honor (verse 2). It is difficult to categorize the two occurrences of "the Jews" in verses 9 and 11. There is no suggestion of hostility or violence on their part (although there is from the chief priests) and nothing explicit concerning officialdom. The temptation is to treat them as generic; after all, this is Jerusalem at Passover time—who else but Jews would one expect to find there? That John has twice specified "Jews" rather than leaving the text as "a large crowd found out . . . many were going over to Jesus" suggests that these were special Jews. Moreover, these were people whom one would expect to be not interested in Jesus and the last to put their faith in him. That so many did put their faith in him so angered the chief priests that, irrationally, they now began plotting to kill innocent Lazarus as well as Jesus. That John uses the term "were going over (*hupēgon*) to Jesus" suggests that the chief priests viewed this as disloyalty or even apostasy; they had expected these "Jews" to remain loyal to their traditional values. Presumably their loyalty was particularly important because these were people who commanded the respect of the general public—they were the trendsetters of Jewish society. The most likely explanation, then, is that they were teachers of the law, especially those who were members of the Sanhedrin, most of whom (like Nicodemus) were Pharisees. As Bethany was within easy walking distance of Jerusalem this was not unreasonable. Because of this these two occurrences are classified as category (ii), authority.

Where I am going, you cannot come

My children, I will be with you only a little longer. You will look for me, and just as I told the Jews, so I tell you now: Where I am going, you cannot come. (John 13:33)

Jesus is addressing the Twelve, apart from Judas Iscariot who has just set off to betray him to the high priests. In John 7:34 Jesus had told an audience variously described as Jews and Pharisees, "You will look for me, but you will not find me; and where I am, you cannot come." In John 8:21: "Once more Jesus said to them, 'I am going away, and you will look for me, and you will die in your sin. Where I go, you cannot come.'" In the next

Hypocrites or Heroes?

verse his audience is described as "the Jews"—see on *Jesus is going away*, p. 97. So Jesus is referring back to one or both of those incidents and the meaning of "the Jews" here clearly depends upon the meaning of "the Jews" there. Both of those sayings were addressed to audiences which had previously been described as Pharisees and were therefore assigned to category (ii), authority and so the same must apply here.

Jesus' arrest

> Then the detachment of soldiers with its commander and the Jewish officials [*hupēretai tōn Ioudaiōn*] arrested Jesus. They bound him and brought him first to Annas, who was the father-in-law of Caiaphas, the high priest that year. Caiaphas was the one who had advised the Jews that it would be good if one man died for the people. (John 18:12–14)

The reference to "Jewish officials" places the instance in verse 12 in category (ii), authority. Similarly, the incident to which verse 14 refers took place in the Sanhedrin (John 11:49f) so that "the Jews" whom Caiaphas advised were also Jewish officials and the same applies.

Jesus before Pilate

> Pilate said, "Take him yourselves and judge him by your own law."
> "But we have no right to execute anyone," the Jews objected.
> ... Jesus said, "My kingdom is not of this world. If it were, my servants would fight to prevent my arrest by the Jews. But now my kingdom is from another place."
> ... "What is truth?" Pilate asked. With this he went out again to the Jews and said, "I find no basis for a charge against him." (John 18:31, 36, 38)

These three occurrences in Jesus' interview by Pilate all denote the group of officials who had arrested Jesus and brought him before the Governor; they are therefore category (ii), authority.

The Jews persuade Pilate to crucify Jesus

> The Jews insisted, "We have a law, and according to that law he must die, because he claimed to be the Son of God."
> ... From then on, Pilate tried to set Jesus free, but the Jews kept shouting, "If you let this man go, you are no friend of Caesar. Anyone who claims to be a king opposes Caesar."
> ... It was the day of Preparation of Passover Week, about the sixth hour. "Here is your king," Pilate said to the Jews. (John 19:7, 12, 14)

The three references to "the Jews" all refer primarily to the officials who had brought Jesus before Pilate, although it is likely that these exchanges were within the hearing of a larger and hostile crowd. They are therefore classified as category (ii), authority.

The Day of Preparation

> Now it was the day of Preparation, and the next day was to be a special Sabbath. Because the Jews did not want the bodies left on the crosses during the Sabbath, they asked Pilate to have the legs broken and the bodies taken down. (John 19:31)

Since these Jews had the authority to approach the Roman Governor directly, they must have been high-ranking officials, probably members of the Sanhedrin. Therefore this instance belongs in category (ii), authority.

Joseph of Arimathea places Jesus' body in his own tomb

> Later, Joseph of Arimathea asked Pilate for the body of Jesus. Now Joseph was a disciple of Jesus, but secretly because he feared the Jews. With Pilate's permission, he came and took the body away. (John 19:38)

The reference to fear places this example in category (iii), hostile.

Hypocrites or Heroes?

The risen Jesus appears to the disciples

> On the evening of that first day of the week, when the disciples were together, with the doors locked for fear of the Jews, Jesus came and stood among them and said, "Peace be with you!" (John 20:19)

The reference to fear places this example in category (iii), hostile.

CONCLUSIONS

The 67 occurrences fit into the four categories as follows:

Neutral or generic. There are 21 such occurrences: 2:6, 13; 3:1; 4:9, 22; 5:1; 6:4; 7:2; 10:19; 11:55; 18:20, 33, 39; 19:3, 19, 20, 21 (three times), 40, and 42.

Authority, referring to Jewish officialdom, sometimes with connotations of cold hostility. There are 29 such references: 1:19; 2:18, 20; 5:10, 15; 7:11, 15, 35; 8:22, 31; 9:18; 10:24; 11:19, 31, 33, 36, 45; 12:9, 11; 13:33; 18:12, 14, 31, 36, 38; 19:7, 12, 14, and 31.

Hostile, the Jews being explicitly the cause of persecution or fear, as in the phrase "for fear of the Jews." There are 12 such occurrences: 5:16; 6:41, 52; 7:13; 8:48, 52, 57; 9:22 (twice); 11:54; 19:38; and 20:19.

Violent, the Jews being explicitly the perpetrators of violence or murder or the threats of these, directed towards Jesus or his disciples. There are five such occurrences: 5:18; 7:1; 10:31, 33; and 11:8.

Despite its crudeness, this analysis helps to explain the apparent anti-Jewish feeling that pervades the Fourth Gospel. Even if all 29 occurrences in category (ii) are reckoned to be neutral, denoting no more than officialdom, there remain 17 occasions in the gospel when "the Jews" are explicitly described as the persecutors of Jesus and his disciples, the ones who seek to kill him; they are a people to be feared. Although these represent only about a quarter of the mentions of "the Jews" in the gospel, they nevertheless cast a sinister shadow over the others, so that the reader's suspicion is aroused instantly on encountering any instance of "the Jews."

"The Jews" in John's Gospel

John's use of the term "the Jews" in this way suggests that he regards Jesus, his disciples, and those who would later become disciples as a special category quite distinct from "the Jews." The evangelist surely knew that Jesus and his closest disciples were themselves Jews—and he certainly appreciated that God's promises were predominantly to the Jews (4:9, 22). In John's Gospel, however, "the Jews" are most often the enemies of Jesus and his disciples. It is understandable, therefore, that throughout church history readers have been tempted to think of the Jews in their own time as the enemies of Jesus and Christians, fostering regrettable and totally undeserved anti-Semitism.

What is most important for this study, however, is the link between "the Jews" and officialdom. In John's Gospel it is Jews in authority who generate fear and who persecute and threaten Jesus and his disciples with violence, in contrast with the masses who welcome him. So we can combine categories (ii), (iii), and (iv) into one super-category representing officialdom. When we do this, we find that 46 out of the 67 instances of "the Jews," about two thirds of them, refer to Jewish officialdom and usually these are the Pharisees, the teachers of the law (most of whom were Pharisees) or the Sanhedrin, which was dominated by the Pharisees. No wonder, then, that Ellis Rivkin wrote of the Pharisees in John that "They appear as hardly more than a synonym for *Jews*."[4] It is therefore reasonable to conclude that in John "the Jews" more often than not refers to the Pharisees, *pace* Saldarini, who draws a distinction between them.[5]

In his comprehensive study of *hoi Ioudaioi* in John Stephen Motyer points out that the Fourth Gospel appeared after 70CE by which time the Temple and its cultus had been destroyed and the successors to the Pharisees no longer used the term. In common with a number of scholars he draws a conclusion similar to that expressed above, as the following three passages show:

> The view, in essence, is that "the Jews" with whom Jesus clashes are *a party within Judaism*, the supremely religious, those whom Bornhäuser calls the "Torafanatiker" ("fanatics for the law"), Blank "die Jerusalemer Kultgemeinde" ("the Temple-party in Jerusalem") and Morton Smith the "Yahweh-alone party": they are the sticklers for the law, essentially the *Pharisees* in the period in

---

4. Rivkin, *Revolution*, 98.

5. "In the Gospel of John the Pharisees, along with the Jews and the chief priests, are the most important opponents to Jesus . . ." (Saldarini, *Pharisees*, 195).

the period before 70, who sought to maintain Temple purity in the home, and the *sages of Yavneh* and their followers in the period after 70, who dropped the title "Pharisees" and sought to reinforce the same piety, as the authentic form of Judaism but now deprived of the Temple cult.[6]

... the *Pharisaioi* form the core and leading group within the *Ioudaioi*. The prominent use of the expression "Pharisees" in John does not reflect contemporary usage, but the influence of historical tradition: for the Yavneh sages seem to have avoided this title. But readers would naturally have twinned the narrative's "Pharisees" and "Jews" with their post-70 heirs, namely the Yavneh sages and the movement they led.[7]

"The Jews" is not a global designation of all Abraham's descendants. We have suggested that the lexicography of the word is complex, but that in essence it would be heard—and its usage in the gospel reinforces this—to refer to a distinct group within Judaism, the Judea-based, Torah-loyal adherents of the Yavneh ideals, the direct heirs of pre-70 Pharisaism.[8]

So Motyer's claim is that the evangelist is reading into Jesus' experiences Jewish associations more appropriate to those that existed after the destruction of the Temple in 70CE. Nevertheless he would surely concur with the conclusions of this study that most instances of "the Jews" in John refer to officialdom and, probably, to Pharisees.

He provides a plausible explanation for the anti-Jewish feeling fostered by the gospel's usage of "the Jews" in a hostile context: "The Fourth Gospel may certainly be called 'anti-Jewish,' if this is defined as a motivation to prove the illegitimacy of the ways in which various Jewish groups sought to be faithful to their heritage. But . . . this motivation is *not at all* hostile to the groups concerned." Motyer appeals to the polemical character of the gospel: "the language of the Fourth Gospel is comparatively mild according to both Graeco-Roman and Jewish standards."[9] He is surely correct, then, that the evangelist is following the tradition of Hosea in using threats and warnings to call the nation to turn back to God.[10]

---

6. Motyer, *Your Father*, 54.
7. Ibid., 56.
8. Ibid., 213.
9. Ibid., 211.
10. Ibid., 212.

4

The Pharisees in Josephus and the Rabbinical Literature

NO APOLOGY IS NECESSARY for the brevity of the treatment given here to the Pharisees' depiction in Josephus and the Rabbinical (Tannaitic) literature. After all, according to its title, this study is concerned with their portrayal in the New Testament which contributes most of the pieces of the jigsaw puzzle. Inevitably, however, the paradoxical nature of that portrayal leads us to enquire how other ancient authorities depicted them—Josephus and the Rabbis being the only other ancient writers to have done so—in the hope of finding clues that will resolve the New Testament's contradictions. Although their descriptions of the Pharisees do provide some useful new information, they are nevertheless of limited value. Josephus mentions the Pharisees a few times, mostly in connection with their involvement in political events, but on three occasions he offers illuminating comparisons of the Pharisees with other Jewish "ideologies." The extensive output of the Rabbis mentions them more often, but because that literature is the product of rigorous later editing, there are usually difficulties in ascertaining either that the subject of the description is indeed the movement known to us as the Pharisees or that what is said about them is appropriate to the movement at the time of Jesus.

Hypocrites or Heroes?

JOSEPHUS

Flavius Josephus was not a contemporary of Jesus, having been born in 37CE. As a Jew from a priestly and aristocratic family who participated in the turbulent events of the second half of the first century, he was, however, ideally placed to document the Jewish society of which Jesus had been a recent part. Moreover, he had personal experience of the three main divisions of Judaism: the Sadducees, the Essenes and the Pharisees. It is widely believed that he was himself a Pharisee. The principal reason for this is a passage in his autobiography[1] in which he apparently describes how, at the age of 19, after observing all three "philosophies," he began to follow the legal system of the Pharisees (*polituesthai tē Pharisaiōn hairesei katakolouthōn*).[2] Clearly Rivkin is uncertain about the meaning of this statement: "he does not even tell us what specifically one did when one decided to govern his life by the system of laws of the Pharisees. But one point must not be overlooked. Josephus does not use any word which means 'to join an association,' or 'to become a member of a confraternity.'"[3] Of course, if the Pharisee movement had no formal membership and therefore no initiation procedure, presumably all that was necessary to become a Pharisee was to begin governing one's life according to their system of laws, as indeed Josephus claims to have done. On this basis, then, he *did* become a Pharisee.

There is, however, another possibility. Professor Steve Mason of the University of Aberdeen, Scotland, argues convincingly that Josephus was *not* a Pharisee, citing as evidence that not only do his works show no Pharisaic bias but also that in places he is openly hostile towards them. Indeed, he points out that after Josephus as a young man investigated all three Jewish "philosophies," he rejected them all, despite effusive compliments for the Essenes. It was only when he "began to take part in public or civic affairs (*politeuesthai*)" that he began "deferring to [perhaps 'following the example/lead of'] the school of the Pharisees." Mason claims that a misunderstanding of this passage has led many scholars to assume that Josephus either became a Pharisee or wished people to believe that he had. The Pharisees dominated first-century Jewish civic life and everyone—even the Sadducees (*Antiquities* 18, see below)—deferred to them, without necessarily agreeing with their views. Mason concludes that Josephus was not

1. *The Life*, an appendix at the end of *Antiquities*.
2. Josephus, *Life* 9–12, as cited in Rivkin, *Revolution*, 66f.
3. Rivkin, *Revolution*, 67.

affiliated to any one school of thought, while retaining an interest in all of them. "Once we read the passage in this way," he writes, "we realize that there is simply no basis, anywhere in Josephus's narratives, for connecting him with the Pharisees. And once we abandon the effort to identify him as a Pharisee, we can place his other remarks about the Pharisees in a more adequate and illuminating context." He proceeds to show how Josephus' various references to himself and to the Pharisees are clarified by this new understanding of that relationship.[4]

Like the New Testament, what Josephus says about the Pharisees is mostly incidental; rarely are they the focus of his writing. In general he confines his mentions of them to their involvement in political events, such as their revolts against John Hyrcanus and later against Alexander Jannaeus and the occasion when Salome Alexandra delegated some power to them. Of most interest to us, however, are the three passages, one in *Jewish War* and two in *Antiquities of the Jews*, in which he compares the main philosophical strands of Judaism. The first is in Book 2 of *Jewish War*:

Josephus: Jewish War 2:8:2, 14

> Now there are among the Jews three schools of thought: one may choose that of the Pharisees, that of the Sadducees or, thirdly, one which seems to practice special dignity, that of the so-called Essenes, who, although they are Jews by birth, seem to love each other more than the others do. They despise pleasure as though it were evil, and they practice self-control and value the virtue of not being disillusioned by life's setbacks. They hold marriage in contempt, treating other people's children as their own families, as long as they are willing to learn, guiding and molding them according to their customs. [121] They do not involve themselves in marriage or human succession because they are wary of the licentiousness of women, convinced that not one of them is faithful. [There follows a more detailed description of the Essenes.]
>
> Of the two previously mentioned groups, the Pharisees consider themselves to be experts in the precise elucidation of legal matters; they are the foremost of the sects and totally devoted to God in every way. They maintain that to practice what is right rather than what most people do is an obligation placed upon humanity, although divine assistance is available to every person.

---

4. Mason, "Flavius Josephus."

Hypocrites or Heroes?

> Each soul is indestructible, only passing into a different body when from a good person; when from an evil person, in contrast, it is punished with everlasting retribution.
>
> As for the Sadducees, the second group, they remove God altogether, setting him outside human evil or achievement. They say that the power to choose between good or evil has been set before humanity and a tally will be kept based upon everyone's experience of these. They abolish the punishment and the reward of the underworld to soul and demon alike. While the Pharisees are friendly to each other and work for a common goal, the Sadducees' attitude towards each other is more brutal, treating each other in the same way as uncouth people would. This is as much as I have to say at present concerning the Jewish schools of thought.[5]

Here Josephus adds little to what the New Testament says about the Pharisees. Perhaps what is most interesting here is his description of them as "the foremost of sects" (*tēn prōtēn apagontes hairesin*). But what does he mean by "foremost"? In numbers? In influence? In popularity with the people at large?

The second, brief comparison is in Book 13 of *Antiquities*:

Josephus: Antiquities 13:5:9

> Now at this time there were three Jewish sects which held different understandings of human experience. These were those who called themselves Pharisees, that of the Sadducees and the third that of the Essenes. The Pharisees for their part say that some but not all events are predestined, while others happen by themselves and so are not. The Essene group, in contrast, contends everything to be divinely predestined, leaving nothing at all to the discretion of humans. The Sadducees maintain that nothing is predestined; they consider that human affairs have no inherent purpose, but everything depends entirely upon us ourselves, so that we become responsible for good deeds and evil ones, depending upon where our stupidity takes us. But concerning these I have given a more detailed explanation in the second book of the Jewish war.[6]

This passage is concerned only with the contrasting ways in which the three groups understand the inter-relationship between divine and

5. Josephus, *War* 2:8:2, 14, author's own translation.
6. Josephus, *Antiquities* 13:5:9, author's own translation.

human involvement in the cosmos. The Essenes represent one extreme, "everything ... divine predestination," with the Sadducees at the opposite extreme, "nothing is predestined ... everything depends entirely upon us ourselves." The Pharisees, then, represent moderation: "some but not all events are predestined," which in some measure preserves the paradox of simultaneous divine sovereignty and human responsibility.

The third, more detailed comparison is in Book 18:

Josephus: Antiquities 18:1:2–6

> Ever since the times of the fathers for the Jews there have been three alternative ideologies: that of the Essenes, that of the Sadducees, and the third which the so-called Pharisees followed. As it happens, I have said something about these in the second book of the Jewish war, but to remind you I shall say a little about them now.
>
> As for the Pharisees, they are modest in their lifestyle, despising luxury. For them reason dictates judgment so that they follow good practice, putting them in the very vanguard contested by the arbiters of personal conduct. They are prompt to pay respect to those in advanced years—moreover they do not contradict them in any topic they have raised. In order to achieve as their reward whatever they consider that they deserve, they disparage human desires, for fear that these will bring God's immediate judgment upon themselves. They give advice concerning this and concerning life to anyone willing to approach them, whether good or evil. Their belief is that souls have an immortal nature and that in the hereafter an assessment is made of the righteous and honorable actions of the good or evil in this life: for some an everlasting prison is prepared, while others will live again, a life of ease. Now because they happen to be the most persuasive, whatever the people do concerning divine worship and the interpretation of holy matters are all in accordance with their practices. The cities testify to their devotion to their ample goodness which is superior to everything in lifestyle and teaching.
>
> The Sadducees reckon that the soul perishes with the body. They have no regard for anything except themselves and their laws. Although they pursue teachers of wisdom with a vengeance, they dispute the validity of their teaching. To a limited extent their principles find a home among the foremost dignitaries, but nothing of their own teaching is practiced. For whenever they try to

give a lead, they are compelled against their will to do what the Pharisees say, because anything else would be intolerable for the masses.

The Essenes teach on one hand that everything is under God's control, while on the other they insist that souls are immortal, so that a righteous man's destiny is contested ground. When they bring offerings into the temple as sacrifices, they are accomplishing the distinctive kind of purity that they practice, and by means of this shutting out what is common from the temple. They also offer other sacrifices: for example, members of the aristocracy completely change their way of life by doing manual labor as farmers. A commendable feature of theirs, one which indeed elicits everyone's amazement, is a virtue in which none of the Greeks or barbarians begins to rival them, not even for a little while despite having pursued it from of old. This is that their property is all held in common, so that a wealthy member of the community does not enjoy any significant advantage over someone who has nothing at all. The number of people who practice this lifestyle is over four thousand. They neither take wives nor do they practice slavery, for fear that these give rise to injustice or threaten some aspect of their status. In contrast, in their dealings with each other they live as though they were in service to one another. From those good men or priests who offer themselves they elect managers to receive whatever produce their land yields: wheat and other foodstuffs. In no respect do any of them deviate from this lifestyle, but for the most part they regard the so-called masses as dangerous beasts.

The fourth of these ideologies was founded by Judas the Galilean. This is marked by an all-consuming passion for freedom, which they believe that God, their only lord and master, has given them, while in all other respects they follow the teachings of the Pharisees. They deliberately expose themselves to many kinds of excruciating death for the least reason, executing revenge for their relatives and friends; they regard no human as lord. When the masses saw how determined they were in their hope, they allowed them to proceed as they wished. I am not afraid that anything that I have said about them might be deemed incredible, because those who opposed them were more numerous than those who received contempt. Reason took away the pain of hard labor. From then on these people, led by Gessius Florus, began to behave mindlessly; by his authority they ran riot, so desperate were they to break away from the Romans. And that is sufficient concerning the ideologies of the Jews.[7]

7. Josephus, *Antiquities* 18:1:2–6, author's own translation.

The Pharisees in Josephus and the Rabbinical Literature

Josephus seems to have added the fourth group as an afterthought: his introduction refers to only "three alternative ideologies" and he has omitted to name the fourth, which presumably is that normally known today as the Zealots. As these were a breakaway movement from the Pharisees, it is not surprising that, apart from their "all-consuming passion for freedom," "they follow the teachings of the Pharisees."

What Josephus tells us here about the Pharisees corroborates and extends the picture given by the New Testament. Such was their reputation for good conduct—"The cities testify to their devotion to their ample goodness"—that the Sadducees, the party to which the chief priests belonged, had effectively lost all credibility: "whenever they try to give a lead, they are compelled against their will to do what the Pharisees say, because anything else would be intolerable for the masses." The picture painted here of "masses"—the majority?—of Jews following Pharisaic teaching as normative Judaism stands in striking contrast with the school that regards Pharisaism as just one of several competing "Judaisms." A point at variance with the New Testament—or at least with Luke who describes the Pharisees as "loving money" (Luke 16:14)—is Josephus' insistence that they were "modest in their lifestyle, despising luxury." It accords, however, with Maccoby's observation that the rabbinic writings show many if not most Pharisees as poor or at best moderate-income working class: Hillel was a manual laborer and Shammai a carpenter. The movement transcended the division between rich and poor.[8]

It is interesting that Josephus singles out the Pharisees' attitude to the elderly: "They are prompt to pay respect to those in advanced years—moreover they do not contradict them in any topic they have raised." It is as though the Old Testament emphasis upon respect for the elderly (for example, Lev 19:32)—which was indeed common to many peoples in the ancient Near East—had been largely forgotten by the Jews until the Pharisees revived it. This stands in contrast with Jesus' accusation of the Pharisees that they neglected their elderly (Mark 7:9–13).

Another passage from Josephus of particular interest in regard to the origins of the Pharisee movement is the following:

8. Maccoby, *Jesus*, 53.

Hypocrites or Heroes?

Josephus: Antiquities 13:10:5f

Now the Jews' success moved some to envy Hyrcanus. The worst towards him were the Pharisees, one of the Jewish ideologies as mentioned previously. They have such influence over the masses that whatever they say even against the king or the high priest is believed immediately. Hyrcanus was one of their followers and greatly respected by them. Now one day he invited them to a feast and welcomed them hospitably. As soon as he saw that they were enjoying themselves he began telling them that, as they knew, he wanted to be righteous and to do everything possible to please God and themselves, for this is how the Pharisees seek to order their lives. He thought that, if they saw him going astray and departing from the righteous path, that they should bring it up in order to correct him. When they had assured him that he was absolutely perfect, he was delighted. But one of the guests, Eleazar by name, a man of unpleasant nature and habits, said, "Since you want to know the truth, if you wish to be righteous, relinquish the high priesthood and be content with governing the people." When he wanted to know for what reason he ought to relinquish the high priesthood, he said, "Because we heard from the elders that your mother was a prisoner of King Antiochus Epiphanes." This statement was untrue and Hyrcanus was annoyed with him and all the Pharisees were very angry with him.

Now amongst those who follow the ideology of the Sadducees, which is the exact opposite of that of the Pharisees, there was a great friend of Hyrcanus named Jonathan. In common with all the Pharisees he derided Eleazar saying, "It ought to be made known to him in order that he might learn from it that he deserves punishment for what he has said." As Hyrcanus was talking to the Pharisees, he asked, "What does he deserve to receive?" For custom dictates that one cannot be tried for the libel of a respected person without some means of knowing what has taken place. They said, "Lashes and bonds," as it did not seem right to inflict death on account of reproaches, otherwise the Pharisees would have imposed a punishment whose nature was inappropriate. In this regard they were very strict although they acknowledged that the man who had committed the libel was guilty. Then Jonathan urged him cogently to join the Sadducees after he had left the Pharisees, abandoned their principles, abolished their rule of the people and punished those who had supported them. Of course, this led to hatred towards him and his sons from the masses. We shall consider these matters later.

> Now I wish to explain something concerning the practices which the Pharisees have handed down to the people from the teachings of the forefathers. These indeed were not written down in the laws of Moses and, for that reason, the Sadducees reject them, saying that in order to be binding these practices must have been written down; those only handed down from the forefathers are not obligatory. And as a result of their striving for these things major disputes have arisen, the Sadducees on one hand persuading only the wealthy and not having any following among the masses, while the Pharisees on the other have the support of the masses. But I have given a more precise explanation of these two and also the Essenes in my second book of Jewish Antiquities.[9]

What is useful here is Josephus' explicit testimony that some of the Pharisees' practices were "handed down to the people from the teachings of the forefathers. These indeed were not written down in the laws of Moses." In contrast, the Sadducees claimed that "in order to be binding these practices must have been written down; those only handed down from the forefathers are not obligatory." It is interesting that the stricter-sounding lifestyle of the Pharisees found favor with the populace, while that of the Sadducees did not; perhaps it was the Pharisees' lifestyle with its acts of charity and philanthropy that lent credence to their teaching, in contrast with that of the Sadducees.

THE RABBINICAL (TANNAITIC) LITERATURE

There are major difficulties in consulting the Rabbinical Literature regarding the Pharisees. One is that the literature was partly compiled from oral tradition over a number of centuries; it consists of sayings of the Rabbis, often with no indication of date. Even when a saying is credited to an individual Rabbi whose dates of birth and death are known, it is not always possible to be certain that the attribution is correct; sometimes a later saying is credited to a celebrated earlier Rabbi to lend it credence. According to Saldarini, uncritical readings of the Rabbinical literature lead to "an illegitimate and unhistorical retrojection of second through seventh century rabbinic Judaism on the first century. Such an uncritical reconstruction invites prejudicial readings."[10] Moreover, since there are hundreds of texts

---

9. Josephus: *Antiquities* 13:10:5f, author's own translation.
10. Saldarini, *Pharisees*, 200.

mentioning the Pharisees, each requiring careful critical analysis, a survey of them is outside the scope of a work of this nature.

Both Rivkin[11] and Saldarini summarize the contribution of the Rabbinical literature to the study of the Pharisees, Saldarini presenting convincing criticisms of the earlier work of Rivkin. For this reason Saldarini's description of the relevant material in the Rabbinical literature forms the basis for the following summary. He considers three categories of this literature which may be helpful in researching the Pharisees: (i) sayings and stories about named pre-70 sages; (ii) anonymous laws attributed to and relevant to the pre-70 period; and (iii) texts which mention the Pharisees (*perushim*) by name.[12]

The pre-70 sages

Hillel is the only pre-70 sage to whom a large body of sayings and stories are attributed. Because the later talmudic rabbis celebrated Hillel as their founder, "he was turned into a larger than life figure and even compared to Moses."[13] So the Hillel depicted in the rabbinic sources may bear little resemblance to the historical person. Shammai, famed as Hillel's opponent, is mentioned only in the Hillel material; no material mentioning him alone has survived. Often the materials that mention him are hostile towards him. A large body of tradition attributed to the "houses of Hillel and Shammai" probably dates from the second century and is not a reliable guide to the views or activities of Pharisees in the first century.

The few other first-century sages mentioned are Gamaliel I, his son Simeon and Gamaliel II, Simeon's son. The claim that Gamaliel was Hillel's son is probably apocryphal, an attempt to establish a dynasty. The stories about Gamaliel I are consistent with his being a member of the Sanhedrin, as mentioned in Acts 5:34–41. Simeon is mentioned in Josephus.[14]

---

11. Rivkin, *Revolution*, 125.
12. Saldarini, *Pharisees*, 201.
13. Ibid., 205.
14. Ibid., 207.

Laws relevant to the pre-70 period

Saldarini follows Jacob Neusner's dictum that material assigned to the pre-70 period

> must be established either by attestations (in which a law is presumed in an argument by a named authority) or by the logical development of the mishnaic law (in which a fundamental principle or generative concept is anterior to a later law) . . . literary criteria can yield no comprehensible, reliable results because the Mishnah has been so thoroughly edited and historical criteria cannot give a social context because the laws have been placed in a timeless ideal synthesis of Jewish life . . .[15]

Using Neusner's criteria most of the material from the Mishnah and Tosefta which are probably typical of the first century and therefore a reliable basis for the reconstruction of the Pharisees prove to be concerned with ritual purity, tithes and other food laws and Sabbath and festival observance. "These laws set out an agenda of holiness for the land and people which was a fitting response for a powerless people dominated by the Romans because these laws pertain to the parts of domestic life which can be controlled by people out of power . . ."[16] It is reassuring that these concerns also appear in New Testament references to the Pharisees, each thereby corroborating the other.

Saldarini's belief that Pharisaism was one of a number of competing forms of Judaism[17] underlies his insistence that Pharisaic law exhibits sectarian interests. For example, he claims that the emphases on strict tithing, the maintenance of ritual purity by non-priests and on observance of Sabbaths and other festivals reflects their "program for a renewed Judaism."[18] He points out that the Rabbinical literature often mentions associations or fellowships, some which have been identified with the Pharisees. Best known are the "associates" in Mishnah Tractate Demai, whose special concerns—tithing and ritual purity—accord well with Pharisaism, although there were other associations with other concerns. The Hebrew terms used,

---

15. Ibid., 212.

16. Ibid., 213.

17. "In the Hasmonean and Herodian periods the Pharisees were one, but only one, well known group, characterized by a distinctive way of living Judaism and constant social involvement." (Ibid., 278).

18. Ibid., 215.

haberim for "associates" and *haburah* for "association," are common words with no technical meanings, despite the attempts of some scholars to insist that they apply to one single grouping.[19]

Saldarini reproduces a brief passage from M. Demai 2:2–3 which is particularly revealing:

> He who undertakes to be trustworthy tithes what he eats, and what he sells and what he purchases and does not accept the hospitality of an am ha-aretz . . . he who undertakes to be a *haber* does not sell to an am ha-aretz wet or dry produce and does not purchase from him wet and does not accept the hospitality of an am ha-aretz and does not receive him as his guest while he is wearing his own clothes.[20]

Even if we assume that "He who undertakes to be trustworthy" is the same person as the *haber*, we still have the problem of identifying the *haber* and the *am ha-aretz* (people of the land). Saldarini offers the following interpretation of the passage:

> This rule means that the associates can confidently buy and sell to one another and also eat together without fear of breaking any of the laws they wish to keep. By contrast, they must take great care in their dealings with the people of the land, the am ha-aretz, because the people of the land do not keep the special priestly laws of purity and do not tithe properly and fully. Their food has not been properly sanctified and cannot be eaten by associates and must be tithed if it is acquired.[21]

Scholars are divided as to the degree with which the *haberim* can be identified with the Pharisees, but if Pharisaism were the normative Judaism of the time, the *haberim* were most likely Pharisees, although there may have been other Pharisees who were not *haberim*. It is tempting to compare this passage with the synoptic account of the feast in Matthew/Levi's house. If we identify the Pharisees, including Jesus, with the *haberim* and the tax collectors and "sinners" with the *am ha-aretz*, it is not surprising that the Pharisees were concerned when Jesus, whom they regarded as one of their own number, not only accepted hospitality from an *am ha-aretz*, but also by

---

19. Ibid., 216.

20. M. Demai 2:2–3, translation adapted from Sarason, as cited in Saldarini, *Pharisees*, 217.

21. Ibid., 217.

eating with *am ha-aretz* risked consuming food that had not been properly tithed and sanctified.

It is a pity that Saldarini offers no comment on the final clause which seems to imply that it would be permissible for an associate to receive as his guest an *am ha-aretz* who was wearing someone else's (the associate's?) clothes. Does this indicate an element of deception: let the neighbors think that the associate is welcoming a fellow associate? If so, it is reminiscent of the Pharisaic legalism that Jesus so frequently castigates in the New Testament.

Saldarini, however, urges caution in the identification of the associates:

> Granted the diversity of first-century Judaism, it is better to keep groups, even nameless groups like the associates, separate from one another, rather than trying to identify them with known groups. Even if associates who kept ritual purity and tithed faithfully were similar to the Pharisees, it is sociologically probable that many such similar groups existed in the first century.[22]

But how diverse was first-century Judaism? If Pharisaism was normative Judaism, much of this diversity was embraced within Pharisaism. The similarities with the New Testament mentioned above are consistent with "associate" being a synonym for Pharisee.

Texts which mention the Pharisees by name

The Pharisees—and also the Sadducees—are mentioned by name in places in the Rabbinical literature, but these texts originated over a period of several centuries and there is evidence that the understanding of who the Pharisees—and Sadducees—were changed over time. Sometimes the term "Pharisee" is used pejoratively. The Hebrew word used is *perushim*, whose original meaning is disputed. The most commonly held view is that it means "separated ones," reflecting the habit of Pharisees of separating themselves from anything that might render them ritually unclean. A possible alternative meaning is "interpreters" from their role as interpreters of the law.[23]

It is significant that the Pharisees did not normally refer to themselves by that name. Indeed, the only person in Jewish literature who ever referred

---

22. Ibid., 219.
23. Ibid., 220f.

to himself as a Pharisee is the apostle Paul.[24] The Pharisees usually referred to themselves as *hakamim*, "sages." Saldarini writes, "They have no name for their movement, but call themselves Israel because they consider themselves to be simply proper Jews."[25] Of course, if Pharisaism was normative Judaism, it *would* identify itself with Israel.

Saldarini rightly dismisses as irrelevant a number of texts which use the term Pharisee pejoratively; these seem not to refer to the group called the Pharisees in the New Testament and Josephus.[26] Of definite interest are others which explicitly contrast the Pharisees with the Sadducees; in these both groups are recognizably those described in the New Testament. Saldarini is emphatic that "In the Mishnah and the Tosefta most of the disputes concern purity and most are controversies in which the Sadducees come out second best."[27] He draws the following conclusion:

> If the Pharisees based much of their program for Jewish life on a revised understanding of the purity laws and an application of them to all Israel, . . . then the conflict between the Sadducees and Pharisees on this issue is comprehensible and probably historical in its general content. The application of purity laws to the people at large was a new mode of understanding Jewish life, law and scripture and it is reasonable and even inevitable that the Sadducees or someone else should oppose them.[28]

The Babylonian Talmud demonstrates that the Pharisees dominated the Sadducees, even in details of temple cultus, such as the lighting of incense. But it is hard to see why Saldarini comments concerning the Talmud's "generalization . . . that the Sadducees feared the Pharisees and so followed their interpretations of the law" that "This later Babylonian view is hardly historical for the first century."[29] It is corroborated by Josephus.[30]

Saldarini's conclusion that

---

24. Acts 23:6; 26:5, Phil 3:5.
25. Saldarini, *Pharisees*, 221.
26. Ibid., 222–5.
27. Ibid., 231f.
28. Ibid., 233f.
29. Ibid., 235.

30. "For whenever they try to give a lead, they are compelled against their will to do what the Pharisees say, because anything else would be intolerable for the masses" (Josephus, *Antiquities* 18:1:2–6).

> From the Rabbinic traditions we can learn a bit about the Pharisees, especially in the first century ... But these texts do not reveal the internal structure of the Pharisaic groups, how demanding membership was, what parts of society were drawn to membership, the size of the groups or many other aspects of group structure[31]

is only valid if Pharisaism is assumed to be a sect like the Essenes with a tightly defined membership and structure. If, in contrast, in the first century it was normative Judaism, the grouping to which ordinary Jews belonged by default, the absence of any reference to these details in the sources is understandable, for they simply did not apply.

---

31. Saldarini, *Pharisees*, 236.

5

Historical Reconstruction 1—The Origin of the Pharisees

UNDERSTANDING HOW A MOVEMENT originated often yields important clues concerning its later agenda and influence. Unfortunately the New Testament gives no information concerning the origins of the Pharisees—it accepts them as an established part of the social scene in first-century Palestine as it also accepts the Mount of Olives as a part of Jerusalem's backdrop. Neither do any other ancient documents explicitly describe how the movement came into being. There may be a clue in the Hebrew word *perushim* meaning "separated ones," which appears in the Rabbinic literature. Hellenized as *Pharisaioi*, "Pharisee" is in turn an anglicized singular version. It is not hard to imagine this originating as the pejorative nickname applied to a group of pious Jews who, deciding that authentic Judaism forbade them from conforming to the norms of their society, to some degree separated themselves from their peers.

Before we can seek the movement's origin, however, we must establish precisely what distinguishes a Pharisee from someone outside the movement. Otherwise, at a tumultuous time in Jewish history when many sects and movements were emerging and disappearing, it is all too easy to find ourselves following the wrong trail.

Historical Reconstruction 1—The Origin of the Pharisees

PHARISEE DISTINCTIVES

Although a parenthetical note in Acts 23:8 highlights some of the principal doctrinal differences between the Pharisees and the Sadducees and Josephus highlights the differences in the way the Pharisees, Essenes, and Sadducees understood "human experience,"[1] surely the most distinctive feature of Pharisaism, as Ellis Rivkin observes,[2] is its concept of the twofold law. Not only did the Pharisees observe the commandments of Torah as written in the Pentateuch, but also a whole compendium of oral law which they had compiled and were continuing to compile. This attempted to extend the principles underlying Torah to circumstances which the written scripture did not explicitly cover. As these oral laws were based upon Torah, they were regarded as equally binding with the written Torah. The intention—that in every possible situation a Jew should know exactly what response would best accord with Torah principles and therefore please God—is undeniably worthy, but had unforeseen repercussions.

The New Testament never mentions this explicitly, probably because its authors were so familiar with it that they assumed that their readers would be also; this was something that "everyone knows." There is abundant evidence in the gospels of its unexplained presence. For example, when Pharisees criticized Jesus for dining with tax collectors and sinners (Matt 9:10f), it was oral law that he had infringed; the written Torah contains no such prohibition. There was, however, a fatal flaw in the oral law. As the Rabbis attempted to cover ever more situations, the oral law so proliferated that no one could know the whole of it and some oral rulings conflicted with others. The extent of this oral law brought Jesus into dispute with mainstream Pharisaism, he claiming that it placed an intolerable burden on ordinary Jews: "They tie up heavy loads and put them on men's shoulders, but they themselves are not willing to lift a finger to move them" (Matt 23:4). In apostolic times the oral law was still causing problems for Christians; when converted Pharisees wanted to impose the Pharisaic legal system on Christian believers, Peter's response: "Now then, why do you try to test God by putting on the necks of the disciples a yoke that neither we nor our fathers have been able to bear?" (Acts 15:10) makes explicit what Jesus' saying had implied. It is this twofold law, undergirding the movement's approach to

---

1. Josephus: *Antiquities* 13:5:9.

2. "the Pharisees were the scholar class of the twofold Law" (Rivkin, *Revolution*, 179).

life, that is unique to Pharisaism and this will be taken as its distinguishing feature in our quest for the origin of the movement.

IDENTIFYING THE ORIGIN OF THE PHARISEE MOVEMENT

Although the origin of Pharisaism itself is lost in antiquity, no document giving any explicit account of it, I am indebted to Ellis Rivkin whose reconstruction makes compelling reading; the following account draws heavily upon his work.

Scholars have postulated a wide range of dates for the emergence of the Pharisees. These range from the Hasmonean period back to the time of Ezra or earlier. An even wider range has been suggested for that of the twofold Law. As Rivkin observes,

> No society can exist . . . with fixed, immutable laws, however divine they may be deemed to be. No sooner was the Pentateuch canonized than exegesis inevitably followed. The divine Law had to be studied with great care so that law might keep pace with life. A class of *Soferim*, Scribes or exegetes, thus sprang up as a necessary consequence of the canonization of the Pentateuch. This class, which looked to Ezra as their prototype, made the study of the Pentateuch their special concern and soon attained such mastery and skill that they replaced the priests as the caretakers of the Law. These *Soferim* were the forerunners, it is alleged, of the Pharisees. Long before the Hasmonean Revolt, so it is reasoned, they had pondered the Pentateuch, wrestled with the text, and drawn inferences that were not explicitly set forth therein.[3]

Historical technique

In his quest for the origin of the Pharisee movement Rivkin employed an eminently logical approach which may be summarized as follows: (i) establish a point in time when neither the Pharisees nor the twofold Law existed; (ii) establish a point in time when the existence of the Pharisees and the twofold Law is explicitly affirmed; and (iii) between their non-existence and

---

3. Rivkin, *Revolution*, 185f.

Historical Reconstruction 1—The Origin of the Pharisees

their existence identify a combination of historical circumstances whose nature seems likely to give rise to such a revolutionary phenomenon.[4]

The earliest date on which it has been demonstrated that the Pharisees existed, according to Rivkin,[5] is the time of Jonathan the Hasmonean. This is attested by Josephus, who states that they, together with the Sadducees and the Essenes, were flourishing at that time (*Antiquities* 13:171–3). To determine the latest date on which we may be certain that the Pharisees had not yet come into existence is less easy because it depends, ultimately, upon silence which is notoriously ambiguous. A given document's failure to mention a subject may be because it had not yet come into existence or because, although it *did* exist, the author had not heard of it or *had* heard of it, but chose not to mention it; silence therefore leaves open a multiplicity of possibilities. The only document whose silence may be taken as reliable evidence for the non-existence of a subject is one written by an author whose interests and knowledge are such that he or she would be *bound* to have heard of it and to mention it, if it existed. Rivkin claims to have identified just such a document[6] which he considers to demonstrate incontrovertibly the *non-existence* of the Pharisees or the twofold law at the time of its composition. This document forms part of the deuterocanonical literature, where it is known variously as Ecclesiasticus, the Wisdom of Jesus Ben Sira or, simply, Sirach. Unfortunately its date of composition is uncertain as this depends upon the disputed identities of a king named Euergetes, mentioned in the Prologue, and a high priest named Simon mentioned in the text (Sir 50:1). These leave a time frame extending from 280 to 180BCE.

The special value of this document is the sheer breadth of topics that it considers:

> Ben Sira roams through all the world that surrounds him, considering nothing too low for a well-turned proverb nor too exalted for an exhortatory maxim. And since everything was raw material for his Wisdom, Ben Sira can be assumed to have been silent only when there was *nothing* of significance to communicate. This holds especially with respect to religious life and institutions, the very leitmotiv of his discourses. For though Ben Sira rambles through

---

4. Ibid., 184.
5. Ibid., 185.
6. Ibid., 188.

all of society and its vagaries, he lavishes his greatest love on the cultus, the Aaronide priesthood and the Written Law.[7]

Rivkin's perfectly reasonable assumption, then, is that if the concept of the twofold law had been formulated or if the Pharisee movement had been in existence when Ben Sira wrote, he would surely have mentioned them somewhere in his document. Somewhat pretentiously Rivkin concludes that "Whatever Ben Sira does not mention specifically has no objective claim to existence."[8] The Jewish society that Ben Sira describes is presided over by Aaronide priests who interpret the written Pentateuch literally. Indeed his book offers such a fascinating insight into the religious conditions prevailing before the Pharisees and the twofold law made their revolutionary appearance that Rivkin devotes a chapter to a reconstruction of that society.[9] That chapter does leave the reader wondering what had happened to the *Soferim* or exegetes that Rivkin mentioned previously. These are the ones who had interpreted the Pentateuch ever since its canonization or since the time of Ezra. Ben Sira certainly writes about *Soferim*, but of a different kind: "Pentateuchalists, hierocratic intellectuals, Aaronide supremacists, and lovers and seekers of Wisdom. They were the devotees of the *onefold* Law, the Written Law, and of its authoritative spokesmen, the Aaronide priests."[10] If *Soferim* of the interpretive kind, forerunners of the Pharisees, did exist in Ben Sira's society, opposition from the Aaronide priesthood would surely have driven them underground.

Factors that triggered the birth of the Pharisee movement

So what can have brought into being a movement whose views were so radically different from those of the religious leaders of Ben Sira's society? Rivkin identifies a number of factors. One was a fundamental change in the structure of Jewish society itself, associated with the takeover of rule by the Seleucids in 197BCE. Their predecessors, the Ptolemies, had not been Hellenizers and under them Palestine had remained a predominantly rural, agricultural society, to which the Aaronide cultus was well suited. The Seleucids, in contrast, were aggressive Hellenizers who saw Greek culture

---

7. Ibid., 188f.
8. Ibid., 189.
9. Ibid., 191.
10. Ibid., 197.

Historical Reconstruction 1—The Origin of the Pharisees

as the ideal medium to unify their empire. Greek culture, however, was essentially urban, based around the city or *polis*. Rivkin writes,

> in the decades following Ben Sira's death, the ongoing process of urbanization had so altered the structure of experience of merchant, shopkeeper, artisan, and peasant alike that the Pentateuch no longer resonated with their deepest needs and their innermost yearnings. For the Pentateuch had been designed for a relatively simple agricultural-priestly society and not a highly complex urban-agricultural society embedded within a world of *poleis*—a world in which each individual was stirred on the one hand by feelings of loneliness, alienation, and insignificance, and on the other by intimations of personhood, self-worth, and immortality.[11]

It is not surprising, then, that Rivkin considers that among the factors that brought the twofold law out of hiding and gave rise to the Pharisee movement were "not only dissatisfaction but a heightened awareness that frustration is both unnecessary and susceptible to remedy."[12]

But most important was:

> a situation involving a catastrophic loss of confidence in the ability of the theocratic system to function effectively in a crisis threatening to extinguish the community itself—a situation jarring every individual out of his reliance on normal expectancies, forcing decision making of a most radical sort on every Jew, prying open the mind to the necessity for contemplating daring and frightening goals. It had to be the kind of situation to bring into question the very principles that underwrote the existing institutions of authority, power, and sanctity and to allow for the formulation of principles justifying novel institutions, elevating new and radical leaders into the positions of authority and power.[13]

Rivkin identifies a crisis of this severity in the effort of the Seleucid emperor Antiochus IV "Epiphanes" (175–163 BCE) to forcibly Hellenize the Jews.[14] Always short of money and facing threats to his empire from all sides, especially Rome, Antiochus was tempted by the wealth of the many temples in his empire. Early in his reign he accepted a large bribe from Jason, brother of Onias III, the legitimate high priest of Jerusalem, to re-

11. Ibid., 206f.
12. Ibid., 212.
13. Ibid., 212f.
14. Ibid., 213.

move Onias from office and install him in his place. Jason was the leader of a faction that favored the Hellenization of the Jews. Although he retained the cultus, the Aaronide priesthood and the authority of the Pentateuch, he introduced a gymnasium, Greek sports and Greek fashions into Jerusalem which profoundly shocked more conservative Jews.

Worse, however, was to come. After only three years in office Jason was outbid by another Hellenizing Jew, Menelaus, who to raise the funds for his bribe began stealing the temple vessels. In 169, on his return from a successful campaign in Egypt, Antiochus with Menelaus' assistance stripped the temple of its remaining treasures; not surprisingly this precipitated considerable unrest. To quell this, early in 167 Antiochus dispatched one Apollonius with a party of mercenaries to Jerusalem on a supposedly peaceful pretext. On arrival, however, he treated the city as an enemy conquest, slaughtering some Jews, taking others as slaves, looting and destroying property and establishing a citadel called the Acra containing a Seleucid garrison. This meant effectively that Jerusalem itself, including the temple, no longer belonged to the Jews, but was Hellenized pagan property. Antiochus' aim was probably to identify Yahweh with Zeus.

The horror with which faithful Jews viewed this incursion led Antiochus to ban the practice of Judaism altogether; this included the abolition of Sabbaths and all feasts. Pagan altars were erected throughout the land and unclean beasts sacrificed on them. An altar to Zeus was set up in the temple itself and pigs' flesh burned on it, the sacrilege reflected in Daniel's "abomination that causes desolation."[15] Jews were forced to eat unclean food and participate in pagan rites. Although some Jews complied with these demands, many resisted and paid with their lives. Far from bringing the Jews to submission, however, this led large numbers of them to take up arms in the Maccabean Rebellion of 167 to 164. Central to the resistance movement was a group of pious Jews known as the Hasidim from whose ranks it is widely believed that the Pharisees, Sadducees and Essenes evolved.[16]

That the Jewish uprising succeeded in overcoming Antiochus' army was due partly to the remarkable skills and courage of its own leaders and partly to the fact that Antiochus was fighting battles on so many fronts simultaneously that he could not commit the forces that would have been needed to subdue the Jews. The organized uprising is generally considered

15. Dan 9:27; 11:31; 12:11.
16. Bright, *History*, 403–408.

Historical Reconstruction 1—The Origin of the Pharisees

to have begun when a priest of Joarib's line named Mattathias not only refused to sacrifice to a pagan god but slew a fellow Jew who did agree to do so and also the emperor's officer who had ordered the sacrifice. Mattathias fled to the hills with his five sons John, Simon, Judas, Eleazar, and Jonathan, where they were joined by many other Jews who were fleeing persecution, including some of the Hasidim. They then began a guerrilla campaign against the Seleucids and those Jews who had complied with their Hellenizing regime. When Mattathias died in 166, he was succeeded by his son Judas, known as Judas Maccabeus, whose bravery was so outstanding that the rebellion is often called by his name. His succession of victories against Seleucid armies, some many times greater than his own, led many disheartened Jews to rally to his banner, regarding him as a God-sent deliverer. In 165 Judas recaptured Jerusalem and cleansed the temple, this event subsequently being commemorated in the annual feast of Hanukkah, "the Festival of Lights."[17] The Jewish struggle to remain independent, however, was destined to continue for some time.

The trail of evidence in the inter-testamental literature

This, then, is the tumultuous *milieu* in the midst of which Pharisaism came into being. Any quest in ancient literature for a single event that might be considered the birth of Pharisaism is, however, foredoomed to failure. As Rivkin puts it, "The Pharisaic Revolution has remained a hidden revolution, but it was a revolution nonetheless."[18] Perhaps "evolution" might be a more apt description, for its emergence was almost certainly a gradual process rather than a single event. The Books of Maccabees in which one might expect an account of this new development seem strangely silent, concentrating on the more dramatic events of the Hasmonean Revolt and suggesting that the Hasmoneans restored Judaism to its former self rather than, through the emergence of Pharisaism, radically changing it for ever. Commenting on this, Rivkin writes, "The sources may have obscured it, but they did not totally erase all its markings. Telltale data have seeped through the cracks and crevices of silence—data that presuppose the revolution not explicitly mentioned."[19]

---

17. Ibid., 410f.
18. Rivkin, *Revolution*, 215.
19. Ibid., 215.

Hypocrites or Heroes?

As an example Rivkin reproduces 1 Macc 14:27–48 which, he claims, records "a truly revolutionary act."[20] This passage relates how a "great congregation" (*sunagōgē megalē*) consisting of "priests, and people, and rulers of the nation, and elders of the country" decided that Mattathias' son "Simon should be their governor and high priest for ever, until there should arise a faithful prophet." Rivkin explains why this is revolutionary:

> The family of Joarib were a priestly family, but not a High Priestly family. Hence, neither Jonathan, who had been serving as High Priest, or Simon, who was now invested with the High Priesthood, had a right to be the High Priest, since they were not direct descendants of Zadok, Phinehas, Eleazar, and Aaron. As far as the Pentateuchal Law was concerned, they were usurpers. The High Priesthood belonged, as of right, only to Zadokites.[21]

Moreover, that such an appointment should be made by a *sunagōgē megalē* is remarkable, indeed unprecedented. There is no mention in the Old Testament of a *sunagōgē megalē*, so that strictly speaking, it had no authority whatever and was effectively subverting the Pentateuch. So, whence did the *sunagōgē megalē* derive its authority? Rivkin claims that this was from "laws not written down in the laws of Moses"[22]—in other words, oral law as binding as the written Torah. And that, as established at the start of this chapter, is the distinguishing feature of the Pharisees. So those who brought the *sunagōgē megalē* into being and declared its decisions in accordance with oral law and therefore with the principles of Torah and with God's will were Pharisees or forerunners of the Pharisees. Rivkin sees a confirmation that this or something very like it marks the origin of Pharisaism in that:

> the Pharisees are umbilically related to the Sadducees (the Zadokites), whose historical origins are indelibly impressed in their name. They came to be called Sadducees because of their insistence that only a descendant of the Aaron-Eleazar-Phinehas-Zadok line could minister as High Priest. And the only time this right was challenged by Jews utterly loyal to God and his revelation and not Hellenists at all was when Jonathan took over the High Priesthood and when a Great Synagogue, *sunagōgē megalē*, publicly proclaimed this transfer of power sacrosanct. The rejection

20. Ibid., 216.
21. Ibid., 217.
22. Ibid., 219f.

Historical Reconstruction 1—The Origin of the Pharisees

of this act by the Zadokites-Sadducees set them in opposition to those who had legitimated this transfer of power on the basis of an authority *not* written down in the Law of Moses. These must have been the champions of the laws not written down, the *paradosis*, the *Soferim* of the twofold Law, in contradistinction to the Aaronide-*Soferim* of Ben Sira's day. And it was these *Soferim* whom the Zadokites-Sadducees, in their wrath, denounced as *perushim*, "separatists," "heretics." The umbilical cord from which neither would be sundered was thus tightly tied. And undergirding the Great Synagogue, the *sunagōgē megalē*, as a creation of Soferim-Pharisees is the fact that while the term *Knesset ha-Gedolah* [that is, Great Synagogue] is nowhere found in the Bible, it is recalled in the tannaitic texts as a body of supreme importance which was so endowed with authority that it canonized the prophets and the Hagiographa.[23]

Rivkin, then, sees the Pharisees and Sadducees as two opposing parties that emerged from the Maccabean Rebellion, whose principal difference appeared outwardly to be their understanding of who was entitled to serve as High Priest. This outward difference, however, was the consequence of a more radical inward difference concerning authority: Sadducees accepted as authoritative only the Pentateuch understood literally, whereas Pharisees accepted a broader canon and reserved the right to interpret scripture liberally, their interpretations retaining the divine authority of the original. Moreover, in that a Great Synagogue, *sunagōgē megalē*, was responsible not only for Jonathan's appointment as High Priest, but also for the canonizing of the Prophets and the Writings as scripture alongside the Pentateuch—another Pharisee distinctive—surely herein lies the core of Pharisee authority.

The evidence in Josephus

It may be significant that the "great congregation" that appointed Simon as High Priest consisted of priests, people, rulers of the nation and elders of the country. This constitution resembles that of the Sanhedrin of Temple times; could it be that the Sanhedrin, dominated as it was by Pharisees, saw its precedent or origin in that "great congregation"? It is interesting that the authority of the "great congregation" that appointed Simon as High Priest was apparently accepted by the Hasmoneans and the general populace. This suggests that at that time the Pharisees had already enjoyed

23. Ibid., 220f.

considerable success in winning the people over to their views and had probably been actively promoting them for some time. This is supported by the earliest mention of Pharisees in Josephus—his brief comparison of the ways in which the three ideologies understood human experience (Josephus: *Antiquities* 13:5:9, reproduced on p. 110)—because he claims that all three were active at the time of Jonathan the High Priest.

Josephus' next reference to the Pharisees confirms their influence. One of those whom the "great congregation" had legitimated was John Hyrcanus, a son of Simon. John regarded himself as a disciple of the Pharisees and sought their approval that he was following the path of righteousness. When the Pharisees imposed too lenient a judgment on a somewhat unpleasant character named Eleazar who made a misguided remark about John's mother, he was persuaded to leave the Pharisees and join the Sadducees. In the process he rescinded the laws which the Pharisees had introduced; these, based on the *paradosis* rather than the written Pentateuch, had been rejected by the Sadducees. Josephus notes that the Pharisaic law had the support of the masses, in contrast with the literalist Torah of the Sadducees (Josephus: *Antiquities* 13:10:5f). Not surprisingly John's actions triggered insurrection, civil war between the *paradosis*-favoring Pharisees and literalist Sadducees. As Sanders comments, "The story about Eleazar's remark puts into the terms of personal drama what was more likely serious religio-political opposition. It may even tell us one of the things that the party held against Hyrcanus: his combining the offices of high priest and king."[24]

The unrest continued through the reigns of Hyrcanus' sons Aristobolus I (104–103) and his brother Alexander Jannaeus (103–76), whose opponents were probably Pharisees. Jannaeus' widow Salome Alexandra succeeded him, becoming Israel's only reigning queen (76–67).[25] As she had become a disciple of the Pharisees, she reinstated the *paradosis*-based laws, effectively restoring power to the Pharisees (Josephus: *Antiquities* 16:1f). During Salome's reign the Pharisees seized the opportunity to execute or banish many of their enemies, many probably being Sadducees, in retaliation for their own persecution by Jannaeus. After Salome's death in 67 little more is heard of the Pharisees until in 37 Herod, backed by Rome and supported by the Pharisees, conquered Jerusalem. The Pharisees no longer enjoyed the same power as under Salome, but were popular and

24. Sanders, *Judaism*, 380.
25. Ibid., 381.

influential, sometimes supporting Herod and sometimes engaging in mild rebellion against him.[26]

The New Testament period

The New Testament finds the Pharisees still effectively in power, subject of course to the Roman political supremacy. As Rivkin summarizes the situation, "The Gospels, Acts, and the Epistles of Paul—all attest to the hegemony of the Pharisees. The overarching framework of presuppositions, laws and modes of communication was so Pharisaic that Jesus, Paul, and the earliest disciples could confront the Pharisees only with tools the Pharisees had devised and fashioned."[27] It seems remarkable that Rivkin stops short of describing Pharisaism as normative Judaism.

Deines, however, is less restrained. He concludes that Pharisaism "is a separate movement *within* the nation *for* the nation, whose legitimacy was indeed *accepted* by large parts of the people, even though its requirements were not *observed* to an equal extent. This provides us in my opinion also with justification to consider Pharisaism as normative Judaism, not because all *lived* according to Pharisaic halakhah, but because Pharisaism was by the majority acknowledged as [the] legitimate and authentic interpretation of the divine will for the chosen nation."[28]

Maccoby also contends that Pharisaism was the dominant expression of Judaism in the first century: "In more recent years, however, a new trend is discernible . . . asserting the existence of a normative Judaism in the first century, and which actually goes back to identifying this normative Judaism with Pharisaism, in accordance with the copious ancient testimony to this effect . . ."[29]

---

26. Ibid., 382–4.
27. Rivkin, *Revolution*, 275.
28. Deines, "Pharisees," 501.
29. Maccoby, *Jesus*, 76.

6

Historical Reconstruction 2—The Pharisees at the Time of Jesus

THIS CHAPTER SEEKS TO build a systematic picture of the Pharisee movement based on the references to them in the New Testament and other sources as considered in the previous chapters.

WHO WERE THE PHARISEES?

At the end of the previous chapter we saw that many scholars have concluded that Pharisaism was not a minority sect, but the normative Judaism of Second-Temple Israel, that is, the form of Judaism to which ordinary Jews belonged by default. As soon as we accept this, however, we find ourselves facing a hermeneutical problem. Whenever the New Testament uses the word *Pharisaios*, as it does 98 times, to precisely whom is it referring? If Pharisaism is normative Judaism, most Jews are by definition Pharisees, so why do the authors not say, instead, "Jews"? Of course, as we established in Chapter 3, in John's Gospel many—indeed probably most—of the 67 occurrences of *hoi Ioudaioi*, "the Jews," *do* refer to the Pharisees.

When, however, we examine the individuals whom the New Testament describes as "Pharisees," we find that they are not typical of the Jewish populace at large. Jesus and his disciples never refer to themselves as Pharisees; indeed the only person in the New Testament who does so is Paul. In the New Testament, "Pharisees" always denotes people who exercise

Historical Reconstruction 2—The Pharisees at the Time of Jesus

authority, officials of some sort. Again, this accords with our analysis of *hoi Ioudaioi* in John in Chapter 3 which concluded that 46 of the 67 occurrences refer to officialdom. For example, "the Jews" in John 9:22, clearly the same people as those described as "the Pharisees" in John 12:42, had enacted legislation to excommunicate Jews who confessed Jesus as the Messiah. Not only do these people wield authority, but in this particular instance they exercise it at Sanhedrin level; they are legislators. Indeed, in these and some other examples, "the Jews" and "the Pharisees" are used as nicknames for the Sanhedrin, perhaps because it was *the* Jewish seat of power and it was dominated by the Pharisees. Saldarini, then, is justified in claiming that the Pharisees act "as official representatives of the governing class."[1]

Paul provides a significant example of a Pharisee who exercised an official role. While still called Saul, he obtained "letters" from the high priest empowering him to arrest Jews in Damascus who had become followers of Jesus (Acts 9:1f). Clearly, then, he was serving as a kind of police officer under the Sanhedrin's authority.

Most occurrences of "Pharisees" or "the Jews," then, refer to officials usually acting with the Sanhedrin's authority. If we ask what kind of function these Pharisaic officials served, even a cursory reading of the New Testament reveals that a frequent duty was the reprimanding of those who flouted the Pharisaic code of conduct, based on both written Torah and oral *paradosis*. So they exercised a kind of policing function. Presumably these official duties constituted paid employment; the Sanhedrin dispatched at least one deputation containing Pharisees to Galilee to observe Jesus; if those Pharisees normally supported themselves and their families by some other kind of paid work from which they had to take leave, such an assignment might have caused them serious financial hardship.

It is surely significant that the New Testament writers sometimes treat *Pharisaios* and *grammateus*, "teacher of the law," as synonyms, substituting one for the other.[2] Ultimately *grammateus* denotes someone who could read and write, skills which were less common in the ancient world than today, but which would have been essential for most officials. That 19 of the 63 occurrences of *grammateus* in the synoptic gospels are in conjunction with *Pharisaios* may accord with Rivkin's conclusion that the Pharisees constituted "the scholar class of the twofold Law."[3] On the other hand, no

---

1. Saldarini, *Pharisees*, 189.
2. See Appendix for further on these substitutions.
3. Rivkin, *Revolution*, 179.

fewer than 24 occurrences of *grammateus* appear in conjunction with the chief priests who were Sadducees rather than the Pharisees; these probably represent their administrative assistants or legal advisors, rather than Pharisaic teachers of the law.

So, while Pharisaism itself was normative Judaism—so that most ordinary Jews were technically Pharisees—in the New Testament the terms "the Pharisees," "the teachers of the law," and (in John's Gospel) "the Jews" most often refer to officials whose primary duty was enforcement of the twofold law.

DIVERSITY

If, as we have established, Pharisaism was the normative Judaism of Palestine at the time of Jesus, it embraces such a diversity of beliefs and practices that almost anything said about it will be true to some extent. Moreover, this means that technically all Jews were Pharisees unless they had "opted out" by becoming Sadducees or Essenes or they had been excommunicated so that they became "sinners" (see later). The diversity of Pharisees is evidenced, for example, in John 9:16. As with any diverse group, allowances must be made. Undoubtedly *some* Pharisees were hypocrites, but others were sincere. Probably *some* Pharisees were lovers of money, as Luke claims (Luke 16:14), but certainly most were not.

PHARISEE BELIEFS

This study deliberately glosses over Pharisee beliefs for two reasons. Firstly, the New Testament tells us little about what Pharisees believed, apart from resurrection, so that the researcher is compelled to look to Josephus, who tells us scarcely more than the New Testament, and the rabbinic literature whose problems of interpretation are beyond the scope of this study. Secondly, since Sanders covers this subject with exemplary scholarship in *Judaism Practice and Belief*,[4] those wishing to learn more about Pharisee beliefs are recommended to the relevant section of that work.

---

4. Sanders, *Judaism*, 413–451.

Historical Reconstruction 2—The Pharisees at the Time of Jesus

PRINCIPAL AGENDA: PURITY

Wright summarizes the agenda of the Pharisees in New Testament times as follows: "the Pharisees, broadly speaking, should be understood in terms of an overriding concern for *purity* . . . but . . . the main issue at stake for a Pharisee was not simply 'how to maintain one's own personal purity,' but 'how to be a loyal Jew faced with pagan oppression from outside and disloyal Jews from within.'"[5] Their concern for purity is reflected in the New Testament only in their approach to Jesus concerning his disciples' failure to wash their hands before eating (Matt 15:1–6; Mark 7:1–13). Wright is surely correct in his implication that that particular issue may have been eclipsed by the circumstances of the times. There were many ways in which Roman rule pressurized Jews to compromise their faith and the external pressure from Rome was exacerbated by that from Jews who abandoned the struggle and compromised, for example, by becoming tax collectors (who worked ultimately for the Romans). In these respects the situation resembled that during Maccabean times when Pharisaism came into being.

Sanders draws attention to an aspect of the Pharisaic concern for purity that is not reflected in the New Testament, namely its practice of purity rituals similar to those specified for the priests in Leviticus. While most Pharisees certainly did not consider themselves to *be* priests,[6] their practice of priestly purity rites adapted to suit their essentially urban lay lifestyle shows that they nevertheless aspired to be *like* them in some respects.[7] Saldarini hints at this phenomenon in his description of the "associates" when he states that "the people of the land do not keep the special priestly laws of purity."[8]

REPUTATION

Luke's Parable of the Pharisee and the Tax Collector (Luke 18:10–14) is particularly useful because its impact depends upon the accuracy of Jesus' portrayal of the two contrasting types—they needed to be sufficiently typical of their *genre* for Jesus' hearers to recognize them and perhaps identify them with individuals whom they knew. So, if the fictitious Pharisee in

---

5. Wright, *Paul*, 83.

6. In fact most priests were Pharisees with the exception of the high priests who were mostly Sadducees.

7. Sanders, *Judaism*, 438–440.

8. Saldarini, *Pharisees*, 217.

the parable was telling the truth and was typical of his peers—and there is circumstantial evidence that both were so—the Pharisees were pious, generous, upright citizens, pillars of Jewish society. Indeed, the individual in the parable exceeded the requirements of Torah: he fasted twice per week, although the annual Day of Atonement was the only obligatory fast in Judaism, and he gave "a tenth of all I get," while Torah demanded a tithe only of agricultural produce. Although the message of the parable is that appearances can be deceptive—even Pharisees may have faults and even tax collectors may change their ways and get right with God—the authenticity of its depiction of the Pharisees and their reputation is confirmed elsewhere in the New Testament.

For example, Acts 5:34 refers to "a Pharisee named Gamaliel, a teacher of the law [*nomodidaskalos*], who was honored by all the people." It is dangerous to argue from the particular to the general—that Gamaliel was held in such high public esteem need not indicate that all, or indeed any, other Pharisees were equally admired. But since Gamaliel was in fact the leader of the Pharisee movement,[9] it is reasonable to assume that his reputation was to some extent derived from that of the people over whom he presided; his popularity was therefore partly a product of the reputation of the Pharisee movement as a whole.

The esteem of the Pharisees with the public at large is confirmed by Josephus[10] and mentioned elsewhere in the teaching of Jesus, who clearly took a keen interest not only in them, but also in the attitude of the populace towards them. For example, on four occasions in the synoptics Jesus alludes to the Pharisees and/or teachers of the law enjoying being "greeted in the market-places."[11] While these greetings may indicate that the public admired them and deferred to them in a manner recalling the adulation of the public for celebrities in western culture in the early 21st century, they may also have been the salutations with which Pharisees addressed each other. Even if it were proven that these greetings were from the populace at

---

9. Maccoby, *Jesus*, 5f.

10. "Now because they [the Pharisees] happen to be the most persuasive, whatever the people do concerning divine worship and the interpretation of holy matters are all in accordance with their practices. The cities testify to their devotion to their ample goodness which is superior to everything in lifestyle and teaching" (*Antiquities* 18:1); "the Pharisees ... have the support of the masses" (*Antiquities* 13:10); author's own translation of both passages.

11. Matt 23:7; Mark 12:38; Luke 11:43; 20:46.

Historical Reconstruction 2—The Pharisees at the Time of Jesus

large, it does not necessarily demonstrate popularity, but polite respect—a schoolboy might address a master as "Sir," without necessarily liking him.

Nevertheless the Josephus passages cited earlier certainly suggest popularity. So why were the Pharisees so popular with the public? Surely there must have been other factors besides their piety and uprightness, commendable though those qualities may be? Probably there are two: their legal acumen and their power.

Legal acumen

According to Josephus, "the Pharisees consider themselves to be experts in the precise elucidation of legal matters."[12] The gospels do not state this explicitly, but imply it *passim*, whenever Pharisees or *grammateis* approach Jesus or his disciples regarding some supposed breach of the law or some legal question.

As we have established, what distinguished the Pharisees from other groups was their concept of the *oral law*—they considered that blind obedience to the literal demands of Torah was insufficient. They sought to ascertain the principles underlying the written commands and apply these in situations not covered by the written Torah, the resulting unwritten laws being regarded as equally binding with the written ones. The arguably worthy intention was that in every conceivable situation Jews should know exactly what course of action accords best with Torah principles and therefore with God's will. The unfortunate by-product of this, a vast and ever-growing compendium of unwritten ordinances with which every pious Jew was expected to comply, is presumably the object of Jesus' criticism in such passages as Matt 23:4: "They tie up heavy loads and put them on men's shoulders, but they themselves are not willing to lift a finger to move them." Jesus' argument was that the myriad of unwritten laws had become an intolerable burden for ordinary people.

Nevertheless, from the earliest days of the movement the Pharisees enjoyed the popularity of the Jewish people and this was surely because, despite Jesus' accusation, they did make an effort to ease the burden of Torah observance, especially in regard to the Sabbath. The archetypal Sabbath law is Exod 20:10: "the seventh day is a Sabbath to the Lord your God. On it you shall not do any work, neither you, nor your son or daughter, nor your manservant or maidservant, nor your animals, nor the alien within

---

12. Josephus, *War*, 2:8:2 (author's own translation).

your gates." Central to the observance of this command is the question as to what constitutes "work," since ultimately this determines what is and what is not lawful on the Sabbath. Jews had become increasingly loath to do *anything* on the Sabbath for fear that if God regarded it as work they would thereby incur divine wrath. The Pharisees devised a system of "boundary extensions" which lessened some of the Sabbath restrictions, enabling the Jews to do more while retaining a clear conscience. It was surely because in this way they made life easier for ordinary Jews that they were hailed as heroes of the people.

Power

Although this is not stated explicitly in the New Testament, surely another reason for the Pharisees' popularity with the people is that they represented *power*; moreover, the way in which they wielded it stood in direct contrast with the other power brokers in first-century Palestine, namely the Romans and the Sadducees. Ultimately, of course, political and military power belonged to the occupying Romans who were hated by the Jews not only on account of their high taxes and cruel punishments (such as crucifixion), but also because they, pagan Gentiles, were interfering with the way in which God's own people conducted their affairs.

Internal Jewish affairs the Romans left to the Sanhedrin, the Jewish high council. This was composed of three subgroups: the chief priests, the chief teachers of the law and the elders of the people, the latter being heads of tribes and clans. The chief priests, occupying the pinnacle of Judaism's hierarchy, represented another power base. They were Sadducees, a small group which comprised a few high-priestly families and wealthy landowners. They were pro-Rome; recognizing them as influential, the Romans granted them privileges in exchange for their co-operation. This together with their reputation for rudeness to everyone, including other members of their own movement,[13] alienated them from the populace.

The other two constituents of the Sanhedrin, the chief teachers of the law and the elders of the people, probably consisted mainly of Pharisees. Consequently the Pharisees effectively dominated the Sanhedrin and decided its agenda and policies, as the Gamaliel incident demonstrates—see *Gamaliel speaks out for Peter and the apostles*, p. 83. Josephus also confirms

---

13. "the Sadducees' attitude towards each other is more brutal, treating each other in the same way as uncouth people would" (Josephus, *War* 2:8); author's own translation.

this: "For whenever they [the Sadducees] try to give a lead, they are compelled against their will to do what the Pharisees say, because anything else would be intolerable for the masses" (*Antiquities* 18:1; author's own translation). John's use of "the Jews" and "the Pharisees" as a synonym or nickname for the Sanhedrin also corroborates this—see *Interpreting the law* below—it was so-called because it was the seat of Pharisee and Jewish power. In contrast with the Romans and the Sadducees, the Pharisees were vehemently anti-Rome—indeed the revolutionary Zealot movement, which sought to restore Israel's self-determination by violent means, was a splinter group from their ranks. Moreover, as Pharisaism was normative Judaism, the Pharisees were non-exclusive, a movement *of* the people and *for* the people, making themselves available to all Jews. Because they used such power as they had to improve the lot of ordinary Jews, even if their oral law seemed overwhelming, their ultimate aim was to make it easier for them to obey Torah. The public at large recognized this and regarded them as the one power base in Palestine that was determinedly "on their side."

NUMBERS AND DISTRIBUTION

The influence or reputation of the Pharisees is to some extent linked to the number of individuals in the movement. Scholars have debated this for years. Wright writes:

> We do not know for sure how many Pharisees there were in the time of Jesus. The figure of six thousand, often quoted in this context from Josephus *Antiquities* 17.42, refers specifically to the Pharisees who refused to take the oath of allegiance to Caesar, some time in the reign of Herod the Great. In the forty years or so between that incident and the time of Jesus several important political events had taken place, which might well have induced many more to join the movement. We may assume that there were in any case plenty of Pharisees who were not involved with the particular event in question, and more again who were generally sympathetic to the movement . . . So, too, we do not know the geographical spread of Pharisaism at this stage. Granted that Jerusalem was almost certainly their base, the idea that they never went anywhere else should now be abandoned.[14]

---

14. Wright, *Jesus*, 377f.

Hypocrites or Heroes?

Of course, if as we have established, Pharisaism was normative Judaism at the time of Jesus, arguably *all* Jews were Pharisees except for those who had opted out to become Sadducees or Essenes or who had been excommunicated—see *Those "put out of the synagogue"—the "sinners,"* p. 155. If, however, we interpret "Pharisees" narrowly—as the evangelists seem to have done—so that we count only those individuals who acted as officials enforcing observance of the twofold law, the number is likely to be far less, perhaps in the thousands as Josephus states.

Their geographical distribution is important because the synoptics record many encounters between Jesus and Pharisees in Galilee; was there such a great population of Pharisees in Galilee? Saldarini considers it unlikely and on this basis questions the historical reliability of the synoptics: "The synoptic gospels place the Pharisees mostly in Galilee and hardly at all in Jerusalem. Rabbinic literature places the pre-destruction sages in Jerusalem and has little to say about Galilee. The historical reliability of the Galilean tradition which derives from Mark and his sources is questionable."[15] Similarly, Rudolf Bultmann is probably right in considering it highly unlikely: "There is an active tendency seeking always *to present the opponents of Jesus as Scribes and Pharisees.*"[16] He presents evidence that in many of the Galilean conflict stories Jesus' opponents are initially unidentified and only later named as Pharisees or teachers of the law; he concludes that the evangelists were seeking to cast the Pharisees in the role of Jesus' enemies. On this basis there may have been few Pharisees in Galilee. If so, this would accord with John 4:1–3 in which Jesus retreats from Judea to Galilee in order to escape the unwelcome attention of the Pharisees. It is surely significant that Jesus, who had spent most of his life in Galilee and so presumably was familiar with its religious ambience, apparently expected to escape the Pharisees by returning there. Nevertheless, the supposedly Galilean audience of Jesus' saying in Matt 5:20, "For I tell you that unless your righteousness surpasses that of the Pharisees and the teachers of the law, you will certainly not enter the kingdom of heaven," would have found it incomprehensible unless they were familiar with Pharisees and teachers of the law. Of course, this assumed familiarity may result either from the presence of *some* Pharisees in Galilee or from encounters with Pharisees in Judea while visiting Jerusalem, for example, for the Passover, as pious Jews were expected to do each year.

15. Saldarini, *Pharisees*, 291.
16. Bultmann, *Synoptic Tradition*, 52.

Historical Reconstruction 2—The Pharisees at the Time of Jesus

In Matt 23:15 Jesus refers to the missionary zeal of Pharisees, implying that sometimes they traveled to spread their faith. Galilee's mixed Jewish and Gentile population might have had special appeal to Pharisaic missionaries: Jews surrounded by paganism might be more amenable than others to the fundamentalist and nationalist emphases of Pharisaism.

Saldarini, considering the evidence that can be gleaned from the letters of Paul, makes the somewhat ambiguous comment: "Since Paul lived and worked in the greater Syrian area as a Pharisee, it is somewhat probable that Pharisaism had some influence there and that some Pharisees lived outside Jerusalem and Judea. However, the evidence that Pharisaic teaching and influence spread beyond the Palestinian borders is very tenuous."[17]

If Pharisees and teachers of the law were so scarce in Galilee, why do the synoptics record so many instances of Jesus encountering them there? Is Bultmann correct in his assertion that the evangelists artificially cast them in the role of Jesus' enemies? In fact there is a solution that reconciles the integrity of the synoptics with the historical evidence that Pharisees rarely visited Galilee. Careful analysis of those encounters reveals that many if not all of them were with a delegation of officials from Jerusalem (and occasionally elsewhere, as in Luke 5:17) sent, presumably by the Sanhedrin, to observe Jesus and especially to test his orthodoxy.[18] That a similar delegation consisting of Pharisees and Sadducees had been sent to investigate John the Baptist (see *Pharisees and Sadducees visit John the Baptist*, p. 14) indicates that the Sanhedrin attached high priority to the scrutiny of new religious developments. It seems most likely, then, that Jesus' frequent encounters with Pharisees in Galilee were the consequence of the special interest that his ministry was attracting at Sanhedrin level and therefore not evidence that Pharisees were normally numerous there.

INTERPRETING THE LAW

In his teaching Jesus acknowledged the role of the Pharisees as interpreters of the law and even enjoined obedience to them: "The teachers of the law and the Pharisees sit in Moses' seat. So you must obey them and do everything they tell you" (Matt 23:2f). Two passages in John's Gospel, which

---

17. Saldarini, *Pharisees*, 138.
18. Matt 15:1; Mark 3:22; 7:1–5; Luke 5:17–21. These verses refer explicitly to officials coming from Jerusalem to observe Jesus; many others imply that Jesus was under surveillance.

need to be studied in conjunction, provide a specific example. According to John 9:22, "the Jews had decided that anyone who acknowledged that Jesus was the Christ would be put out of the synagogue." John 12:42 reads, "But because of the Pharisees they would not confess their faith for fear they would be put out of the synagogue." Note that "the Jews" in the first passage has become "the Pharisees" in the second. Considering each in the light of the other, these verses suggest that the Pharisees had introduced legislation to excommunicate any Jew who acknowledged that Jesus was Messiah. Moreover, they imply that the Pharisees had the authority to administer such excommunications (for further see *Those "put out of the synagogue"— the "sinners,"* p. 155). If so, the Pharisees could to some extent determine who was and who was not a member of the Jewish community, a weighty responsibility indeed. How had they acquired such power? As we have established, in John's Gospel some instances of "the Pharisees" and "the Jews" refer in fact to the Sanhedrin, which was effectively under Pharisee control. It was the Sanhedrin that had enacted this legislation and which administered the excommunications; it was almost certainly a session of the Sanhedrin that John's Gospel reports in vivid detail in chapter 9. Although the Pharisees had no constitutional role in the Sanhedrin, two of its three constituent bodies, the chief teachers of the law and the elders of the people, probably consisted mostly of Pharisees. As the Gamaliel incident— see *Gamaliel speaks out for Peter and the apostles,* p. 83—demonstrates, the Sanhedrin was to all intents and purposes a committee of Pharisees.

ENFORCING THE LAW

The Pharisees' duties in regard to the law, however, did not stop at its interpretation and enactment. Many NT references to the Pharisees show them as responsible for its enforcement; they therefore acted as a kind of police force. Saldarini describes the Pharisees as having a "supervisory role" in Jewish society.[19] The gospels show them reprimanding the public for various offenses. For example, they challenged Jesus' disciples when Jesus dined with tax collectors and "sinners" in Matthew/Levi's house (Matt 9:11–13 and parallels). Similarly they approached Jesus when his disciples allegedly profaned the Sabbath by plucking heads of corn (Matt 12:2 and parallels) and when they ate without first washing their hands (Matt 15:1–6; Mark 7:1–13). Since the first and third of these incidents did not infringe Torah,

19. Saldarini, *Pharisees*, 189.

Historical Reconstruction 2—The Pharisees at the Time of Jesus

it appears that their role was enforcement of Pharisaic *paradosis*, the oral law, which, as an interpretation of Torah, they regarded as equally binding with it.

This Pharisaic policing function was probably controlled, ultimately, by the Pharisee-dominated Sanhedrin, which legitimated it. All three synoptists report that Pharisees and teachers of the law were sent from Jerusalem to Galilee to observe Jesus.[20] Their purpose was to investigate his ministry, recalling a similar delegation's earlier investigation of John the Baptist (Matt 3:7, *c.f.* John 1:19, 24). Presumably local community leaders had become so concerned about Jesus' ministry that they had notified the Sanhedrin which sent its own investigators to Galilee to assess him for themselves. Although their official brief would have been to establish whether Jesus' teaching conformed to the Torah tradition, it is possible that there were other reasons—might Jesus pose some kind of threat to the Pharisee movement itself? From this time onwards Jesus was kept under surveillance. The incident of the man with the shriveled hand in the synagogue (Matt 12:9–14 and parallels) is significant in this respect; Luke states explicitly that the Pharisees contrived the situation in the hope of finding grounds on which Jesus could be arrested (Luke 6:7). Indeed, it was partly because Jesus was aware of this surveillance that he stopped teaching in plain language and began preaching exclusively in parables (Mark 4:33f); it would be difficult to find grounds for a charge of heresy or sedition in these innocuous stories.

John's Gospel shows that the surveillance continued when Jesus was in Jerusalem. For example, after Jesus healed the lame man at Bethesda (John 5:1–18) on a Sabbath, that in the eyes of the Pharisees constituting a serious violation of Sabbath law, Jesus refers to what may have been a formal warning in respect of this (John 7:21); if so this suggests that they had agents watching him. After this the Pharisees tightened the observation to see if he profaned the Sabbath again. No doubt they considered this surveillance justified when the healing of the man blind from birth also took place on a Sabbath (John 9:14). Their special interest in him is confirmed by the meticulous detail with which they investigated that healing, even interrogating the healed man's parents (John 9:18) and subjecting the man himself to a second round of questioning (John 9:24). Although it seems unlikely that the Pharisees *per se* had the authority to subject people to interrogation and summon witnesses, if the investigating body was the Sanhedrin itself,

---

20. Matt 15:1; Mark 3:22; 7:1; Luke 5:17.

effectively in Pharisee hands, it had the necessary authority—it was the highest court in the land, apart from the Roman authorities. The Pharisees had arrogated the functions of legislature, judiciary, legal profession and police. One might summarize the situation in vernacular English as, "They ran the whole show."

FAULTS OF THE PHARISEES

Self-importance

It seems as though the Pharisees had appropriated nearly all the limited power that the Romans delegated to the Jews and, as we have seen, it was on account of this, together with their piety and desire to ease the burden of Sabbath observance that they were popular with the Jewish public at large, as evidenced by the greetings in the marketplace. Jesus might have condoned this adulation if he had considered the Pharisees worthy models, but he recognized flaws in their piety (Matt 5:20). He saw that corruption had found inroads through the deference the public paid them: they—or some of them at least—enjoyed this so much that they had begun to encourage it by ostentation. Dressing in "flowing robes" (Mark 12:38; Luke 20:46) made them more conspicuous, attracting greetings from more admirers. The wide phylacteries and long tassels that supposedly symbolized piety (Matt 23:5) served the same purpose. This adulation fostered self-importance, shown in their preference for the VIP seats in synagogues.[21] The admiration of the public was becoming more important to them than God's approval: as Jesus expressed it, "Everything they do is done for men to see" (Matt 23:5).

Hypocrisy

It may be significant that a whole section of Jesus' Sermon on the Mount is concerned with the same danger (Matt 6:1–18). Its teaching is summarized succinctly in the opening verse: "Be careful not to do your 'acts of righteousness' before men, to be seen by them. If you do, you will have no reward from your Father in heaven." So Jesus considered that unworthy motives for religious observance nullified any benefit that it might have brought. Presumably it was witnessing such malpractice that prompted Jesus to deliver

21. Matt 23:6; Mark 12:39; Luke 11:43; 20:46.

this teaching. Unlike his broadly similar diatribe against hypocrisy in Matt 23/Luke 11, this passage does not name the guilty individuals or groups. Nevertheless, the similarities between the two passages leave little doubt as to whom Jesus had in mind.

It is sometimes pointed out that the Greek word *hupokritēs* with which Jesus so vehemently castigated the teachers of the law and Pharisees in Matt 23:15–33 was the regular Greek word for "actor." So was Jesus accusing his hearers of acting out a role like players on the stage—in reality they were not the same people that they purported to be? They claimed to be pious, but their preference for human approbation rather than divine approval invalidated their piety.

However, the situation is not as simple as it might seem. In the LXX *hupokritēs* is used with its later meaning of "one who fails to observe the standards he advocates" in Job 34:30 and 36:13; the cognate *hupokrisis* was used meaning "hypocrisy" by Phocylides in the 6th century BCE, by Polybius in the 2nd century BCE and in the LXX in 2 Maccabees. Because it is possible—if not probable—that Jesus was familiar with this usage of these words, his denunciation of the teachers of the law and Pharisees as "hypocrites" in Matt 23:15–33 may not have had actors in mind, despite the immediate appeal of that suggestion.

Self-righteousness

In the Parable of the Pharisee and the Tax Collector the fictitious Pharisee commends his own righteousness: "God, I thank you that I am not like other men—robbers, evildoers, adulterers—or even like this tax collector" (Luke 18:11). In other words, he had compared his own conduct with that of his peers and judged himself superior to most if not all. Moreover, he assumed that God would share his estimation of himself.

As was said earlier, the parable's immediacy depends upon the accuracy of its portrayal of the two characters. The parable suggests, then, that such self-righteousness was a common failing among Pharisees. Indeed, as mentioned earlier, much of the teaching of Jesus, especially in the Sermon on the Mount (for example, in Matt 6:1–18), is intended to eliminate this fault. Jesus repeatedly urges his hearers to shield their piety from their peers in order to preclude the possibility of such false motives and thereby ensure that obedience to God's will is their sole priority.

Hypocrites or Heroes?

Each of the three faults enumerated above—self-importance, hypocrisy, and self-righteousness—blurs into the others. Moreover, they are by no means peculiar to the Pharisees. The inevitable consequence of human fallibility and the unattainable ideals of theism is surely that all religious people throughout the ages have struggled with them to some extent. The Pharisees themselves were certainly aware of this problem, as Maccoby observes:

> The rabbis were well aware of the danger of hypocrisy and were constantly on their guard against it. Many rabbinic passages show their abhorrence of it. Their nomenclature in this regard is interesting. They use more than one designation to denote "hypocrite," but a particularly interesting expression used for this purpose is "someone whose inside is not like his outside." . . . attacks on hypocrites were a familiar rabbinic topos, and Jesus is here treading well-trodden ground, though the editors of the Gospels, in their hatred of the Pharisees, extend these attacks to the whole Pharisee movement, rather than to individuals.[22]

Maccoby is surely correct in his final statement. The evangelists' portrayal of Jesus as castigating all Pharisees as hypocrites is certainly an exaggeration. None would doubt that some and perhaps even most Pharisees were guilty of hypocrisy to some extent; inevitably the same is true of Christian believers today who claim to follow a Lord who enjoined perfection (Matt 5:48). The evangelists do, however, acknowledge that there were some Pharisees whose sincerity and integrity were exemplary, as is clear from the example of Nicodemus.

THE PLOTS AGAINST JESUS

Surely the most serious accusation that the New Testament makes about the Pharisees is that they plotted against Jesus. One such plot, while Jesus was in Galilee, is mentioned in Mark and Matthew:

> Then the Pharisees went out and began to plot with the Herodians how they might kill Jesus. (Mark 3:6)
> But the Pharisees went out and plotted how they might kill Jesus. (Matt 12:14)

---

22. Maccoby, *Jesus*, 84f.

Historical Reconstruction 2—The Pharisees at the Time of Jesus

A later plot when Jesus was in Jerusalem is mentioned in Mark and Luke:

> Now the Passover and the Feast of Unleavened Bread were only two days away, and the chief priests and the teachers of the law [*grammateis*] were looking for some sly way to arrest Jesus and kill him. (Mark 14:1)
>
> Every day he was teaching at the temple. But the chief priests, the teachers of the law [*grammateis*] and the leaders among the people were trying to kill him. (Luke 19:47)
>
> and the chief priests and the teachers of the law [*grammateis*] were looking for some way to get rid of Jesus, for they were afraid of the people. (Luke 22:2)

In John's Gospel, following the healing of the crippled man at Bethesda we read that:

> For this reason the Jews tried all the harder to kill him; not only was he breaking the Sabbath, but he was even calling God his own Father, making himself equal with God. (John 5:18)

In John "the Jews," as demonstrated in chapter 3, usually refers to the Pharisees. In John 8:40 Jesus addressing "the Jews" states, "you are determined to kill me." This claim might seem justified by the following passages:

> At this, they picked up stones to stone him, but Jesus hid himself, slipping away from the temple grounds. (John 8:59)
> Again the Jews picked up stones to stone him, (John 10:31)
> So from that day on they plotted to take his life. (John 11:53)

The New Testament's claims seem a serious charge against the Pharisees, but was the intention of the plots described in these passages to *kill* Jesus? Neither the Pharisees nor any Jewish authority could have executed Jesus lawfully because the Romans had abolished Jewish death sentences. So any such alleged plots would of necessity be conspiracies to kill Jesus unlawfully, that is, to murder him.

Let us consider the first plot mentioned in the synoptics. Mark alone in Mark 3:6 records the detail that that plot was "with the Herodians." The Pharisees and the Herodians had so little in common that for them to act in concert would certainly have attracted attention. It might have been only because of this that Mark became aware that the meeting had taken place. But how did Mark (whose gospel was copied by Matthew) *know* that it concerned "how they might kill Jesus"? It is hardly likely that a meeting of this sort was open to the public. So Mark's assertion is sheer conjecture. Indeed, the Greek text of Mark 3:6 is ambiguous: *kai exelthontes hoi Pharisaioi euthus meta tōn Hērōdianōn sumboulion edidoun kat' autou hopōs auton apolesōsin*, literally, "And when they went out, the Pharisees at once took counsel with the Herodians against him as to how they might destroy him." The verb rendered "kill" in the NIV and "destroy" in the KJV and RSV is *apollumi* which occurs no fewer than 92 times in the New Testament and has a broad range of meanings. Although Liddell and Scott's lexicon does list "kill" and "slay" among its meanings, Thayer's New Testament lexicon gives its primary meaning as "destroy *i.e.* to put out of the way entirely, abolish, put an end to, ruin." Undoubtedly it is used sometimes in the New Testament to mean "kill" (for example, in John 18:14) and intransitively to mean "perish." Nevertheless it would be unsafe to assume that because this verb *can* mean "kill" that is what it *does* mean in this passage. As we shall see, a more appropriate rendering in the present context might be "ruin."

That the Pharisees of all people understood and respected Torah with its prohibition of murder hardly needs saying. Despite the faults mentioned earlier in this chapter, they are not the kind of people whom we should expect to find conspiring to commit cold-blooded murder. It is inherently more likely—especially in view of their legal expertise—that the meeting considered the lawful remedies available to alleviate the threat that Jesus posed. That this was indeed their agenda is made explicit in Mark 3:2, paralleled in Matt 12:10 and Luke 6:7: "Some of them were looking for a reason to accuse Jesus, so they watched him closely . . ." That this was still their intention after the healing is evident from Luke 6:11: "But they were furious and began to discuss with one another what they might do to Jesus." This is exactly the kind of action that we should expect from the Pharisees—and the close surveillance under which Jesus was kept during the later part of his ministry[23] may have been the outcome of that meeting. Interestingly, the only other occasion in the New Testament in which the Pharisees and the Herodians are reported as co-operating is Mark 12:13 where they set out "to catch him [Jesus] in his words." If, as the involvement of the Herodians suggests, this is part of the same conspiracy, here is confirmation that the intention was not to kill Jesus, but to destroy his reputation; if he lost his following, he would cease to be a threat to the establishment. All the

---

23. For example, the synoptic gospels mention deputations from Jerusalem travelling to Galilee to hear Jesus, probably to investigate him, in Mark 3:22; Luke 5:17; Matt 15:1f/ Mark 7:1–5.

Historical Reconstruction 2—The Pharisees at the Time of Jesus

evidence suggests, then, that the meeting mentioned in Mark 3:6 decided to keep Jesus under close surveillance in the hope of observing some offense for which he could be arrested and thereby lawfully removed from circulation, his reputation "ruined." Ultimately, of course, the fact remains that the Pharisees did *not* kill Jesus—see *Jesus' trial and passion: the unexpected twist in the tale*, p. 193.

There is another possibility that must be considered. The alleged reason for these plots against Jesus is that he violated the Sabbath by healing on it. Maccoby believes that the officials with whom Jesus debated concerning his (or his disciples') breaking of the Sabbath were not Pharisees, but Sadducees. He suggests that in the relevant texts the original word was "Sadducees" which some editor has changed to "Pharisees"; for a detailed evaluation of this theory see later under *Sabbath breaking*, p. 197. Maccoby cites in support of this theory Mark's statement concerning the alliance between the Pharisees and the Herodians; this he describes as "quite impossible," while an alliance between the Sadducees and the Herodians is entirely feasible—those two groups had much in common and often collaborated.[24] There is much to commend Maccoby's theory; indeed in many ways it is more consistent with what is known about the Pharisees and the Sadducees than the traditional belief that Jesus argued with the Pharisees about Sabbath observance. If Maccoby's theory is true, it was not Pharisees who plotted against Jesus, but Sadducees. All other aspects of the plot as discussed above remain true—it was not a plot to kill Jesus, but to ruin his reputation and therefore his influence. And eventually, of course, it was the Sadducees—in the persons of the chief priests—who *did* kill Jesus, inasmuch as they blackmailed the Roman Governor into crucifying him.

The later Jerusalem plots in Mark and Luke and the plots mentioned in John, which also take place in Jerusalem, are somewhat different. Apart from the two Lucan passages which use the ambiguous *apollumi* (see above), the Greek verb used is *apokteinō* whose definitive meaning is "kill." Mark's reference to "some sly way" heightens the sinister atmosphere. In the Marcan and Lucan passages the conspirators are consistently described as "the chief priests and the teachers of the law [*grammateis*]," although "the leaders among the people" are appended in Luke 19:47, making this possibly refer to the whole Sanhedrin. It is surely significant that the Pharisees whom Jesus had so frequently engaged in debate during his ministry are not mentioned by name. The chief priests are always listed first, presumably

---

24. Maccoby, *Jesus*, 125.

because they were seen as the prime instigators. The *grammateis* may have been their administrative assistants or legal advisers rather than Pharisee teachers of the law. So there is no evidence that Pharisees were involved in this later plot.

The perpetrators in John 5:18 are described as "the Jews." Although John often uses this term as an alternative to "the Pharisees," this is by no means its only possible meaning. Often—and clearly in this instance—it carries connotations of authority: so these were Jewish officials. Although those officials are often Pharisees, in Jerusalem they might also be Sadducees. Moreover, this plot is the consequence of another Sabbath breach and, as Maccoby has demonstrated (see above), there is evidence that it was Sadducees rather than Pharisees with whom Jesus debated about Sabbath observance. Furthermore, Sadducees are more likely than Pharisees to object to Jesus' addressing God as "Father" as they do here. This was not a practice that Jesus originated—it is not uncommon in the later Old Testament scriptures,[25] as Pharisees would have known well. Since Sadducees, in contrast, accepted only the Pentateuch as scripture, to them the practice would indeed have seemed heretical or even idolatrous.

In John 8 and 10 while Jesus accuses "the Jews" of *wanting* to kill him, the two episodes in which they picked up stones sound more like instances of extreme anger: the stones may indeed have been picked up, but John does not state that any were actually thrown—surely this was a threatening gesture rather than a calculated attempt to kill Jesus. The evangelists, who with the possible exception of Luke have an anti-Pharisee bias, have escalated threats into a murderous conspiracy presumably to blacken the Pharisees; this not only adds drama to their story, but also makes Jesus a more acceptable alternative to the Jewish establishment. Similar techniques are used by 21st-century chroniclers to upgrade minor incidents into seemingly significant events in order to engage the public's interest and thereby sell more newspapers or attract more television viewers.

Although John 11:53 clearly reports a plot to kill Jesus within the context of a meeting of the Sanhedrin, the conspirators themselves are not identified. The plot is depicted as the response to a speech by the high priest Caiaphas who prophesied that it was expedient for one man to die for the nation (John 11:50). As the Pharisees and Sadducees were long-standing adversaries, it is most likely that the "they" who plotted to kill Jesus were the Sadducees following the lead of the high priest; it is unlikely that Pharisees

---

25. For example, Hos 11:1; Jer 3:4, 19; 31:9; Mal 1:6; 2:10.

would have responded in this way. It is possible that the Pharisees agreed to Jesus' arrest (John 11:57) in the hope that they might then persuade the Sadducee members of the Sanhedrin to adopt a less drastic course of action.

Only Luke among the evangelists seems warmly disposed towards the Pharisees. He alone mentions no plots by *Pharisaioi* to kill Jesus; he is also the only one to record the three occasions when Jesus was invited to dinner by Pharisees (Luke 7:36; 11:37; 14:1) and to report the Pharisees' warning to Jesus to flee from Herod Agrippa's territory (Luke 13:31).

Overviewing these passages, we are forced to conclude that there is no clear evidence of Pharisee involvement in any plot to *kill* Jesus. Pharisees probably were involved in one or more plots to find grounds on which Jesus could be arrested; that, however, would have been a perfectly lawful course of action.

THE PHARISEES' ATTITUDE TO OTHERS

Gentiles

The attitude of the Pharisees to those outside their movement is a complex subject. Even their attitude to Gentiles shows ambivalence. In general Jews were wary of Gentiles and the Pharisees were probably no exception to the rule. Matt 23:15, however, suggests that Pharisees engaged in some form of missionary activity that targeted them: "Woe to you, teachers of the law and Pharisees, you hypocrites! You travel over land and sea to win a single convert (*prosēluton*)." Although the expression "travel over land and sea" may be hyperbole, equivalent to the colloquial English phrase "go to great lengths," and the convert a Jew, *prosēlutos* generally denotes a Gentile convert and this certainly is how Keener understands the passage. It was, however, not necessary for Jews to travel in order to proselytize Gentiles: Luke 7:1–10 reports the healing in Capernaum of the servant of a Roman centurion of whom the local Jewish elders testify, "he loves our nation and has built our synagogue." It is surely a reasonable conclusion, then, that this centurion was a convert to Judaism; if so, it is inherently more likely that those instrumental in his conversion were Pharisees than Sadducees or Essenes. The Pharisees, then, apparently targeted Gentiles as potential converts to their form of Judaism.

Hypocrites or Heroes?

Sadducees and Essenes

There is even greater ambiguity in the New Testament's depiction of the attitude of the Pharisees towards Jews who were outside their movement. This is probably a consequence of uncertainty concerning precisely who were deemed to be outside the movement, that of course being the complement of those considered to be *inside* it. After all, if Pharisaism was the normative Judaism of first-century Palestine, having no formal membership and therefore being "the grouping to which ordinary Jews automatically belonged,"[26] *all* Jews except Sadducees and Essenes were technically Pharisees—unless, of course, they had been "put out of the synagogue," to use the Johannine term. We shall return to that particular category shortly.

Although Sanders has argued cogently that Pharisaism was just one of several competing "Judaisms" and that it had no particular influence,[27] he sagely draws attention to the importance of "Common Judaism," that is, those elements of Judaism that Pharisees, Sadducees, and Essenes shared. These include the temple cult, the payment of taxes and tithes to the temple and priests, the observance of the commandments, circumcision, food laws, charitable works, and the Sanhedrin. Deines, commenting on Sanders' analysis, observes that,

> The connecting element among all the groups is the knowledge of the divine establishing of the priesthood and the temple cult in the Torah. . . . Sanders rightly calls into question this splintered portrait of Judaism . . . He is therefore to be thanked for placing the concept of what was "common" to Judaism so prominently in the center of his works. What Sanders has persuasively shown is that Judaism is to be understood as *one* religion, and was perceived as such by outsiders."[28]

On this basis, then, Pharisees would certainly have acknowledged Sadducees and Essenes as fellow Jews and, when necessary, would have co-operated with them for the benefit of the nation; in the Sanhedrin, for example, they served alongside Sadducees. At another level, however, the Pharisees and Sadducees both regarded the other as to some extent heretical and heated arguments between the two groups concerning their

---

26. Maccoby, *Jesus*, 74.
27. Sanders, *Judaism*, 380–412.
28. Deines, "Pharisees," 452f.

differences probably occurred frequently; Paul deliberately incited such a dispute in Acts 23:1–10.

Those "put out of the synagogue"—the "sinners"

That there was at least one category of Jew with whom Pharisees preferred to have no social contact is evident from the occasion when they criticized Jesus for dining with tax collectors and "sinners."[29] That incident raises a host of issues. While the nature of those designated "tax collectors" and the reason for their disfavor is well understood (for further on this see under *Dining with tax collectors and "sinners,"* p. 20), the same cannot be said for the people whom the evangelists describe as "sinners"; the scholars offer a diversity of understandings of this term as used in the gospels.[30]

---

29. Matt 9:10–13; Mark 2:16f; Luke 5:30–32.

30. Keener's 1999 commentary on Matthew contains an excursus—"Who Were the 'Sinners'?"—surveying Jewish literature from New Testament times, but ironically this leaves the title question largely unanswered. He concentrates on the relationship between "sinners" and the *ʿam haʾarets*—the "people of the land"—the common people whom the Pharisees despised for failing to observe food laws. Keener regards the term *ʿam haʾarets* as denoting all Jews who were not members of such sects as the Pharisees or the Essenes. Some claimed that Pharisees did not despise the common people; others that they did. The distinction between the observant *haberim* and the non-observant *ʿam haʾarets* overrode class distinctions. There was, however, no total separation between Pharisees and any other Palestinian group; even Pharisees did business deals with the *ʿam haʾarets*. In contrast, the term "sinners" probably specifies blatant violators of the law. "Pharisees were concerned about with whom they ate, and if they were careful merely about meals with *ʿam haʾarets*, one can be certain that they would suspect a teacher who ate with blatant 'sinners'" (Keener, *Matthew*, 294–296).

France's 2007 commentary on Matthew agrees broadly with Keener (France, *Matthew*, 353, 355). Commenting on 9:10–13 he writes, "'Sinners' has been taken here to mean simply the *ʿam haʾarets*, the common people who did not observe the scribal laws of tithing and purity, but the term usually carries a more clearly moral sense, as in Luke 7:36–50, and the recent focus on the forgiveness of sins in 2–8 points that way." To demonstrate the distinction between the two groups France states, "Jesus and his disciples themselves apparently belonged to the *ʿam haʾarets*, yet they are expected to keep away from *hamartōloi*" (France, *Matthew*, 353, fn 16). Presumably he considered that Jesus and his disciples belonged to the *ʿam haʾarets* because, on the basis of such passages as Matt 15:1f, Jesus did not require his disciples to observe the scribal purity laws. Despite this, evidence will be presented later that Jesus and his first disciples were themselves Pharisees.

Keener and France agree that the sinners not only neglected scribal tithing and purity laws, but also were guilty of more serious violations of Torah. W. D. Davies and D. C. Allison concur: "They are . . . the 'wicked', the *reshaʿim*, those Jews who, in the eyes of

Hypocrites or Heroes?

While the New Testament writers never explain the identity of these "sinners" whom Pharisees took such pains to shun—they probably assumed that their readers would be familiar with the term—they have left sufficient clues to allow a reconstruction. In Matt 9:13 and parallels Jesus' juxtaposition of "righteous" and "sinners" ("I have not come to call the righteous, but sinners") implies that they are antonyms. From the context it is clear that "the righteous" in this saying refers to the Pharisees, so that the "sinners" must be in some sense the opposite of Pharisees; could "sinner" then be a technical designation for a Jew outside the Pharisee movement? J. D. G. Dunn believes so; he points out that the Pharisees and the Essenes

> regarded those *outside their group* as effectively apostates. To disagree with their understanding and practice of the law was to disagree with the law. To be outside the group was to be outside the boundary marked by the law, to be "sinners." . . . "sinners" are not just Gentiles, or those who break the law in ways that any Jew would recognize. They are Jews who disagree with the group's sectarian interpretation of the law; sinners, not in some absolute sense, but in the judgment of those who thought that their understanding of righteousness was the only correct one. Those who were unacceptable to them, "sinners," they naturally assumed were unacceptable to God.[31]

Wright holds a similar view: "It is very likely that the Pharisees of the pre-70 period regarded ordinary non-Pharisaic Jews as in some ways second-class citizens who, because they did not adhere to the Pharisaic way, were *technically*, in their eyes, transgressors of the Torah."[32] Although he

---

others, have abandoned the law and denied God's covenant with Israel" (Davies *et al*, *Matthew*, 1:100).

Joachim Jeremias offers a rather different meaning in his *New Testament Theology* of 1971. Although dated, this is still a useful source of background information. He states: "In the world of Jesus, the term 'sinner' had a quite definite ring. It was not only a fairly general designation for those who notoriously failed to observe the commandments of God and at whom, therefore, everyone pointed a finger, but also a specific term for those engaged in despised trades. . . . These are in part trades which were generally thought to lead to immorality, but above all those which by experience led to dishonesty: the second category included gamblers with dice, usurers, tax collectors, publicans and herdsmen (these last were suspected of leading their herds on to other people's land and pilfering the produce of the herd). When the gospels talk of 'sinners,' they are thinking of those occupied in despised trades as well as those whose way of life was disreputable" (Jeremias, *Theology*, 109f).

31. Dunn, *Discipleship*, 69f.
32. Wright, *Jesus*, 266.

Historical Reconstruction 2—The Pharisees at the Time of Jesus

does not use the word "sinners," the thought is surely implied in "transgressors of the Torah." Within a sectarian context, then, "sinners" could simply denote those outside the sect.

On this basis, then, within a Pharisaic context a "sinner" is not necessarily a violent or evil person, but one who does not follow Pharisaic beliefs or practices and who is therefore regarded as outside the Pharisee community. A difficulty with Dunn's and Wright's interpretations is that they regard the Pharisees as a sect like the Essenes, which had a tightly defined membership. Having established that Pharisaism was normative Judaism, how much of these interpretations is still applicable? Pharisaism had no formal membership; Jews were Pharisees by default, unless they opted out in order to join the Essenes or Sadducees.

But although Pharisaism kept no list of members, it did presumably keep a record of those whom it "put out of the synagogue." The Sanhedrin, which as we have established was dominated by the Pharisees, used excommunication as a penalty for many offenses, which included becoming a tax collector or a prostitute. The Pharisees probably saw a precedent for this in the use made of excommunication by the reformers Ezra and Nehemiah, whom they may have regarded as their illustrious forbears:

> Anyone who failed to appear within three days would forfeit all his property, in accordance with the decision of the officials and elders, and would himself be expelled from the assembly of the exiles. (Ezra 10:8)
> When the people heard this law, they excluded from Israel all who were of foreign descent. (Neh 13:3)

Since under Roman rule the death penalty was unavailable to the Jews, exclusion from the community served as a substitute. Indeed it *was* a symbolic death sentence inasmuch as victims forfeited all the benefits of living in the Jewish community. The victim's family was compelled to disown him or her, bringing disgrace on them as well. Not only was the victim's property forfeit, but victims were denied access to the synagogue, respectable employment and probably the regular markets. This is reflected in the use of "the lost" or "the perished" (*ta apolōlota* or *to apolōlotos*) as an alternative designation for the "sinners."[33]

Because of the extensive use made of excommunication, every Jewish town and city would inevitably have an underclass of excluded folk living

---

33. For example in such passages as Matt 10:6; 15:24; Luke 15:4, and 19:10. In Luke 19:10 the context is the conversion of Zacchaeus, a chief tax collector.

on the fringes of its society, recalling the shadowy existence supposedly eked out by the dead in Sheol. It must have frequently happened that an excluded person encountered a loved one in the street, convention demanding that no recognition be shown by either party. Nolland hints at this interpretation when, explaining the word "sinner," he states that "The term should be understood sociologically as identifying those publicly known to be unsavory types who lived beyond the edge of respectable society . . ."[34] In some ways, however, this underclass mirrored regular society. If excludees were denied access to the regular markets, they would of necessity have set up their own alternative ones. Although barred from "respectable" employment, they could be employed by other members of the underclass. Although banned from the synagogues, some religious participation was still available to them: they could enter the outermost court of the Temple (the Court of the Gentiles) and they could and did attend open-air rallies such as those at which Jesus and John the Baptist preached.

Evidence in the gospels suggests that it is these folk excluded from the Jewish/Pharisaic community whom the epithet "sinner" usually designated. For example, the declaration by the Pharisees to the man blind from birth, "We know this man [Jesus] is a sinner" (John 9:24) may reflect the fact that Jesus, having been found guilty twice of profaning the Sabbath by healing on it, had now been excommunicated, that is, officially declared a "sinner"—for further details see *Jesus' expulsion from Pharisaism*, p. 181. The phrase "tax collectors and sinners," which appears to have entered everyday usage in first-century Palestine[35] as a designation for the underclass, denoted the "sinners" among whom the tax collectors were prominent, because being literate and wealthy they became the natural leaders in this alternative society, able to employ other "sinners." This explains the presence of the many "sinners" at the dinner in Matthew/Levi's house (Matt 9:10 and parallels): while the tax collectors present were surely Matthew/Levi's former work colleagues, the "sinners" would have been his associates in the alternative community, such as the tradespeople who supplied his food and other household needs.

What if an excluded Jew, a "sinner," felt remorse for his or her offenses and wished to return to the fold of Judaism/Pharisaism? Would the Pharisees welcome back a person whom they themselves had excommunicated?

---

34. Nolland, *Luke*, 1:246.

35. It occurs eight times in the gospels (Matt 9:10, 11; 11:19; Mark 2:15, 16; Luke 5:30; 7:34; 15:1).

Historical Reconstruction 2—The Pharisees at the Time of Jesus

The New Testament gives no explicit answer, but the teaching of Jesus certainly implies that such people were offered little or no hope of restoration. For example, in the Prodigal Son the elder brother who represents the Pharisees disowned the returning prodigal ("this son of yours" rather than "my brother"), who portrays the repentant "sinners" (Luke 15:28–30). Indeed Jesus' primary motive in telling this parable is to highlight the error of this attitude, contrasting it with the extravagant welcome for the repentant prodigal shown by the father who represents God. The same concern underlies his severe declamation in Matt 23:13: "Woe to you, teachers of the law and Pharisees, you hypocrites! You shut the kingdom of heaven in men's faces. You yourselves do not enter, nor will you let those enter who are trying to." The unfortunates whose attempts to enter the kingdom the Pharisees were hindering cannot be Gentile converts, because as we have seen they were welcomed.[36] This leaves only Jewish "sinners," those who had been excommunicated. Jesus may have had in mind especially the tax collectors and prostitutes, large numbers of whom apparently had responded to the ministry of John the Baptist (Matt 21:31f; Luke 7:29). It is possible that those excommunicated for less serious crimes could be reinstated—see later on *The Pharisees' attitude towards "sinners,"* p. 206.

---

36. See *Gentiles*, p. 153.

7

Historical Reconstruction 3—Jesus and the Pharisees

As WE HAVE SEEN, the New Testament paints an ambiguous picture of Jesus' dealings with the Pharisees. Sometimes they seem to have been on friendly terms[1] and at other times at such loggerheads that some passages speak of Pharisee plots against him,[2] prompting Jesus to denounce them as the devil's offspring (John 8:44). Maccoby explains these apparent discrepancies as follows:

> The explanation that was offered at one time was straightforward. These passages [praising and reverencing the Pharisees] belong to an earlier version of the Gospels and have survived the extensive re-editing to which the Gospels have been subjected. Since these passages go so much against the grain of the Gospels as a whole, they could not have been added at a later stage of editing, but must belong to the earliest and most authentic layer.[3]

---

1. For example, in Matt 5:20 and 9:10–13 Jesus acknowledges that Pharisees have righteousness of a kind and on three occasions he accepts dinner invitations from them (Luke 7:36; 11:37; 14:1).

2. For example, in Matt 23:13–29 Jesus refers to them as "hypocrites" six times; for the Pharisee plots against Jesus see *The plots against Jesus*, p. 148.

3. Maccoby, *Jesus*, 156.

Historical Reconstruction 3—Jesus and the Pharisees

On this basis, then, later anti-Pharisee redactors failed to expunge or at least tone down the legacy of their pro-Pharisee predecessors. But Maccoby does not leave the matter there:

> It began to be argued that the pro-Pharisee and pro-Torah passages of the Gospels were not the earliest but the latest elements in these documents. This conclusion was reached through a more generalised theory known as form criticism, which proposed that large portions of the Gospels were written, shortly after the lifetime of Jesus, to meet the doctrinal and communal needs of various Christian communities . . . Now some of these communities were what were called "re-Judaizers," that is, communities that could not face the radical revisions of Judaism which Jesus had demanded, and wished to return to a more Jewish way of life in accordance with the Torah . . . It was these "re-Judaizers" who were responsible for the introduction of pro-Jewish passages into the Gospels which made Jesus seem a more Jewish figure than he actually was.[4]

Maccoby's failure to provide citations supporting the arguments to which he alludes in both these extracts might lead readers to suspect that these arguments are his alone. Furthermore, his understanding of form criticism is questionable. He proceeds to refer to Bultmann's extreme version of form criticism which left little historical truth about Jesus in the gospels, before returning to the "re-Judaizing" theory which he apparently favors:

> How then . . . are we to explain the passages in which Jesus pays tribute to the Pharisees and to the Torah and declares himself an adherent of traditional Judaism? It seems that for these passages the expedient of "re-Judaization" is still held to work. The historical Jesus could never have uttered these passages.[5]

Maccoby surely needs to apply Occam's principle that "entities should not be multiplied unnecessarily." It seems that he has borrowed the idea of "extensive re-editing" of the gospels from the Rabbinical literature which is indeed the product of such a process. No other New Testament scholar has suggested that the gospels were repeatedly re-edited to change their emphasis. Today most believe that the only editing they received was when the evangelists compiled them from oral tradition or written sources;

---

4. Ibid., 157f.
5. Ibid., 160.

consequently they present a reasonably accurate picture of Jesus. So we must seek an alternative explanation for the apparent discrepancies in their portrayal of Jesus' relationship with the Pharisees.

"READING BETWEEN THE LINES" IN THE GOSPELS

If, as claimed above, the gospel records are reasonably accurate, Jesus' relationship with the Pharisees must have undergone at least one radical change, which it is our task to identify. In order to do so we need to "read between the lines" in the gospels—the evangelists do not always explain everything.

To return to the jigsaw puzzle analogy, effectively what the gospels present is a loosely bound assemblage of individual snippets which we might compare with the pieces of the puzzle. The trouble is that when we try to complete the picture, we find that some pieces are missing. To complete the picture (or the particular part of it in which we are interested) sometimes we have to fill in a gap ourselves by reconstructing a missing piece. Usually this requires us to postulate that some event happened which the evangelists have not recorded explicitly. To do this involves a precarious tightrope walk: on the one hand, guided by the context—that is, the surrounding pieces—we exercise our imagination in order to establish *what* happened, while on the other we use all our knowledge of the relevant people, places, and times to keep our imagination within the bounds of reason; we should not wish to reconstruct something that could *not* have happened. If the piece that we reconstruct in this way confirms and even explains other gospel material, this suggests that it is *possibly* correct, although we can never be absolutely certain; at best it will remain a theory. The process is similar to the well known "hermeneutical circle"[6] and, arguably, an extension of it.

---

6. This is a process which can—with patience—reconstruct the prior knowledge that authors assumed their readers would have, explaining obscure passages in ancient documents. It involves repeatedly reading the relevant texts, on each successive cycle reconsidering their meaning in the light of findings or conjectures made in earlier cycles. D. E. Nineham describes it as follows: "The full interpretation of an ancient document is thus very often a laborious business requiring great skill and sensitivity... The procedure must be to begin by interpreting the words on the basis of the best guesses we can make as to the original assumptions and presuppositions. In the light of the interpretation which that yields we may hope to refine our understanding of the presuppositions and then re-read the text on the basis of our new understanding of its assumptions. The process may have to be repeated many times and it may seem circular—it is in fact often referred to as the 'hermeneutic circle'" (Nineham, *Use*, 26).

Historical Reconstruction 3—Jesus and the Pharisees

Explaining Jesus' changing relationship with the Pharisees is complicated by the fact that the gospels do not always adhere to chronological order. Nevertheless, an overarching trend is discernible: in general the friendly episodes are early in Jesus' ministry and the hostile ones later. The reconstructed "missing piece of the puzzle" proposed here is that Jesus' ministry divides into two distinct phases in which it is not only his dealings with the Pharisees that change, but also his aims and the methods he uses. The weakness of the traditional view—that is, that Jesus followed the same agenda throughout his ministry—is apparent as soon as we ask what that agenda was. Did he intend to reform Judaism? Or did he intend to start a new religion? Surely the answer to both questions is "yes," but he could hardly pursue both simultaneously. So he tried first one and then the other. The evangelists hint at a change of agenda when they pointedly mention his change of teaching methods, for example, in Mark 4:33f.

During the earlier phase Jesus' aim was to reform Pharisaic Judaism. Although reformers are usually unpopular with their peers—human nature tends to resist change and religious human nature especially so!—Jesus appreciated that Pharisees, who generally encouraged theological debate, would be more likely to listen to one of their own number than to an outsider. So at this time he enjoyed friendly relations with the Pharisees and shared their ideals; he was unmistakably a Pharisee himself. It is possible to identify the incident which precipitated the change in the relationship and in his agenda, thereby bringing the first phase to an end and initiating the second. During this second phase Jesus, having abandoned his attempted reform of Pharisaism, began building a new faith community mainly from the repentant "sinners," although all were welcome. His relations with the Pharisees now deteriorated, he becoming increasingly critical of them and they of him; indeed so suspicious of him were they that they kept him under surveillance in the hope of finding grounds on which to arrest him.

The evangelists never refer explicitly to these two phases, probably because their existence was so well known when they wrote that they assumed that their readers would be equally familiar with them and able to fit individual gospel incidents into the framework that they provide. The two-phase theory explains so many paradoxical elements in Jesus' ministry that it is surely worthy of consideration. The overview of Jesus' ministry that follows assumes that the two-phase theory is correct and highlights his changing relationship with the Pharisees.

WAS JESUS A PHARISEE?

The commonly held notion that Jesus and the Pharisees were arch-rivals results from a superficial reading of the gospels; careful study reveals that the relationship between them was complex. Of course, if Pharisaism was normative Judaism—so that all Jews were technically Pharisees—there is no need to prove that Jesus was a Pharisee. But this question uses the word "Pharisee" in the same specialized sense that the New Testament writers use, denoting a Jew who not only observed the law fastidiously himself, but also had a responsibility to encourage others to do so and to reprimand those who failed to do so. In the conjectural first phase of his ministry Jesus himself and some of his disciples were Pharisees and enjoyed friendly relations with other Pharisees. The evidence to support this is as follows.

Firstly, the Pharisees expected Jesus and his disciples to observe the Pharisaic code of conduct based on the *paradosis*—the oral law. Surely the clearest example of this is the occasion when Pharisees criticized Jesus for dining with tax collectors and "sinners."[7] Another is the incident concerning the disciples' failure to wash their hands before meals (Matt 15:1–6; Mark 7:1–13). Significantly neither action infringes the written Torah, so the code of conduct which the Pharisees considered that Jesus and his disciples had violated must have been based on oral law. Their expectation that Jesus and his disciples would behave as they themselves did is reasonable only if they regarded them as members of their own movement—that is, as Pharisees. Moreover, as Jesus had acquired a reputation as a teacher with exceptional authority (Matt 7:28f), they may have been especially concerned that his unconventional behavior might bring their movement into disrepute.

Secondly, Pharisees apparently recognized Jesus as a teacher. In Matt 9:11, addressing his disciples, they referred to Jesus as "your teacher." When they approached Jesus about his disciples plucking grain on the Sabbath, by referring to "your disciples" (Matt 12:2) they were implicitly acknowledging that as their teacher Jesus was responsible for their actions. Pharisees sometimes address Jesus directly as "Teacher."[8] It is unlikely that they would have accorded him the honorific title of "teacher" if he were not a Pharisee himself—how could a heretic or a "sinner" (see *The Pharisees' attitude to others*, p. 153) be trusted to teach others?

---

7. Matt 9:10–13; Mark 2:16f; Luke 5:30–32.
8. Matt 22:15f, 34ff; Luke 7:40.

Historical Reconstruction 3—Jesus and the Pharisees

Thirdly, Jesus' core beliefs were the same as those of the Pharisees. Although he engaged in polemical debates with them, these generally concerned personal matters. Pharisees accused him of unauthorized absolution (Matt 9:2f),[9] breaking the Sabbath (Matt 12:1f), and exorcizing using demonic power (Matt 12:24), but they did not criticize his theology. He accused them of failing to practice the ethics they taught (Matt 23:2f) and of neglecting major commandments while observing trivial ones to the tiniest detail (Matt 23:23f). He never, however, declared their theology incorrect—as he did that of the Sadducees (Matt 22:23–33). Jesus' teaching on such fundamentals as the nature of God, the spiritual realm, resurrection, and the canon of scripture is the same as that of the Pharisees and was subsequently adopted by the Christian movement.

Fourthly, the debates themselves are, ironically, further evidence that Jesus *was* a Pharisee; Pharisees would surely have dismissed someone from outside their movement as an unworthy opponent. Polemical debates between various factions *within* Pharisaism—such as the rival schools of Shammai and Hillel—were, however, commonplace.[10] As Maccoby comments, "Amicable disagreement was an essential ingredient in Pharisaism, and the Pharisee literature is full of disagreements between the various sages of the movement."[11] By "the Pharisee literature" Maccoby means the rabbinic literature, the rabbinic movement being in his opinion—and that of many scholars—a continuation of the Pharisee movement of Temple times.

Fifthly, Jesus often uses characteristically Pharisaic language, such as his derogatory sayings about tax collectors in Matt 5:46f and 18:17. His frequent use of "kingdom" terminology is also typically Pharisaic, as is his use of parables.

Lastly, in Matt 23:2f Jesus enjoins his hearers to obey the Pharisees' teachings. Presumably Jesus obeyed them himself—if he did not, he would be every bit as guilty of hypocrisy as the Pharisees whom he was about to accuse! If Jesus himself followed the Pharisees' teachings, surely this makes him a Pharisee.

Interestingly, Rivkin acknowledges the similarities between Jesus and the Pharisees:

---

9. The accusers in this incident are described as "teachers of the law," but most of these belonged to the Pharisaic party.
10. Wright, *Jesus*, 378.
11. Maccoby, *Jesus*, 135.

> Jesus was, like the Pharisees, a *didaskalos*, a teacher. He taught by word of mouth and example, even as did the Pharisees. So like them was he that on occasion he is addressed by them as Teacher (*didaskalos, rav*). He frequented their synagogues, read from the prophets on the sabbath, indulged in their mode of exegesis, regarded all three divisions of scripture as co-equal, firmly believed in eternal life and resurrection.[12]

Sadly he stops short of drawing what is surely the obvious conclusion. Maccoby, in contrast, following a more detailed comparison, concludes that: "Jesus . . . himself is the most recognizable Pharisee in the whole of first-century Jewish literature."[13] Furthermore, Maccoby points to corroborating evidence in the rabbinic literature: he claims that Jesus is mentioned in the Babylonian Talmud and some other rabbinic sources and was regarded by the rabbis for a short time as a "fully fledged member of the rabbinic movement known in his day as the Pharisees," albeit a disgraced member.[14]

In contrast, Deines argues that Jesus was *not* a Pharisee:

> The Pharisees' interest in Jesus (and previously in John the Baptist), which is attested in the Gospels, can be explained by their essentially open understanding of tradition: they are prepared to listen to Jesus, even to learn from him, as long as he establishes his teaching in continuity with Torah tradition. The ways part, however, as soon as Jesus places his authority *above* that of Torah tradition. For this reason Jesus cannot be called a Pharisee, because he is *not* one at the decisive point, i.e. *kata nomon*.[15]

But Jesus upheld the authority of Torah as fervently as any rabbi (for example, Matt 5:17–19). Perhaps it is on the basis of such sayings as "I and the Father are one" (John 10:30) that Deines regards Jesus as claiming a higher inherent authority, disqualifying himself from his definition of a Pharisee. The Christian movement, especially under the influence of Paul—despite his claim to be a Pharisee!—became suspicious of law in general and it is easy to see why Pharisaism rejected the Christians as *minim* (accursed heretics) as it did not reject the Sadducees or the Essenes.

---

12. Rivkin, *Revolution*, 275.
13. Maccoby, *Jesus*, 141.
14. Ibid., 144, 148.
15. Deines, "Pharisees," 494.

Historical Reconstruction 3—Jesus and the Pharisees

The evidence, then, is substantial. Furthermore, re-reading the gospels with the pre-understanding that Jesus is a Pharisee introduces no difficulties. On the contrary, it explains some details that are otherwise puzzling. A trivial example is Jesus' adherence to the convention of wearing tassels (*kraspedon* in Matt 9:20 and 14:36) as a reminder of Torah, although in Matt 23:5 he criticizes the long *kraspeda* worn by some Pharisees!

While even Rivkin acknowledges the similarities between Jesus and the Pharisees (see above), in one respect Jesus *did* differ from them. Moreover, this was the one respect that Rivkin and others consider to epitomize the Pharisees—observance of the *paradosis* or oral law. Jesus seems to have had scant regard for the *paradosis*. The Pharisees criticized Jesus for failing to observe commands in the *paradosis* when he dined with tax collectors and "sinners" (Matt 9:10f) and when his disciples failed to wash their hands before eating (Matt 15:2). Jesus criticized the Pharisees for so multiplying *paradosis*-based commandments that they made life intolerable for ordinary Jews (Matt 23:4, *c.f.* Matt 11:28) and for allowing their *paradosis* to subvert Torah commandments relating to family welfare (Matt 15:3–6). While in his cynicism regarding the oral law and his reverence for Torah Jesus resembles the Sadducees, he certainly regarded the whole of the Old Testament canon as scripture and he believed in angels, spirits and the resurrection, which were Pharisee beliefs not shared by the Sadducees.

But even if Jesus rejected much of the *paradosis*, he certainly believed in exegesis of the Torah, as the Pharisees did and the Sadducees did not. The Antitheses (Matt 5:21–48) provide examples of Jesus' exegesis of Torah commandments: he sought to extract the core principles underlying the written commandments and reapply them in other life situations, as the Pharisees did. Jesus' interpretation of Torah is, however, even more stringent than that of most of the Rabbis. For example, it is not unduly difficult to refrain from the literal act of murder, but in Matt 5:22 Jesus focuses God's judgment instead on the anger that is the root cause of murder, even when it leads to no outward action. The same principle applies in the second antithesis when Jesus condemns the "looking lustfully" that gives rise to adultery (Matt 5:27f) even when confined to looking. Przybylski refers to this process as "fencing Torah," that is, banning lesser indiscretions so that people never have an opportunity to commit the more serious offenses.[16] The ultimate example of Jesus' extraction of core principles is surely the Double Commandment of Love (Mark 12:28–32)—one who sin-

---

16. Przybylski, *Righteousness*, 81f.

cerely loves God and his or her neighbors will automatically observe all the commandments. And, as Maccoby points out, "Jesus' singling out of these two verses from the Hebrew Bible (one from Deuteronomy and the other from Leviticus) as the greatest of the commandments was not an idea of his own creation, but an established part of Pharisee thinking."[17] We are forced to conclude that Jesus *was* a Pharisee, albeit a radical one. This explains the presence in the gospels of reports of Jesus having friendly dealings with his fellow Pharisees.

Jesus was, however, a most unusual Pharisee, as evidenced by his concern for "sinners." It is not surprising that he aroused the suspicions of his fellow-Pharisees or that Maccoby refers to him as a "disgraced member" of the Pharisee movement. The gospels attest to Jesus' growing criticism of the Pharisaic movement (as exemplified by his diatribe against them in Matthew 23) and it with him, as evidenced by the Pharisee plots against him (Matt 12:14; Mark 3:6; John 8:40–44) and by his eventual excommunication from the movement—see *Jesus' expulsion from Pharisaism*, p. 181.

INFLUENCES ON JESUS' MINISTRY

We have established that Jesus was a Pharisee and that Pharisaism was the normative Judaism of his day. It is presumably safe to conclude, then, that Jesus was brought up in a Pharisaic environment and it would be natural for him to feel a certain loyalty towards this as "the rock from which he was hewn." The childhood incident recorded in Luke 2:41–52 demonstrates not only the piety of his family background, but also that even at twelve years old Jesus apparently showed prodigious religious insight.

Nevertheless, the fact that the first of the two phases of his ministry aimed to reform Pharisaism demonstrates that he recognized in it flaws in need of amendment. Cynicism is often the product of age and experience; it would not have been easy for Jesus as a comparatively young and uneducated person from a rural province—despite his special gifts—to discern the faults of the society of which he was a member, especially when many aspects of it were admirable and its faults subtle. Surely he must have received a "prompt" from some outside agency which drew his attention to the deficiencies in his society. If so, who or what provided it? As so often, the New Testament gives the answer to this question, but without stating that it is the answer or even acknowledging that there is such a question

17. Maccoby, *Jesus*, 121.

Historical Reconstruction 3—Jesus and the Pharisees

needing an answer. To return to the jigsaw puzzle analogy, on this occasion instead of a piece missing we find ourselves holding a piece whose proper location in the overall picture is hard to identify. This particular piece shows John the Baptist.

John the Baptist

The Baptist is an enigma. Tantalizingly the evangelists hint at an importance that they never explain, perhaps out of fear that to do so might elevate John above Jesus himself. They credit him only as Jesus' herald or forerunner, a role afforded scriptural sanction by the prophecy of Mal 3:1. But he was so much more than that! If Jesus accomplished the plan of salvation, it was the Baptist who initiated it. If Jesus built a new church, it was on foundations that John had laid down. France hints at this:

> Their careers run parallel in significant ways: both are popularly regarded as prophets, opposed by the Jerusalem authorities, eventually rejected and executed, but given burial by their disciples. So Jesus will take up where John leaves off, and this is just what John has said must happen.[18]

And Wright takes the argument a step further:

> There is good reason to think that John himself did indeed prophesy a coming figure who would complete the work that he had begun, and that Jesus applied this to himself. Though John seems at a later stage, while in prison, to have been puzzled by what Jesus was doing (and more particularly, it appears, by what he was not doing), Jesus continued to regard him as the advance guard for his own work, both as the chronological and theological starting-point for his own ministry, and as in some senses the role model for his own style, the pattern with which he would begin.[19]

So what do the gospels tell us about John? According to Luke 1:36, he was a cousin of Jesus on his mother's side and, since his mother Elizabeth was expecting him at the time of Jesus' conception, John can have been no more than a few months older than Jesus.

Luke also reveals that John had been born into a priestly family (Luke 1:5–25, 57–80). It is therefore reasonable to ask why as an adult John was

---

18. France, *Matthew*, 98.
19. Wright, *Jesus*, 161f.

not ministering in the Temple. A tempting conjecture is that more males were being born into priestly families than the cultus needed, so some selection process was employed and John was one of those whom it rejected. Aware of a divine calling and frustrated by the Temple establishment, John sought an alternative ministry. The vivid eschatological motifs in the snippet of his preaching preserved in Matt 3:7–12 suggest the influence of one of the apocalyptically oriented sects.[20] If John had joined one of those, that and his experiences of the Temple hierarchy might explain his radical, anti-establishment stance.

References in the New Testament to the "disciples of John the Baptist"[21] indicate that John became the leader of a community which continued to exist long after his death (Acts 19:1–6). This community may have been a form of Pharisaism inasmuch as its mission was to all Jews to prepare them for God's imminent judgment, itself a tenet of Pharisee beliefs. To this end John held open-air rallies at which he addressed large crowds, preaching the necessity of repentance and administering "a baptism of repentance for the forgiveness of sins" (Mark 1:4).

The Baptist's influence on Jesus

All three synoptics state that Jesus submitted to John's baptism[22] and John implies it (John 1:32–34). Although a literal reading of the synoptic accounts gives the impression that Jesus arrived at the scene of John's ministry, was baptized immediately and went off at once into the wilderness to be tempted, this is unlikely. The evangelists have summarized a sequence of events that would surely have extended over many days and possibly many weeks. Certainly John would have expected his baptismal candidates to undergo a period of preparation, which probably involved becoming temporary members of his community.

This is supported by the somewhat different account in John's Gospel which implies that Jesus spent some time in the company of the Baptist (John 1:29f, 35f). At least two of Jesus' earliest disciples had been disciples of the Baptist until he redirected them to follow Jesus (John 1:35–37). Since one of these was Andrew (John 1:40f), it is possible that his brother Simon

---

20. Jossa clearly regards the "apocalyptic currents" as a significant component of Judaism at the time of Jesus; see the citation on page 5, fn 13.

21. For example, Matt 9:14; 11:2–7; 14:12.

22. Matt 3:13–17; Mark 1:9–11; Luke 3:21f.

Historical Reconstruction 3—Jesus and the Pharisees

was present as well. Simon and Andrew worked in partnership with Zebedee's sons James and John (Luke 5:10), who according to one theory[23] were Jesus' first cousins, so it is possible that James and John were also with the Baptist at this time. Had some or all of these Galilean fishermen traveled together from Galilee to Judea with the express intention of becoming temporary members of the Baptist's community and receiving his baptism? (It is interesting that the gospels do not mention any of Jesus' disciples receiving John's baptism.) If so, did Jesus travel with them? It would be natural for this extended-family group to travel together to visit and support the Baptist, to whom some of them were related and who was making what was, in those days, the equivalent of headline news.

What is most significant about the time that Jesus spent with the Baptist is that this would have exposed him, perhaps for the first time, to radical teaching which was probably quite unlike that which he would have received each Sabbath in the synagogue at Nazareth. For example, John proclaimed that even pious Pharisees needed to repent:

> But when he saw many of the Pharisees and Sadducees coming to where he was baptizing, he said to them: "You brood of vipers! Who warned you to flee from the coming wrath? Produce fruit in keeping with repentance. And do not think you can say to yourselves, 'We have Abraham as our father.' I tell you that out of these stones God can raise up children for Abraham." (Matt 3:7–9)

This speech demonstrates that John did not baptize indiscriminately, but insisted upon evidence ("fruit") of repentance. John's baptism was a ritual cleansing from sin, recalling the ablutions required of Gentile proselytes entering the Jewish community. Although these "Pharisees and Sadducees" were almost certainly a deputation sent by the Sanhedrin to investigate his ministry,[24] when he saw them in the crowd, John assumed that they too were presenting themselves for baptism. Consequently he

---

23. If Matt 27:56 and Mark 16:1 refer to the same group of women, the mother of James and John, Zebedee's sons, was named Salome. If John 19:25 also refers to this group, Salome was the sister of Mary, Jesus' mother. This would make James and John Jesus' first cousins, sharing the same priestly descent as Mary. Furthermore, this would explain the unlikely circumstance that a Galilean fisherman (if the "other disciple" is John) was "known to the high priest" (John 18:58).

24. C.f. John 1:19 in which "the Jews of Jerusalem sent priests and Levites to ask him who he was" and John 1:24 which seems to indicate that there were also Pharisees in this delegation. The "Jews of Jerusalem" is probably a Johannine appellation for the Sanhedrin. For further see *Pharisees and Sadducees visit John the Baptist*, p. 14.

was appealing to prominent Jewish leaders to come to God on the same terms as Gentile proselytes, implying that all were equally estranged from God. This message would have been so deeply offensive to them that it is not surprising that later they refused to endorse John's ministry.[25] But such forthright teaching must have made a deep impression upon Jesus.

Another way in which John's ministry was radically different from Pharisaism was its inclusiveness. John welcomed all, including "sinners" of the most despised kinds, such as tax collectors and prostitutes, who apparently responded to his ministry in large numbers.[26] Consequently Jesus and some of his first disciples were eyewitnesses of a revival taking place amongst the very people whom Pharisees generally dismissed as under God's curse and with whom they refused to associate. This influenced him, showing that there was indeed no curse on the "sinners"; on the contrary, many of them were more open to God than some respected Jewish leaders. Through his demonstration of the flaws in Pharisaism and the possibility of redemption for the "sinners" whom the Pharisees so despised John paved the way for both phases of Jesus' ministry.

The wilderness

The synoptics are unanimous that after his baptism Jesus spent forty days in the wilderness being "tempted by Satan" (Mark 1:13) before he began his public ministry. Whatever other spiritual experiences Jesus underwent in the wilderness, he would surely have needed time alone to contemplate the implications of what he had seen and heard during his period with the Baptist. He had to work out his own theological stance and the form that his ministry should take. His upbringing had been solidly Pharisaic, but John's ministry had revealed serious flaws in Pharisaic Judaism as practiced at that time. Moreover, Jesus had witnessed God at work amongst the very people whom Pharisees dismissed as worthless and strenuously avoided. Which route should he follow—the conservative faith of his upbringing or the radical faith of his cousin the Baptist? Or might there be some way in which he could combine the two?

Jesus decided at first to remain with the Pharisaism of his upbringing. His intention was reform, purging Pharisaism of its hypocrisy and theological error. In some ways this role resembled that of many Old Testament

25. Matt 21:25–27; Mark 11:30–33; Luke 20:4–8.
26. Matt 21:32; Luke 3:12f; 7:29.

Historical Reconstruction 3—Jesus and the Pharisees

prophets, calling God's people back to a simple, personal faith in Yahweh. He recognized that this would be difficult, possibly fruitless and certainly dangerous. But, if he succeeded in this part of his mission, there would be no need for the second part; properly reformed, the Pharisees would willingly reach out to the "sinners" and welcome those who repented.

But what if his mission to Pharisaism failed? Probably in the wilderness of temptation Jesus decided that if his attempt to reform Pharisaism failed, he would abandon it, writing off the Pharisees as they had written off the "sinners." Then he would adopt a more radical stance and build a new faith community mainly from the "sinners," whose sincere repentance he had witnessed while with the Baptist and who, like himself, had been rejected by Pharisaism. How he would recognize that his attempted reform of Pharisaism had failed was, of course, uncertain. Perhaps he assumed that he *would* recognize it if it happened, while hoping that it would not.

THE EARLIER PRO-PHARISEE PHASE OF JESUS' MINISTRY

Jesus appreciated that he could reform Pharisaism only by continued involvement in it. Accordingly, he observed its conventions, such as wearing tassels as a reminder of the Torah (Matt 9:20; 14:36) and he taught in the synagogues.[27] His first disciples were, like himself, pious Pharisees.

In fact the evangelists record few encounters between Jesus and "Pharisees" in this first phase of his ministry which was spent mostly in Galilee. Although Pharisaism was normative Judaism, so that Jesus' disciples and most of those who listened to his preaching were technically Pharisees, they would not normally have referred to themselves as such. Similarly, the evangelists reserve the term "Pharisees" for officials whose primary function appears to be the enforcement of the Pharisaic twofold Law. These officials seem to have been seldom seen in Galilee.[28] That Jesus' references to them—for example in the Sermon on the Mount (see below)—were apparently understood by his Galilean audience suggests that they were nevertheless not only familiar with Pharisees, but also regarded them as models of righteousness. Although this familiarity may be the consequence

---

27. For example, Matt 4:23; Mark 1:21; Luke 4:16.

28. Jesus thought that he could escape the attention of the Pharisees by returning from Judea to Galilee—see *The Pharisees hear about Jesus' ministry overtaking that of the Baptist*, p. 72.

Hypocrites or Heroes?

of occasional visits by Pharisees to Galilee, it is perhaps more likely that it was gained from encounters with them when visiting Judea, such as during the annual pilgrimage to Jerusalem for the Passover. Although the gospels record Jesus as having many encounters with Pharisees in Galilee in the later phase of his ministry, most if not all of those Pharisees were members of one or more delegations sent from Jerusalem especially to observe him.

During this first phase of his ministry Jesus preached in plain language—in contrast with the parables that he used almost exclusively later—to congregations consisting of fellow Pharisees. The Sermon on the Mount in Matt 5–7 probably consists of summaries of several such sermons; its content is clearly oriented to those already pious with a view to purging error and deepening commitment; France aptly describes it as "an anthology of the teaching of Jesus relating to discipleship."[29] In it Jesus roundly denounces the hypocrisy that was one symptom of the need for reform. For example, Matt 6:1–18 focuses on malpractice in the alms, prayer, and fasting that were the pillars of Jewish piety. It is surely significant, however, that he refrains from naming any particular guilty individuals or groups and thereby offending them; during this phase of his ministry he needed to remain on friendly terms with his fellow Pharisees. When he condemns similar errors in the later phase of his ministry (Matt 23), he repeatedly names the teachers of the law and Pharisees as the perpetrators. Jesus upheld the authority of Torah as fervently as any Rabbi would have done (Matt 5:17–20) and in the Antitheses his reinterpretations of the familiar commandments prohibiting murder and adultery make more stringent demands than the originals did.

One injunction to his disciples may indicate that during this phase Jesus admired the Pharisees:

> For I tell you that unless your righteousness surpasses that of the Pharisees and the teachers of the law, you will certainly not enter the kingdom of heaven. (Matt 5:20)

If Jesus intended this saying to be understood literally, he meant: "The Pharisees and the teachers of the law are excellent examples of righteousness, but you must do even better than they." This implies some admiration for them, although, as 6:1–18 shows, he was clearly aware of their shortcomings.

---

29. France, *Matthew*, 155.

Historical Reconstruction 3—Jesus and the Pharisees

One remarkable feature of this first phase of his ministry is the harsh language that he uses regarding "sinners" and tax collectors:

> If you love those who love you, what reward will you get? Are not even the tax collectors doing that? And if you greet only your brothers, what are you doing more than others? Do not even pagans do that? (Matt 5:46f)
>
> If you love those who love you, what credit is that to you? Even "sinners" love those who love them. And if you do good to those who are good to you, what credit is that to you? Even "sinners" do that. And if you lend to those from whom you expect repayment, what credit is that to you? Even "sinners" lend to "sinners," expecting to be repaid in full. (Luke 6:32–34)

The point that Jesus was making depends upon the fact that both he as a Pharisee and his audience of Pharisees despised tax collectors and "sinners," regarding them as the worst kinds of Jew, on a par with pagan Gentiles. None of the scholars provides a convincing explanation for these passages which stand in striking contrast with the compassion for tax collectors and "sinners" that Jesus exhibited later—for example, "I have not come to call the righteous, but 'sinners'" (Matt 9:13)—and for which he received criticism.

France, for example, attempts to dismiss this reference to tax collectors and pagans as hyperbole, an extreme illustration used to drive home a point: "By using traditional Jewish terms for those whom they regarded as at the bottom of the moral scale Jesus underlines how basic a human instinct this is: everyone looks after their own."[30] This may be true, but it does not alter the fact that those who heard Jesus refer in this way to tax collectors and "sinners" would assume that he despised them as Pharisees were expected to do; moreover, as a teacher renowned for his special authority (Matt 7:28f), he promoted this attitude.

We must remember, however, that this teaching was delivered during the early phase of Jesus' ministry when he did indeed follow traditional Pharisaic beliefs and practices, which included this obligation to shun sinners and Gentiles; these views are typical of Pharisaism. Perhaps at this stage Jesus was concentrating upon winning the confidence of his fellow Pharisees in the hope that when he had done so he could persuade them to adopt a more compassionate attitude towards repentant "sinners."

---

30. Ibid., 227.

Hypocrites or Heroes?

Another occasion when Jesus implies that the "sinners" should be treated in the same way as Gentiles is recorded in Matt 18:17: "If he refuses to listen . . . , treat him as you would a pagan or a tax collector." Although this saying occurs in the second half of Matthew's Gospel, it surely belongs in the early phase; as mentioned earlier, the gospels do not always present material in strict chronological order. It is unthinkable that Jesus would have equated a tax collector with a Gentile in this way after the calls of Matthew/Levi or Zacchaeus, which happened in the later phase of his ministry.

Although this first phase of Jesus' ministry took place mainly in Galilee, news of it must have reached the Sanhedrin in Jerusalem. The most likely *scenario* is that one or more local community leaders who had become concerned about Jesus' attempted reform of Pharisaic Judaism and his growing reputation sent a message about him to the Sanhedrin. The Sanhedrin scrutinized new Jewish religious developments; one of its functions was the maintenance of the precarious balance between Roman political supremacy and the freedom of the Jews to practice Judaism in all its various forms. Since these included Pharisaism which had a nationalist and therefore anti-Rome element, the Sanhedrin was probably afraid that a reformed Pharisaism might be so nationalistic as to destabilize the tense political situation. Accordingly, just as it had sent a deputation to investigate John the Baptist when his ministry began attracting attention (see *Pharisees and Sadducees visit John the Baptist*, p. 14), the gospels record that it did the same with Jesus. Moreover, that deputation was instrumental in bringing this early phase of Jesus' ministry to its conclusion.

THE TURNING POINT

The gospels do not state explicitly that Jesus did a *volte-face* in the middle of his ministry. This is one of the missing pieces of the jigsaw puzzle: we deduce that it happened from its consequences which the evangelists did record; probably they assumed that their readers would be so familiar with the two-phase division of Jesus' ministry that they would understand what had changed and why.

Jesus had prepared himself for such a mid-ministry change of agenda, perhaps when in the wilderness of temptation. So, when he recognized that his attempted reform of Pharisaism had failed, he did as he had planned then—he abandoned that agenda and switched to the alternative.[31] Jesus'

---

31. It may be significant that Paul in Corinth followed the same procedure: on arrival

Historical Reconstruction 3—Jesus and the Pharisees

alternative course adopted the radical theology if not the radical clothing of his cousin the Baptist; he began building a new faith community largely from the repentant "sinners" who had responded in great numbers to the Baptist's ministry (Matt 21:32), but whom the Pharisees had refused to re-admit to the Jewish community (Matt 23:13).

It was the first appearance and the reaction of the delegation of officials sent by the Sanhedrin to observe him that led Jesus to conclude that his reforming mission to the Pharisees had failed and that the time had come for the change of agenda. The delegation first appears on the occasion of the healing of the paralyzed man let down through the roof.[32] In all three synoptics this episode is followed immediately by the call of the tax collector Matthew/Levi.[33] Although the connection between these two events is not obvious, the second is nevertheless an indirect consequence of the first.

According to Luke, the healing of the paralytic was attended by "Pharisees and teachers of the law, who had come from every village of Galilee and from Judea and Jerusalem." This suggests that the deputation sent from Jerusalem to observe Jesus was augmented on this first surveillance session by selected community leaders from Galilee, perhaps the same ones who had reported Jesus to the authorities. This investigative deputation resembles the one sent by the Sanhedrin to investigate John the Baptist—see *Pharisees and Sadducees visit John the Baptist*, p. 14. Its official purpose would have been to establish whether or not Jesus' ministry complied with Torah; if it observed any breach of Torah tradition, it could denounce him as a false teacher, a heretic. Effectively, therefore, its brief was to "pick faults" in Jesus' teaching if it possibly could.

Moreover, it found a fault, giving Jesus his first experience of opposition from the Jewish hierarchy. The deputation claimed that his pronouncement of the paralyzed man's sins as forgiven constituted blasphemy, since only God had the authority to grant such absolution. Jesus recognized in this not only the hopelessness of his intention to reform Pharisaism, but also the beginnings of the plot—strictly the first in a series of many plots—against him that would culminate in the cross. From this time onwards

---

he first sought to evangelize his fellow Jews; it was only when they rejected his ministry that he turned to the Gentiles (Acts 18:1–6). Was he deliberately following the precedent set by Jesus?

32. Matt 9:1–8; Mark 2:1–12; Luke 5:17–26.

33. Matt 9:9–13; Mark 2:13–17; Luke 5:27–32.

there are so many references in the gospels to spies, observers, and tests of Jesus' orthodoxy that the only safe assumption is that Jesus' public ministry was kept under constant surveillance, the anti-Jesus stance of the Pharisee-dominated establishment growing apace.

Further evidence in the synoptic gospels that Jesus radically changed his methods in the middle of his ministry is that he stopped teaching in synagogues and taught instead mainly in the open air. More significant, perhaps, is his change from teaching in plain language to the exclusive use of parables (Mark 4:33f). The reasons for these changes will be considered shortly.

John's Gospel also refers to a change of target audience in the middle of Jesus' ministry:

> I have other sheep that are not of this sheep pen. I must bring them also. They too will listen to my voice, and there shall be one flock and one shepherd. (John 10:16)

John gives no indication of the setting or occasion of this saying, but from verse 19 it appears to have been addressed to "the Jews," which, as we saw in Chapter 3, often denotes the Pharisees. Some commentators, such as Beasley-Murray[34] and J. H. Bernard,[35] claim that these "other sheep" are Gentiles, but there is no record in the gospels that Jesus ever intentionally targeted Gentiles. It is more likely that he was referring to the "sinners." Here Jesus is telling the Jewish leaders, which almost certainly means the Pharisees, that, because they rejected his attempted reforms, he is now rejecting them and building a new community, although he stops short of specifying that he is building it from the "sinners," the very folk whom they themselves have excommunicated.

THE LATER PRO-"SINNER" PHASE OF JESUS' MINISTRY

In all three synoptic gospels the episode immediately following the healing of the paralyzed man—that is, the occasion when the deputation from the Sanhedrin made its first appearance and accused Jesus of blasphemy—records him as performing a radical and highly significant act: he called the tax collector Matthew/Levi as a disciple.[36] Until now his closest disciples

---

34. Beasley-Murray, *John*, 171.
35. Bernard, *St John*, 2:361.
36. Matt 9:9; Mark 2:14; Luke 5:27.

had been pious Pharisees like himself; he appears to have avoided contact with tax collectors and "sinners." As a tax collector, Matthew/Levi was a pariah, an outcast from Jewish society—see *Dining with tax collectors and "sinners,"* p. 20. In calling Matthew/Levi Jesus was effectively making a statement: "Even those commonly dismissed as the very dregs of society are welcome as my disciples, for I see worth in them." Because Pharisees were expected to distance themselves from such folk, it is not surprising that when the tax collector held a dinner—presumably so that his friends could meet this teacher who so unusually was willing to spend time with their sort—the Pharisees in the deputation observing Jesus, the same group that had been present at the healing of the paralyzed man (Luke 5:17), criticized Jesus for attending.[37]

Jesus had now abandoned his attempt to reform the Pharisaism that represented the normative Judaism of his day. Deines hints at such a change of agenda when he writes, 'In Matthew's eyes the Pharisees are mainly responsible for the failure of Jesus' mission among his own people.'[38] From now on he would concentrate instead on the "sinners," those Jews whom the Pharisaic leadership had excommunicated and considered accursed, even though the ministry of John the Baptist had demonstrated their readiness to respond to God's call to repent. His aim now was to build a new faith community, the church, in which repentant "sinners"—and others—would find support and encouragement to develop their discipleship and eventually to transform the world.

Surveillance

The official surveillance of Jesus continued. Even the three occasions recorded in Luke's Gospel when Jesus accepted dinner invitations from Pharisees[39] formed part of this surveillance and therefore belong in this later phase of Jesus' ministry. Since, however, their very nature presupposes a measure of friendliness between Jesus and the Pharisees concerned, they presumably took place early in this phase; they certainly could not have happened after Jesus' expulsion from Pharisaism (see later). Throughout this later phase Jesus—or at least his public ministry—was constantly observed by a team of Jewish officials whose purpose ostensibly was to discover whether his min-

37. Matt 9:10–13; Mark 2:15–17; Luke 5:29–32.
38. Deines, 'Good Guys,' 22.
39. Luke 7:36; 11:37; 14:1.

istry conformed to Torah tradition. In practice, because of the Sanhedrin's fear that Jesus might destabilize the tense political situation, their hidden agenda was to obtain evidence of some offense that would provide grounds for his arrest. Even while in Galilee this team—like that which investigated John the Baptist—appears to have included Sadducees as well as Pharisees (Matt 16:1). This confirms that it was an initiative of the Sanhedrin which contained both Sadducees and Pharisees.

Moreover, this surveillance was neither passive, mere observation in the hope that Jesus might make some "unforced error," nor unbiased. It is impossible to ignore the impression given by the evangelists that the observers actively played the role of *agent provocateur*, repeatedly attempting to trick Jesus into some self-incriminating statement or action. A favorite technique was to ask him a question cunningly contrived so that whatever answer he gave would land him in trouble, either providing grounds for arrest by the Jewish or the Roman authorities or so disillusioning his followers that they would desert him, thereby depriving him of his influence. Examples include the question of tribute to Caesar[40] and that concerning the woman caught in the act of adultery (John 8:2–11). Another favorite ruse was to confront him with a needy person who presented some form of ethical challenge to see how he would react. Examples are the sinful woman in the Pharisee's house (Luke 7:36–50), the man suffering from dropsy in another Pharisee's house (Luke 14:1f), the man with the shriveled hand in the synagogue,[41] and the woman caught in the act of adultery (John 8:2–11). Yet another kind of test was the demand for a miraculous sign (Matt 12:38); if Jesus failed to perform one, he could be denounced as a charlatan, but if he obliged, his supernatural powers could be attributed to demonic assistance.[42] For further on the Pharisees' plot to have Jesus arrested see *Did the Pharisees really plot to kill Jesus?*, p. 205.

Hostility

Needless to say, what begins as a mild and tentative hostility towards him on the part of the deputation—which the evangelists sometimes identify as the Pharisees—grows steadily (Matt 9:3–6; Mark 2:6f). Similarly Jesus' disillusionment with them is reflected in his increasingly forceful dealings

---

40. Matt 22:15–22; Mark 12:13–17; Luke 20:19–26.
41. Matt 12:9–14; Mark 3:1–6; Luke 6:6–11.
42. Matt 9:34; 12:24; Mark 3:22.

Historical Reconstruction 3—Jesus and the Pharisees

with them (Matt 12:24–32; 23:1–36); now, of course, he no longer needed to remain on friendly terms with them. John's Gospel records an exchange that may have taken place soon after the beginning of this second phase:

> It was winter, and Jesus was in the temple area walking in Solomon's Colonnade. The Jews gathered round him, saying, "How long will you keep us in suspense? If you are the Christ, tell us plainly."
>
> Jesus answered, "I did tell you, but you do not believe. The miracles I do in my Father's name speak for me, but you do not believe because you are not my sheep. My sheep listen to my voice; I know them, and they follow me." (John 10:22–27)

In John's Gospel, the phrase "the Jews" often refers to the Pharisees. So this passage may portray Jesus as dissociating himself from them ("you do not believe because you are not my sheep") and claiming that others ("My sheep," the "other sheep" of John 10:16) do listen to him and follow him.

Despite this saying, Jesus did not abandon Pharisaism at once. For a while he continued teaching in the synagogues, the last such occasion recorded in the gospels being that when he was rejected by the congregation at Nazareth.[43] The synoptists do not explain why Jesus stopped teaching in synagogues, perhaps because they were embarrassed by it. The most likely explanation[44] is that he was banned from synagogues when he was excommunicated from Pharisaism, that is, when he was formally declared to be a "sinner" himself.

Jesus' expulsion from Pharisaism

We have already noted that the Pharisees introduced legislation to excommunicate ("put out of the synagogue") any Jew who professed belief that Jesus was the Messiah (John 9:22; 12:42—see *Interpreting the law*, p. 143). With such legislation in place Jesus himself could hardly remain a Pharisee in good standing. In fact a sequence of passages in John's Gospel appears to trace possible stages in his excommunication. The first was Jesus' healing

---

43. Matt 13:54–58; Mark 6:1–6; Luke 4:16–30.

44. It is possible, of course, that Jesus continued teaching in synagogues, but the evangelists had no reason to record any such occasions. It is also possible that he chose to stay away from them. Since his main mission now was directed to the "sinners" who were themselves banned from the synagogues, for Jesus to continue teaching in them would not serve his purpose.

on a Sabbath of the lame man at Bethesda (John 5:1-18). The second was Jesus' reference to a formal warning relating to that healing or possibly a similar one (John 7:21). The third focuses on Jesus' healing—also on a Sabbath—of the man blind from birth (John 9:1-14); the Pharisees took a special interest in this healing—perhaps they had intensified their surveillance to ensure that if Jesus broke the Sabbath again, they would have incontrovertible evidence (John 9:15f). The fourth and final stage was the Pharisees' telling the formerly blind man, "We know this man [Jesus] is a sinner" (John 9:24). This may reflect Jesus' recent expulsion from the Pharisee community—his formal declaration as a "sinner"—for healing on the Sabbath after a warning.

Although a repeated breach of the Sabbath was more than sufficient grounds for excommunication,[45] Jesus' case was aggravated by the fact that he was attracting many followers (John 12:19), some of whom had begun acclaiming him as Messiah. In Pharisaic piety the Sabbath was sacrosanct, so that the notion of a Sabbath-breaking Messiah was a particularly dangerous heresy. This presumably is why the Pharisaic authorities introduced legislation to excommunicate Jews who believed in Jesus. In apostolic times this legislation severely affected the Christian community in Jerusalem, causing its members such hardship (since, as "sinners," they found it difficult to obtain employment) that Paul raised funds from the diaspora to relieve them.[46] The ruling must have applied only in Jerusalem or Judea, because Paul was able to teach openly about Jesus in synagogues elsewhere in the Roman Empire.[47]

Some scholars have questioned the authenticity of John's references to excommunication, claiming that they reflect the situation prevailing at the time that John wrote his gospel rather than that of Jesus' ministry. C. K. Barrett, for example, writes, "That the synagogue had already at that time applied a test of Christian heresy is unthinkable."[48] Similarly J. L. Martyn has argued that the wording of John 9:22 suggests the formal decision of an authoritative body such as the Council of the Pharisees at Jamnia which

---

45. Excommunication seems lenient compared with the death penalty prescribed for breach of the Sabbath in Exod 31:14f, but the Roman authorities had outlawed Jewish death penalties.

46. Rom 15:26; 1 Cor 16:1-4; 2 Cor 8:1-9:15. A famine at this time would have exacerbated the hardship faced by the Jerusalem church.

47. Pisidian Antioch (Acts 13:14f), Iconium (14:1), Thessalonica (17:1f), Berea (17:10), Corinth (18:4), Ephesus (19:8).

48. Barrett, *St John*, 361.

Historical Reconstruction 3—Jesus and the Pharisees

led to the formulation of the *birkath ha-minim*, the cursing of the heretics, probably during the last 20 years of the first century.[49] Beasley-Murray, however, demonstrates that from the time of Jesus his followers experienced opposition from Judaism, including expulsion from synagogues, and that the *birkath ha-minim* drew upon an earlier decision to exclude Christians from synagogues.[50] There is therefore no reason to doubt the veracity of John's references to excommunication.

Accounts of Jesus' excommunication probably circulated in oral tradition amongst the earliest Christian congregations. When compiling their gospels, however, the evangelists were reluctant to mention it, perhaps because it appeared to cast Jesus in a derogatory light. Consequently the synoptists do not mention it at all and John implies it, rather than stating it explicitly; this is another reconstructed missing piece of the jigsaw puzzle. Nevertheless all three synoptists pointedly relate Jesus' healings on the Sabbath,[51] as well as other infringements of the Sabbath, as though they expect their readers to recognize their special significance, namely the penalty that Jesus paid for them. Apparently Jesus' closest disciples were not excommunicated at the same time, for he later told them, "They *will* put you out of the synagogue" (John 16:2).

Although as a "sinner" Jesus was banned from synagogues, the outermost court of the Temple—the "Court of the Gentiles"—was still open to him. The gospels record Jesus as still teaching there during the last week of his ministry (for example, Matt 21:23).

The new format of Jesus' ministry

From now on Jesus' public teaching took place mostly in the open air, because both he and the "sinners" whom he now sought to reach were banned from the synagogues. Moreover, in the open air he probably felt less constraint to adhere to the conventions of Pharisaic Judaism. His mentor, the Baptist, had also preached in the open air.

Another major change in Jesus' *modus operandi* at about this time was from teaching in plain language to the use of parables:

---

49. Martyn, *History and Theology*, 46–68.
50. Beasley-Murray, *John*, 153f.
51. Matt 12:9–14; Mark 1:21–27; 3:1–6; Luke 6:6–11; 13:10–17; 14:1–6.

> With many similar parables Jesus spoke the word to them, as much as they could understand. He did not say anything to them without using a parable. But when he was alone with his own disciples, he explained everything. (Mark 4:33f, paralleled in Matt 13:34)

There were two reasons for this change. Firstly, Jesus knew that his open-air meetings were being attended by members of the surveillance team sent by the Sanhedrin, who were monitoring his teaching for heresy in the hope of finding grounds on which to arrest him.[52] By deliberately concealing his spiritual teaching in innocuous stories Jesus ensured that the spies would find no offensive content in his teaching. Secondly, parables provided an easily memorable vehicle for conveying spiritual truth, especially when addressing people who may have had little previous religious instruction; their ability to shock their hearers into reflection concerning their own spiritual condition made them a particularly effective tool in this new phase of his ministry.[53] Ironically, in his use of parables Jesus was following a well established Pharisaic tradition.[54]

Jesus' preaching ministry was, however, a means to an end. His aim now was to build a radical new community willing to respond to God's word. His pronouncement to Peter, "I tell you that you are Peter, and on this rock I will build my church" (Matt 16:18), implies the beginning of a new movement with Peter as the prototype member. During their time with John the Baptist, Jesus and some of his disciples had witnessed a religious revival amongst the "sinners" and had recognized this as a genuine work of God. So Jesus' agenda now built upon foundations that the Baptist had laid down by creating a new faith community largely from the "sinners" whom the Pharisees so despised. Paradoxically, the fact that Jesus had now been declared a "sinner" was an advantage; he was himself officially one of the people whom he sought to reach. Because he, like they, was a victim of Pharisaic oppression (Matt 23:13), they should be more disposed to accept him as an ally than if he had remained a Pharisee in good standing.

John the Baptist was now dead, executed by Herod Antipas (Mark 6:17–29). In many ways, however, Jesus' reoriented ministry closely resembled John's. For example, Jesus and his disciples now exercised a ministry of baptism. Only John's Gospel mentions this explicitly (John 3:22–26; 4:1f), but the instruction to his disciples in the Great Commission to baptize

52. For example, Mark 12:13; Luke 11:53f; 20:20f.
53. Thiselton, "Hermeneutics," 85.
54. Maccoby, *Jesus*, 103.

Historical Reconstruction 3—Jesus and the Pharisees

converts (Matt 28:19) would have been startling if those disciples had not been already conversant with the administration of the rite.[55] The absence of any explicit reference in the synoptics to this aspect of Jesus' ministry is probably because early Christian congregations were well aware that their own conspicuous baptism of converts was a continuation of the routine practice of Jesus and his disciples.

Because Jesus baptized his converts, because he welcomed the "sinners" (Luke 15:2) and because he found himself in frequent debate with the leaders of Judaism, it is not surprising that some of the public thought that he was the Baptist returned from the dead (Matt 16:14). Even Herod Antipas surmised that Jesus was John come back to haunt him (Mark 6:14–16; Matt 14:1f); popular superstition maintained that those who had suffered an unjust death were likely to return to haunt their killers.

Building a new community from the "sinners"

In this second phase of his ministry, then, Jesus sought to build a new faith community, the church, chiefly from the "sinners," although others were welcome.[56] So when Jesus called Matthew/Levi, the tax collector, he was not simply adding another recruit to his retinue of disciples—he was making a radical statement: even these most despised of outcasts were now welcome as his followers. Jesus later befriended another tax collector, Zacchaeus, and dined in his home too, again attracting criticism (Luke 19:1–10). During this period the gospels record Jesus as gaining a reputation as "a friend of tax collectors and 'sinners:'"

> The Son of Man came eating and drinking, and they say, "Here is a glutton and a drunkard, a friend of tax collectors and 'sinners.'"[57]

It may be significant that this report does not apparently brand Jesus as a "sinner" himself. It probably originated early in this later phase of Jesus' ministry, before his excommunication, when he was still commonly regarded as a Pharisee, but a renegade one who had a concern for "sinners."

---

55. ". . . now the full-blown rite of Christian baptism is introduced without any indication that this is something new. For Matthew's readers it was probably so familiar as to need no explanation, but its sudden appearance right at the end of the gospel is surprising in the narrative context." (France, *Matthew*, 1116).

56. For example, Acts 15:5 refers to Pharisees who were members of the Jerusalem church.

57. Matt 11:19; Luke 7:34, *c.f.* Luke 15:2; 19:7.

Hypocrites or Heroes?

Matthew alone records a significant detail in Jesus' instructions to his twelve disciples before sending them out on a preaching mission:

> Do not go among the Gentiles or enter any town of the Samaritans. Go rather to the lost sheep of Israel. As you go, preach this message: "The kingdom of heaven is near." Heal the sick, raise the dead, cleanse those who have leprosy, drive out demons. Freely you have received, freely give. Do not take along any gold or silver or copper in your belts ... (Matt 10:5–10)

Here Jesus describes his target people as "the lost sheep of Israel" (*ta probata ta apolōlota oikou Israēl*, literally "the lost [or perished] sheep of the house of Israel"). The imagery of lost sheep may refer back to Matt 9:36 where Jesus described the crowds as "harassed and helpless, like sheep without a shepherd," drawing upon the traditional imagery of Ezek 34, verse 34 of which mentions the "house of Israel."

Precisely whom did Jesus consider to constitute "the lost sheep of Israel"? Clearly he is referring to Jews as opposed to Gentiles and Samaritans, but does he regard all Jews as "lost sheep" or just a portion of them? Most scholars prefer the first interpretation: France and Hagner are typical, maintaining that the phrase denotes Israel as a whole rather than any specific group within Israel.[58] Perhaps their understanding of the saying has been influenced by doctrinal considerations, such as belief that Jesus' mission targeted all Israel. Some scholars, however, have taken the alternative viewpoint: David Hill refers to K. Stendahl's conviction that the "lost sheep" are the *'am ha-'ares*, the "common people" who did not follow Pharisaic law,[59] although he (Hill) maintains that the Old Testament imagery of Ezek 34 demands that it is all Israel that is scattered on the mountains.[60] Interestingly, Nolland concedes that "it is unlikely that Matthew wants to insist here that all of Israel were lost sheep ... it is best to take the genitive as partitive (so: those of the house of Israel who were lost) rather than explicative (so: all of the house of Israel constitute the lost)." He then qualifies this as follows: "Nonetheless, Matthew does not intend to focus ministry here to some marginalised subsection of Israel, but rather to need in Israel wherever that was evident."[61] But focusing on a marginalized subsection of Israel—the "sinners"—is precisely what Jesus is doing in this later phase of

---

58. France, *Matthew*, 382; Hagner, *Matthew*, 1:270.
59. Stendahl, "Matthew," 683, as cited in Hill, *Matthew*, see below.
60. Hill, *Matthew*, 185.
61. Nolland, *Matthew*, 416f.

Historical Reconstruction 3—Jesus and the Pharisees

his ministry, as evidenced in his dining with tax collectors and in the parable of the Wedding Feast (particularly the Lucan version)—see *The Pharisees in the parables of Jesus*, p. 188. Moreover, in Luke's three parables about the "lost" (Luke 15:3–32) the same verb *apollumi* is used consistently of the "lost" who clearly represent the "sinners"—it is as though "the lost" were another technical designation for the "sinners"—see *Pharisees and teachers of the law complain about Jesus befriending sinners*, p. 64. And if we accord the flexible verb *apollumi* a stronger meaning—so that *apolōlota* becomes "perished," a perfectly valid rendering—it is hard to escape the conclusion that this saying refers to that portion of the population of Israel that had become disenfranchised through excommunication, namely the "sinners."

The wording of the gracious invitation in Matt 11:28–30 suggests that that appeal was addressed to pious Jews who found Pharisaic Judaism with its multitude of oral laws an intolerable burden. If so, during this period Jesus still occasionally used plain-language preaching to address folk who were conscious of struggling to observe the twofold law. France concedes that those burdened by the unreasonable demands of the teachers of the law may be the intended target, but has reservations: "the wording in this passage does not make that application explicit, and a wider reference to life's difficulties cannot be ruled out."[62] When this speech is considered in the context of this second phase of Jesus' ministry, however, such an appeal to those disillusioned with Pharisaic Judaism seems possible, to say the least.

That Jesus' cleansing of the Temple—a blatant act contrived deliberately to force a confrontation with the Jewish hierarchy—together with the consequent challenge by a deputation from the Sanhedrin concerning Jesus' authority (or "sign" in John's Gospel) is recorded in all four gospels[63] indicates that the evangelists considered this a signal episode in Jesus' ministry. His typically Rabbinic countering question, "John's baptism—where did it come from? Was it from heaven, or from men?" (Matt 21:25, paralleled in Mark 11:30; Luke 20:4) is cunning in that either answer would have embarrassed the deputation; ironically here Jesus is turning the surveillance team's own tactics against this deputation! Although he had apparently declined to respond to the deputation's original question, his invocation of the Baptist had answered it by analogy. The Jewish authorities had failed to endorse John's ministry, despite the religious revival which it

---

62. France, *Matthew*, 448.
63. Matt 21:23; Mark 11:28; Luke 20:2; John 2:18.

sparked, and they would do the same with Jesus' ministry. Because of the sheer incompetence revealed in this failure to recognize the hand of God when it was manifest in their midst, the present Jewish leadership was to be removed from office and replaced by others who had demonstrated their openness to God by genuine repentance, namely, the "sinners." This is the message of The Parable of the Wicked Tenants,[64] which all three synoptics present at this point, although in Matthew's Gospel it is preceded by The Two Sons (Matt 21:28–32) and followed by The Marriage Feast (Matt 22:1–10), both carrying the same message coined in different imagery. The Pharisees' depiction in Jesus' parables is considered below.

The Pharisees in the parables of Jesus

Only one of Jesus' parables mentions the Pharisees by name: the Pharisee and the Tax Collector (Luke 18:10–14). This has already been considered— see *The Parable of the Pharisee and the tax collector*, p. 66, and *Reputation*, p. 137.

In view of the Pharisees' dominant position in the social and religious scene of Palestine at the time and their influence on the ministry of Jesus, it is not surprising that several other of Jesus' parables refer to them under the veil of parabolic form. All are of the triadic type, that is, they feature three main characters, one of whom represents God and, in these examples, another represents the Pharisees (or the Jewish leadership generally), and the third the (repentant) "sinners." In Matthew's Gospel these include the three polemical parables which appear in succession in Jesus' reply to the challenge by the deputation from the Sanhedrin concerning his authority to cleanse the temple. Using different imagery each presents essentially the same message: that God is about to oust Israel's present incompetent leaders, including the Pharisees, from office and replace them with others who will serve him more faithfully, such as the repentant "sinners."

The first of the three, the Two Sons (Matt 21:28–32), occurs only in Matthew. It resembles the Prodigal Son (Luke 15:11–32, see below) in that both are about two contrasting sons, one a repentant sinner and the other self-righteous. Jesus' hearers would have recognized the vineyard which forms the story's setting as a traditional symbol of Israel.[65] The Father represents God; the two sons sent to work in the vineyard represent respectively

---

64. Matt 21:33–46; Mark 12:1–12; Luke 20:9–19.
65. Isa 3:14; 5:7; 27:2; Jer 2:21; Ezek 15:1–6; Hos 10:1.

Historical Reconstruction 3—Jesus and the Pharisees

the "sinners," who at first rebelled but later repented, and the Jewish leaders, such as the Pharisees, who professed obedience but failed to deliver it. When Jesus forces his distinguished audience to think about the parable by asking them a question about it, they give him the correct answer, although the question is hardly difficult. What is significant, however, is that the hearers apparently fail to recognize that *they are* that second son who, despite protestations of loyalty, disobeyed his father. Unusually the shock element so characteristic of Jesus' parables comes in the interpretation rather than the parable itself when Jesus makes the audacious statement:

> I tell you the truth, the tax collectors and the prostitutes are entering the kingdom of God ahead of you. For John came to you to show you the way of righteousness, and you did not believe him, but the tax collectors and the prostitutes did. And even after you saw this, you did not repent and believe him. (Matt 21:31f)

Jesus uses the conjunction of "the tax collectors and the prostitutes" to underline his message: contrary to popular belief, even these—the most despised kinds of "sinner"—are closer to God's kingdom than the distinguished religious leaders in the deputation. The proof of this is that those sinners recognized divine authority in John's ministry and responded to his preaching, demonstrating their repentance by submitting to his baptism. In contrast, the leaders in the deputation are not willing even to say whether or not John's ministry was "from heaven."

The Wicked Tenants appears in all three synoptics.[66] So many of its details have counterparts in the real world that many have treated it as an allegory, focusing on the climactic killing of the son as a passion prediction. Although the parallels with Jesus' own experience are certainly suggestive, they are nevertheless incidental—the story is a simple parable whose message is centered around Jesus' question and answer:

> What then will the owner of the vineyard do? He will come and kill [*apolesei*] those tenants and give the vineyard to others. (Mark 12:9)

As in the Two Sons, the vineyard represents Israel and its creator and owner is God. The tenants are the Jewish leaders such as the Pharisees and Sadducees; their refusal to yield the agreed share of the produce to the landowner represents their failure to fulfill their obligations to God. The succession of servants sent by the landowner represents the prophets

---

66. Matt 21:33–46; Mark 12:1–12; Luke 20:9–19.

whom God sent to call Israel back to obedience, many of whom were persecuted or even killed by the Jewish establishment. As a consequence of the murder of the son whom he sends as a last resort those tenants are now to be removed from office and replaced by others. But although intellectually Jesus' hearers know what is bound to happen—significantly in Matthew's version they themselves correctly answer Jesus' question—once again spiritual blindness prevents them at first from recognizing that *they are* those tenants in the story, it is *they* who within days will hand over the Son of God to be crucified, and consequently it is *they* who face being ousted from office. Although *apolesei*, part of the ubiquitous verb *apollumi*, is translated "kill" by the NIV and "destroy" by the RSV and KJV, perhaps the most appropriate rendering would be "get rid of." The more violent renderings may have been influenced by identification of the death of the son in the parable with the death of Jesus.

In the original Marcan version Jesus ends the parable with a statement contrived to provoke a question: "He will . . . give the vineyard to others." Aware that his hearers will be wondering who these "others" might be, Jesus gives a cryptic clue by launching at once into an Old Testament parable from Ps 118:22f:

> "Haven't you read this scripture: 'The stone the builders rejected has become the capstone; the Lord has done this, and it is marvelous in our eyes'?" (Mark 12:10f)

The symbolism has changed, the sharecroppers becoming builders who sent back an oddly shaped stone that had lain around on the construction site only to discover that it was the very cornerstone or keystone intended to anchor the whole structure together, arguably the most important stone in the building. Many recent commentators identify this stone with Jesus, rejected by the Jewish hierarchy when they crucified him, but resurrected to become head of the church.[67] That, however, cannot be the

---

67. For example, "The citation . . . focuses on one element of the preceding parable, namely the rejection of the son, now clearly the rejection of Jesus" (Hagner, *Matthew*, 2:622). Cranfield (*St Mark*, 369) is similar. "Probably Luke sees the resurrection vindication of Jesus as preparatory to the emergence of the new Christian leadership of the people of God" (Nolland, *Luke*, 3:953). France alludes to the assonance of "son" and "stone" if Jesus was speaking in Aramaic: "just as the builders rejected the stone only to find that their judgment was overturned and the stone given the place of highest importance, so you will see that the son you have rejected and killed is the one God has chosen to take your place." But he also sees a role for the Church of "sinners": "But instead of a single new tenant, or even a new ruling group to replace the current Jewish leadership,

Historical Reconstruction 3—Jesus and the Pharisees

meaning that Jesus intended, because his hearers could not have understood it that way before his death and resurrection; moreover, in Matthew it takes no account of the context (the other two polemical parables). So, who else had the Jewish leaders rejected? The "sinners"—excommunicated Jews—now repenting in large numbers (Matt 21:32) but meeting with obstruction from the Jewish establishment (Matt 23:13) will form the basis of Jesus' new faith community, the church, which is to replace the Jews as God's chosen people. In 1915 A. H. M'Neile hinted at this interpretation: "If the quotation is by Jesus himself . . . the pious members of the Jewish race oppressed and misused by their religious leaders will be advanced to honour."[68]

The third in the trio, the Marriage Feast (Matt 22:1–10, Luke 14:16–24), has elements in common with the Wicked Tenants. For example, the successive deputations of slaves (although Luke mentions only one) recall the successive deputations sent in the Wicked Tenants to receive the produce. Both represent the prophets whom God sent to Israel to persuade the people to serve him faithfully and enter His salvation. The king of course represents God and the originally invited guests the leaders of Israel. The meaning comes at the end:

> Then he said to his servants, "The wedding banquet is ready, but those I invited did not deserve to come. Go to the street corners and invite to the banquet anyone you find." So the servants went out into the streets and gathered all the people they could find, both good and bad, and the wedding hall was filled with guests. (Matt 22:8–10)

As in the Wicked Tenants, the privilege originally offered to Israel's leaders, who included the Pharisees, is withdrawn and extended to a different set of beneficiaries who prove satisfactory. Luke's account describes those gathered in as "the poor, the crippled, the blind and the lame" (Luke 14:21), in other words, the marginalised, who were popularly believed to be accursed. In both versions the irony of the situation is well to the fore: the very people whom pious Jews despised as under God's curse now enter his salvation, while those for whom it was originally intended forfeit the privilege.

One other parable clearly depicts the Pharisees: the Prodigal Son (Luke 15:11–32), which could be regarded as an elaborate version of the

---

Jesus speaks of a 'nation'" (France, *Matthew*, 815f).

68. M'Neile, *Matthew*, 311.

Hypocrites or Heroes?

Two Sons. Although the Pharisees are not mentioned by name, Manson's summary, "the father represents God, the elder brother those scribes and Pharisees who criticized Jesus, and the younger brother the publicans and sinners whom Jesus befriended,"[69] fits the storyline and many recent commentators have reached the same conclusion, as will be seen. So the prodigal's humiliating homecoming represents the sinners' repentance and the Father's unrestrained welcome for him God's joy when any wanderer returns to the fold, a common theme in Jesus' teaching (for example, Matt 18:12-14; Luke 15:3-7). The elder brother's resentment of the Father's welcome for the returned prodigal portrays the Pharisees' refusal to accept repentant "sinners," which is the principal message in the story. Consequently Bultmann's suggestion[70] that the parable should end with verse 24 indicates that he has completely missed its point. Indeed, that the parable is more about the elder brother than the younger is eloquently expressed by G. B. Caird:

> "*There was a man who had two sons*," and he lost them both, one in a foreign country, the other behind a barricade of self-righteousness. The elder contrived, without leaving home, to be as far away from his father as ever his brother was in the heathen pigsty.... The selfishness of the elder brother was less obvious and less vulnerable. He asked for nothing, desired nothing, enjoyed nothing. He devoted himself dutifully to his father's service, never disobeying a command of his father, and thought, no doubt, that he was the model of unselfishness; yet he himself was the centre of his every thought, so that he was incapable of entering sympathetically into his father's joys and sorrows.[71]

Although Caird's exegesis of the parable does not explicitly mention the Pharisees, he was surely as aware as Manson that the elder brother is a beautifully observed representation of them. Leon Morris is of the same

---

69. Manson, *Sayings*, 286.

70. "Surely the narrator's purpose, to make plain the fatherly goodness of God, which unconditionally forgives self-condemning remorse, is already attained in verse 24? And is not the point of the parable shifted when God's forgiveness is defended against the charge of injustice? Yet verses 25-32 are not an allegorical fabrication, but remain completely within the parable so far as formal features are concerned. But neither does this second half of the parable really differ in context from the first, but rather makes plain by contrast the paradoxical character of divine forgiveness." (Bultmann, *Synoptic Tradition*, 196.)

71. Caird, *Saint Luke*, 182.

opinion: "The likeness to the Pharisees is unmistakable."[72] Similarly Nolland states, "The prodigal and the elder brother of the parable are to be linked on the one hand to the tax collectors and sinners and on the other hand to the Pharisees and scribes . . ."[73]

Although the elder brother appears to exhibit the admirable traits of loyalty, industriousness, unselfishness, and patience, his reaction to the return of his brother demonstrates that he has "lost the plot." He wants God for himself and is not willing to share him with those whom he considers unworthy. If the younger brother had not returned and instead news had arrived that he had starved to death in the distant country, surely the elder brother would have approved on the grounds that this was what he deserved. While God's loving welcome for repentant sinners is undeniably an essential element in the parable, it is nevertheless secondary to its main intention: to show that God's people have a duty to co-operate with God in mediating his love and forgiveness to repentant sinners, which according to Jesus the Pharisees were failing to do (Matt 23:13). As Caird astutely concludes, "The parable was told not to offer a generous pardon to the nation's prodigals, but to entreat the respectable Jews to rejoice with God over the restoration of sinners, and to warn them that, until they learnt to do this, they would remain estranged from their heavenly father and pitifully ignorant of his true character."[74] Morris states explicitly what Caird implies: "The parable says something to 'the tax collectors and sinners.' But it also has a message for 'the Pharisees and the scribes.'"[75] Surely, then, Jesus told this parable as an appeal to the Pharisees to welcome repentant "sinners" instead of excluding them permanently from the Jewish community.

JESUS' TRIAL AND PASSION: THE UNEXPECTED TWIST IN THE TALE

The parables that contrast the Pharisees with the "sinners" are not hard to understand. At the end of the Wicked Tenants Mark reports that the deputation from the Sanhedrin "looked for a way to arrest him because they knew he had spoken the parable against them. But they were afraid of the crowd; so they left him and went away" (Mark 12:12). Even if they would

72. Morris, *Luke*, 261.
73. Nolland, *Luke*, 2:780.
74. Caird, *Saint Luke*, 184.
75. Morris, *Luke*, 257.

not admit it openly, surely at some level they recognized the truth in Jesus' implicit accusation that they were incompetent and divine judgment inevitable. Several courses of action were open to them: they could "lose face" by admitting that Jesus was right and resigning *en masse*. Alternatively they could brazenly continue their persecution of Jesus, taking whatever measures might be necessary to suppress the unpalatable truth.

In fact the Pharisees amongst them took a third course, although once again the New Testament leaves the reader to fill in the gap left by a piece missing from the puzzle. Although the clues to what happened are there in all four gospels, no evangelist directs attention to them or draws any conclusions. What is clear, of course, is that Jewish leaders blackmailed the reluctant Roman Governor into crucifying Jesus as an insurgent against Rome. But precisely who were those Jewish leaders? This aspect of the passion narrative is so totally unexpected that most scholars gloss over it as though what happened is exactly as they expected; only Maccoby draws attention to the startling element.[76] The Pharisees, who were so prominent as the party with whom Jesus debated and, moreover, who had been so avidly plotting his downfall and monitoring his ministry in the hope of finding grounds to arrest him, vanish from the scene without a word of explanation. The last appearances of *Pharisaios* in the synoptic gospels before Jesus' arrest are in the series of approaches made to Jesus in the Temple by various groups posing loaded questions in the hope that his replies might incriminate him. The only subsequent occurrence of *Pharisaios* is in the curious incident, peculiar to Matthew, in which Pharisees and chief priests approach Pilate and request that a guard be placed on Jesus' tomb (Matt 27:62–66). Throughout Jesus' arrest, interrogation by the Jewish leaders and his interview with Pilate the prime instigators are the chief priests, sometimes accompanied by *grammateis* who were surely their own administrative assistants rather than Pharisaic teachers of the law. The pattern is repeated in John's Gospel: despite the evangelist's informant inside the Sanhedrin, John's last use of *Pharisaios* before the arrest is in John 12:42f and his use of it in John 18:3 is in a phrase denoting the Sanhedrin. Moreover, most of the instances of *hoi Ioudaioi* in his Passion narrative are generic, relating to the Jewish people as a whole rather than to the Pharisees.

Maccoby summarizes the paradoxical situation as follows:

---

76. Sanders refers to Maccoby's views and agrees that "Jesus was executed at the behest of the high priest" (Sanders, *Judaism*, 400f).

Historical Reconstruction 3—Jesus and the Pharisees

> Although throughout his career Jesus is alleged to have been criticized by the Pharisees, ... no Pharisee is represented as having appeared as a witness at Jesus' alleged trial to press these points...[77]

It is as though, when the final showdown began, the Pharisees quietly withdrew themselves from the plot and hoped that in the ensuing drama no one would notice their absence. So why did they do this? There are several possibilities.

Let us first eliminate the possible objection that, as an inference from silence, the veracity of the claim is dubious. In other words, an objector might argue that the Pharisees *were* involved in the trial and passion of Jesus and it is only by some strange mischance that none of the evangelists has recorded any instance of this. That is highly unlikely. Most of the evangelists had an anti-Pharisee bias; surely they would have delighted in recording instances of Pharisees perjuring themselves in order to bring false evidence against Jesus. That even John with his spy inside the Sanhedrin has failed to produce any evidence of Pharisaic involvement at this critical stage of the proceedings can only indicate that there was none. So the lack of references to the Pharisees at the trial of Jesus need not be an oversight—it may accurately reflect the truth: they were not involved.

If so, why did the Pharisees absent themselves from the interrogation and trial of Jesus? The situation is extraordinarily complex with interwoven currents and counter-currents; the Pharisees were a diverse group. Any or all of the following may be true; individuals may have acted from a variety of motives.

Firstly, some may indeed have been afraid of the crowd, as Matt 21:46 states. The New Testament attests that the Pharisees, or some of them at least, enjoyed the adulation of the people (Luke 11:43). Maybe they feared that if they were seen to be complicit in the execution of this man popularly acclaimed as a prophet, the people might desert them and seek other heroes.

Secondly, some who heard Jesus' reply to the deputation from the Sanhedrin may have accepted the truth of the Parable of the Wicked Tenants and recognized the enormity of what they were on the brink of doing—enacting the role of the villains who slew the Master's son. So they decided to take no further part in it. By all accounts, most Pharisees had a keen sense of justice and, even if they themselves did not believe that Jesus was

---

77. Maccoby, *Jesus*, 71.

Hypocrites or Heroes?

Messiah or even a prophet, they would surely have recognized that he had done nothing deserving the death penalty.

Thirdly, the gospels record that at least one *grammateus* was deeply impressed by Jesus during that series of approaches in the Temple in the last week of his ministry (Mark 12:28–34). Perhaps Mark's concluding remark, "And from then on no-one dared ask him any more questions," reflects some consensus among the Pharisees that Jesus was, after all, a genuine teacher from God and not to be subjected to further persecution.

Fourthly, undoubtedly some Pharisees were secretly followers of Jesus and they, of course, would not wish to be associated with his arrest, trial or execution. Examples are Nicodemus, possibly John's unidentified "spy" in the Sanhedrin, and the "many leaders" of John 12:42.

Lastly, the "Gamaliel incident" of Acts 5:34–41 may shed some light on this matter. Gamaliel, the leader of the whole Pharisee movement according to the Rabbinic writings,[78] ordered the Sanhedrin to spare the lives of Peter, John and some other apostles who had been arrested for preaching about Jesus—paradoxically, the same Jesus whose downfall the Pharisees had allegedly been plotting not long previously. What brought about such a complete reversal of Pharisee policy? Could it be that there had been a significant undercurrent in the Pharisee movement that, while not necessarily accepting Jesus as a prophet or Messiah, nevertheless recognized his persecution as unjust? Could it perhaps be that Gamaliel had received so many deputations about this that at the last possible moment he ordered or advised all Pharisees to take no further part in the arrest, trial or execution of Jesus? This would certainly explain their unexpected absence from the legal proceedings. It is, of course, true that Pharisees were involved in the request for a guard on the tomb of Jesus (Matt 27:62–66), but to guard a tomb in order to forestall an act of deception is hardly a crime.

Of course, if the Pharisees, as described above, chose at the critical moment to pull out of the conspiracy against Jesus and if, as shown earlier, the Pharisees dominated the Sanhedrin, why did they not intervene by persuading the chief priests to spare Jesus? Again there are several possible reasons.

Firstly, there was no opportunity. There was no further assembly of the Sanhedrin before the trial itself.

Secondly, although they sought to work together in the Sanhedrin, the Pharisees and the Sadducees had been adversaries ever since the emergence

---

78. Ibid., 5f

of their respective movements during the Maccabean Revolt. Consequently the Pharisees' sudden decision to spare Jesus might well have exacerbated the chief priests' (who were Sadducees) determination to kill him.

Thirdly, since the Romans had abolished Jewish death penalties, they alone had the power to perform an execution and that only for crime against Rome. The Sadducees were the only Jews who had the ear of the Roman authorities and sufficient influence to persuade them. The Pharisees had little influence on the Romans—indeed, on account of their nationalist tendencies, the Romans probably regarded them as potential troublemakers. It was therefore a more or less unilateral initiative on the part of the chief priests (Sadducees), not a decision of the full Sanhedrin, that handed Jesus over to Pilate.

This places the onus for Jesus' crucifixion fairly and squarely on the Sadducees. They, like the Pharisees (earlier in Jesus' ministry at least), regarded Jesus as a threat to Judaism and to national security. But, unlike the Pharisees, the Sadducees were not afraid of the people. They had never enjoyed public popularity; their power resided in their wealth, the high offices that they held in the Temple hierarchy and their Roman patronage. They could afford to ignore the crowds and the Pharisees; they could do whatever they wished. Or, at least, usually they could. Paradoxically, the execution of Jesus was an exception to this rule. Such was his popularity that if it became known that the chief priests were responsible for his death, that might trigger severe unrest which would be in the interests of neither the Sadducees nor their patrons, the Romans. They overcame this with a scheme of Machiavellian cunning: by arresting Jesus at night, interrogating him in secret in the chief priest's home rather than in a public courtroom and handing him over as an insurgent to Pilate in the early morning, they could effectively acquit themselves. No one need know that this was a priestly initiative. The hated Romans would take the blame for the execution of the popular prophet Jesus as an insurrectionist, while they, the chief priests, could deny any involvement in the process.

8

Hypocrites or Heroes—Explaining the Paradox

THIS CHAPTER SEEKS TO answer the questions raised in chapter 1 concerning the paradox of the Pharisees, drawing upon our findings in chapters 2 to 7. The paradox is chiefly concerned with the related issues of the accusation that Jesus—or his disciples—infringed the Sabbath and the nature of the Pharisees' plots against Jesus.

SABBATH BREAKING

The occasions when Jesus or his disciples were accused by the Pharisees of breaking the Sabbath account for what is perhaps the most difficult to resolve of the apparent discrepancies in the gospels' portrayal of the Pharisees. The rabbinic sources depict the Pharisees as working to *relax* the Sabbath regulations by devising legal loopholes known as the *'erub*[1] (boundary extension) system to reduce the inconvenience which the Sabbath restrictions imposed on Jews. Sanders describes an example: "By constructing doorposts and lintels, they 'fused' several houses into one, so that dishes could be carried from one to the other"[2] on the Sabbath. This kind of provision, however, is not reflected in the gospel passages in which Jesus

---

1. France, *Matthew*, 456.
2. Sanders, *Judaism*, 425.

argues about the Sabbath with Pharisees; instead they are portrayed as rigorously enforcing a literal understanding of the Torah Sabbath regulations, including an absolute ban on Sabbath healings.

Two such incidents appear in all three Synoptics: the disciples' plucking heads of grain[3] and the healing of the man with the shriveled hand.[4] Luke adds two further Sabbath healings: one of a crippled woman in a synagogue (Luke 13:10–17) and one of a man suffering from dropsy in a Pharisee's house (Luke 14:1–6). Each except the last of these elicits an accusation by Pharisees that the Sabbath has been violated; Jesus then proceeds to defend his (or the disciples') actions. The exceptional last-mentioned incident elicits no recorded response at all, but that it was contrived as a test is evident in Luke's note that Jesus was "being carefully watched" (Luke 14:1). John records two Sabbath healings: the lame man at Bethesda (John 5:1–16) and the man blind from birth (John 9:1–14). These may be the reason for Jesus' excommunication from the Jewish/Pharisee community (for further see *Jesus' expulsion from Pharisaism,* p. 181). The inclusion of so many such incidents in the gospels surely indicates that the evangelists regarded them as a significant feature of Jesus' ministry.

Maccoby summarizes the inconsistency, especially in regard to Sabbath healings, as follows:

> It is an amazing fact that, when we consult the Pharisee law books to find out what the Pharisees actually taught about healing on the Sabbath, we find that they did *not* forbid it, and they even used the very same arguments that Jesus used to show that it was permitted. Moreover, Jesus' celebrated saying, "The Sabbath was made for man, not man for the Sabbath," which has been hailed so many times as an epoch-making new insight proclaimed by Jesus, is found almost word for word in a rabbinic source (*Mekhilta Shabbeta* 1, on Exod 31:13), where it is used to support the Pharisee doctrine that the saving of life has precedence over the law of the Sabbath. So it seems that whoever it was that Jesus was arguing against when he defended his Sabbath healing, it cannot have been the Pharisees.[5]

It must be pointed out that when Maccoby refers to "the Pharisee law books" he means the Rabbinical literature; Maccoby in common with

---

3. Matt 12:1–8; Mark 2:23–28; Luke 6:1–5.
4. Matt 12:9–14; Mark 3:1–6; Luke 6:6–11.
5. Maccoby, *Jesus,* 124.

many scholars considers the Rabbinic movement to be a continuation of the Pharisee movement.

Before considering Maccoby's ingenious solution to the problem, let us examine the "conventional" explanation. France considers that the *'erub* provisions "are the product of the rabbis who represented the continuing Pharisaic leadership after the destruction of the temple." They belong therefore to a later period; in Jesus' time the "Pharisaic party existed to promote and practice the most rigorous observance of the Torah."[6] On this basis, then, the gospel text is sacrosanct and Sanders is misleading in giving the impression that the *'erub* system was in place in Temple times. Despite Maccoby's implication that Jesus' memorable saying, "The Sabbath was made for man, not man for the Sabbath," was originally a rabbinic saying[7] that Jesus adapted for his own use, surely the converse could be true: could not Jesus have originated the saying and the Rabbis copied it so that it found its way into the Talmud? It is notoriously difficult to date material in the Talmud; if, as Maccoby also asserts, Jesus is mentioned and at least one of his sayings is reproduced elsewhere in the Babylonian Talmud,[8] why should not this saying be one of his?

The principal difficulty with the "conventional" approach is that it requires the Pharisees to make a complete *volte-face* from rigorous literal interpretation of the Torah during Jesus' days to the more lenient approach of the *'erub* system not long afterwards. Moreover, if in Jesus' day the Pharisees' interpretation of Torah's demands was effectively no different from the Sadducees', why do the New Testament and Josephus agree that the Pharisees enjoyed the popularity of the Jewish populace while the Sadducees did not? Surely it was because the Pharisees with their exegesis and *paradosis* sought to ease the burden on ordinary Jewish people by making Torah observance easier, in contrast with the Sadducees who rigorously insisted on its literal interpretation? Those who favor the "conventional" understanding are in danger of abolishing the distinction between the Pharisees and the Sadducees altogether.

Maccoby's ingenious solution to the problem is not without difficulties, but it *is* nevertheless plausible. He suggests that it was not Pharisees, but *Sadducees* with whom Jesus argued concerning Sabbath breaking and

---

6. France, *Matthew*, 456.

7. "The Sabbath was handed over to man, not man to the Sabbath." (Maccoby, *Philosophy*, 87.)

8. Maccoby, *Jesus*, 144.

Hypocrites or Heroes—Explaining the Paradox

especially Sabbath healing. Although no Sadducee documentation survives, it is known that the Sadducees favored the kind of literal interpretation of Torah, including its Sabbath regulations, that the supposed Pharisees were seeking to enforce in the gospel passages mentioned. Maccoby finds support for his theory in Mark's statement that after a Sabbath healing the supposed Pharisees conspired with the Herodians concerning what they should do about Jesus (Mark 3:6). Such co-operation, he claims, is "quite impossible," the interests of those two groups being too different. But it is perfectly credible that Sadducees might conspire with Herodians, who had generally similar interests; moreover, those groups are known to have collaborated on other occasions. What Maccoby is suggesting, then, is that the officials with whom Jesus debated concerning Sabbath breaking were in fact Sadducees and some editor has amended the gospel text replacing the original reading "Sadducees" with "Pharisees" in those passages "in which Jesus is inexplicably arguing a Pharisee viewpoint about the Sabbath *against* the Pharisees."[9]

Indirect evidence in support of Maccoby's theory is provided by several other gospel passages which would be more credible if the present reading "Pharisees" had been substituted for an earlier reading "Sadducees." For example, in John 7:49 unidentified Pharisees are reported as saying "But this mob that knows nothing of the law—there is a curse on them." This sounds like a typical Sadducee remark; Pharisees would have blamed themselves for not educating the "mob" in the law. Indeed the action in that whole pericope is more typical of the Sadducees than the Pharisees. Another such passage is Luke 16:14: "The Pharisees, who loved money, heard all this and were sneering at Jesus." There is no evidence elsewhere that the Pharisees "loved money"; indeed some prominent Pharisees such as Hillel lived in poverty without apparently seeking to improve their circumstances. The Sadducees, in contrast, enjoyed both wealth and power, so they arguably "loved money."

There is, then, circumstantial evidence in the New Testament that substitutions of the kind that Maccoby describes may have taken place. But why should anyone wish to make this kind of change? And who could such an editor be? Maccoby believes the gospels to have been subjected to multiple layers of editing as happened in the formation of the rabbinical literature, which would allow many such opportunities. Most gospel critics, however, believe that the gospels came into existence in a rather different

---

9. Ibid., 125.

manner—the only editing was by the evangelists themselves as they compiled the gospels from their source materials.

There are, however, several possible explanations for such a change. Maccoby argues, "The Pharisees were known to be the chief religious authorities of the Jews, not the Sadducees . . . it was of utmost importance to the Gospel editors to represent Jesus as having been a rebel against the Jewish religion, not against the Roman Occupation."[10] While this is certainly possible, it forces a questionable level of political motivation on to the evangelists. Alternatively, the evangelists may simply have wished to blacken the Pharisees in order to make Jesus a more attractive religious figure than they. While the evangelists seem to have taken care to depict Jesus himself accurately, they may have allowed themselves some license in their portrayal of the opposition.

Another possibility is that the changes were accidental, the result of ignorance or negligence. Although the gospels were not subjected to multiple layers of editing, they were repeatedly copied by scribes and occasionally scribes make mistakes. Because the Greek words *Pharisaioi* and *Saddukaioi* are similar in appearance, it is conceivable that a weary scribe or one whose attention had wandered might write one in mistake for the other.[11] Alternatively, when reading *Saddukaioi* in the original, a scribe might decide that this was a mistake, *Pharisaioi* being intended; he might then deliberately amend the text mistakenly believing that he is correcting a previous scribe's error. We must remember that these scribes may have been confused about the Pharisees and Sadducees themselves. By the time the gospels were first written the Sadducees had ceased to exist and Pharisaism, which hardly ever referred to itself by that name, had become effectively the only surviving form of Judaism. So a scribe copying a gospel manuscript some centuries later might be unfamiliar with the subtle distinctions between those two groups which effectively were now lost in antiquity.

It seems unlikely, however, that the changes we are considering are the result of scribal error, because if following a scribal error both the original and the corrupted MSS are used to make further copies, variant readings may result. As Maccoby's theory requires that several instances of "Pharisees" originally read "Sadducees," we should expect there to be numerous

10. Maccoby, *Jesus*, 126.

11. A similar scribal error is believed to have resulted in the well-known variant readings *ōrgistheis* and *splagchnistheis* in Mark 1:41.

textual variants involving those words. There is, however, only one textual variant in the New Testament that involves the word *Pharisaios*. This concerns John 7:32 where in place of the first instance of *hoi Pharisaioi* some manuscripts have *hoi archiereis*, "the chief priests," and the second instance of *hoi Pharisaioi* is omitted by some manuscripts. This solitary example does have the virtue of showing that the proposed substitution is feasible, as the chief priests were mostly Sadducees. The lack of textual variants need not indicate that no substitution occurred, but that if it did happen it was at author level rather than scribal level, so that no manuscripts ever existed with the word "Sadducees" in the appropriate places.

One seemingly solid objection to Maccoby's conjectured substitution of "Pharisees" for "Sadducees" is that it introduces a *geographical* inconsistency. Let us consider the two Sabbath-breaking incidents that are common to all three synoptics: the disciples' plucking the heads of grain and the healing of the man with the shriveled hand. If Maccoby's theory is correct, the persons with whom Jesus argued were Sadducees. Now the Sadducees were a small group consisting of the chief priests and a few wealthy aristocratic families based in Jerusalem. But these two incidents happen early in the gospel narrative and the setting is almost certainly Galilee. That the disciples were walking through cornfields also suggests a rural rather than an urban location. It is most unlikely that Jesus and his disciples would repeatedly encounter Jerusalem-based Sadducees so far from home in Galilee, especially on a Sabbath.

There is, however, a plausible counter-argument. Jesus might have had repeated encounters with Sadducees even in Galilee on a Sabbath, *if they had been sent there especially to observe him*. The deputation sent, presumably by the Sanhedrin, to investigate John the Baptist (Matt 3:7) consisted of "Pharisees and Sadducees."[12] It is understandable that such a deputation would include members of both groups, as both were represented in the Sanhedrin; France refers to it as a "cross-party delegation."[13] We have already noted the abundant evidence in the gospels that a similar deputation was sent to Galilee to investigate Jesus. Although the principal passages[14] referring to this describe its constituents as Pharisees and *grammateis*, by

---

12. That deputation might also be the one described in John 1:19: "when the Jews of Jerusalem sent priests and Levites to ask him who he was." This need not conflict with Matt 3:7. The "Jews of Jerusalem" is probably a reference to the Sanhedrin. Pharisees are mentioned in John 1:24, probably forming part of the same delegation.

13. France, *Matthew*, 110.

14. Matt 15:1; Mark 3:22; 7:1; Luke 5:17

analogy with the earlier deputation it would be reasonable to expect it also to include Sadducees; perhaps the *grammateis* were the chief priests' administrators sent to protect the special interests of the Sadducee members of the Sanhedrin—after all, in the New Testament *grammateis* are more frequently associated with the chief priests than with the Pharisees. If so, it might have been the Sadducee members of the deputation who criticized Jesus for infringing their rigorous literal interpretation of the Sabbath laws, causing him to respond with typically Pharisaic arguments for a more lenient interpretation.

Evidence in support of this counter-argument appears in Matt 16:1–12 where Jesus is approached and tested *in Galilee* by a group which according to Matthew consisted of "Pharisees and Sadducees." Afterwards he warns his disciples about "the yeast of the Pharisees and Sadducees," suggesting that, even in Galilee, he was concerned about the teaching of the Sadducees and the effect that this might have on his disciples. It is tempting to surmise that the evangelist himself added the detail about Sadducees to tradition such as the similar Matt 12:38f which mentioned only Pharisees, but why should he do this unless it were true? The sheer unexpectedness of the pairing bespeaks the authenticity of the tradition[15] and the presence in Matthew of other unique incidents whose veracity is generally accepted suggests that his unique sources were reliable.

In summary, both theories present difficulties. Although Maccoby's may seem the more farfetched in requiring someone to have substituted "Pharisees" for "Sadducees," this theory nevertheless seems to the present author to be the more consistent with the situation presented in the New Testament and other ancient sources. The "conventional" theory may preserve the integrity of the gospel text, but it requires there to have been effectively no difference between Pharisees and Sadducees at the time of Jesus and therefore no reason for the general popularity of the Pharisees with the Jewish populace.

---

15. A chronicler who wished, for whatever reason, to fabricate an incident would surely make it sound as ordinary—and therefore credible—as possible in order to minimize the likelihood of critical readers questioning its claims and subjecting them to scrutiny. On this basis an improbable story, such as one in which Pharisees and Sadducees act in concert, is unlikely to have been invented.

DID THE PHARISEES REALLY PLOT TO KILL JESUS?

The plot against Jesus is inseparably bound up with the question of Sabbath breaking (see above), for it was Jesus' (or his disciples') breaches of the Sabbath that led to the meeting—with the Herodians according to Mark—which supposedly plotted to kill him.

The situation is complicated by three factors. Firstly, Jesus was already under surveillance when the Sabbath breaking occurred—even at the healing (not on a Sabbath) of the paralyzed man let down through the roof, there were officials from Jerusalem and elsewhere present, sent presumably by the Sanhedrin to investigate Jesus in much the same way that the earlier deputation had been sent to investigate John the Baptist.

Secondly, this deputation is likely to have contained Sadducees as well as Pharisees. According to Maccoby's theory (which has much to commend it—see above) it was Sadducees and not Pharisees with whom Jesus argued concerning the observance of the Sabbath; an editor amended the relevant texts in the gospels to "Pharisees" either accidentally out of confusion or deliberately to blacken the Pharisees. Sadducees were far more likely than Pharisees both to take exception to breaches of the Sabbath and to enlist the support of the Herodians. So those plotting the downfall of Jesus may have been Sadducees or possibly a mixture of Sadducees and Pharisees.

Thirdly, as explained earlier in *The plots against Jesus*, p. 148, it is unlikely that the conspirators plotted to *kill* Jesus, at least in the early stages. Whether the conspirators were Pharisees or Sadducees or Herodians or some combination of these, to kill Jesus would have been illegal under Roman law as well as unethical and, in view of Jesus' popularity with the public at large, liable to incite unrest that was in no-one's interests. It is far more likely that the conspirators "were looking for a reason to accuse Jesus" as stated in Luke 6:7; in this way they could remove him from circulation legally, putting an end to his ministry and his influence. Moreover, while the Greek verb *apollumi* which is translated "kill" in the NIV of both Mark 3:6 and Matt 12:14 can have that meaning, it can also mean "lose," "get rid of," or "destroy." Perhaps in this context "ruin" might be the most appropriate rendering.

Where the verb *apokteinō*, which definitely means "kill," is used in connection with later plots against Jesus, the plotters are never described as Pharisees. Usually, as in Mark 14:1 and Luke 22:2, they are the chief priests and the teachers of the law [*grammateis*], the latter referring probably to the priests' administrative assistants rather than Pharisaic teachers of the law. Consequently, it is impossible to find unequivocal evidence in the New Testament that Pharisees ever plotted to *kill* Jesus, although they may have conspired to ruin his reputation. The plot to have him killed, which of course eventually succeeded, was a priestly (and therefore Sadducee) initiative.

THE PHARISEES' ATTITUDE TOWARDS "SINNERS"

Jesus' most serious complaint against the Pharisees concerned their refusal to reinstate repentant "sinners" (Matt 23:13). As a consequence of this those who had been excluded from the Jewish community were condemned to a lifetime on the margins of society (see *Those "put out of the synagogue"—the "sinners,"* p. 155). Indeed, Jesus founded the Church as an alternative faith community to provide a spiritual home for the repentant "sinners." He told the Parable of the Prodigal Son (Luke 15:11–32) to urge his peers to emulate God in welcoming those who repented and thereby avoid the error of the prodigal's merciless elder brother who represents the Pharisees.

But how accurately does this picture reflect Pharisee attitudes towards repentant sinners? Although Wright argues that first-century Judaism attached national significance to the forgiveness of sins, he does not deny that it was still important at the individual level.[16] Pharisees regarded all three parts of the Old Testament as authoritative scripture and all three emphasize Yahweh's concern for forgiveness of sins at the individual level: it is implicit in the levitical sin offerings, still offered in Second Temple times, and in such passages as Ps 32:1–5 and Isa 55. Sanders produces abundant evidence that in "Common Judaism"—and therefore in Pharisaism—repentance was regarded as leading to forgiveness of sins at the individual level: "Repentance is straightforward: God will forgive those who repent of their sins and who make restitution (if the sin is against another human)."[17]

---

16. "From the point of view of a first-century Jew, 'forgiveness of sins' could never simply be a private blessing, though to be sure it was that as well, as Qumran amply testifies. Overarching the situation of the individual was the state of the nation as a whole; and, as long as Israel remained under the rule of pagans, as long as Torah was not observed perfectly, as long as the Temple was not properly restored, so Israel longed for 'forgiveness of sins' as the great, unrepeatable, eschatological and national blessing promised by her god. In the light of this, the meaning which Mark and Luke both give to John's baptism ought to be clear. It was 'for the forgiveness of sins,' in other words, to bring about the redemption for which Israel was longing." (Wright, *Jesus*, 271.)

17. Sanders, *Judaism*, 271.

Hypocrites or Heroes—Explaining the Paradox

Moreover, Sanders emphasizes the *leniency* of the Pharisees, especially as contrasted with the harshness of the Sadducees. He refers to Josephus' account of Eleazar's opposition to John Hyrcanus (see Josephus: *Antiquities* 13:10:5f) and the Gamaliel incident when the Sadducee party wished to prosecute Peter and John (Acts 5:17), while Gamaliel as leader of the Pharisees secured their release (Acts 5:34–41). Sanders goes on to point out that the "Mishnah tractate *Sanhedrin*, which deals with courts and offenses, especially those for which the Bible prescribes death, is remarkably lenient. . . . *Sanhedrin* and the following tractate, *Makkot* ('stripes'), which discusses cases for which the penalty was thirty-nine lashes, contain so many rules requiring accusations to be thrown out of court that it is difficult to imagine a conviction." Although Sanders stresses that "the courts of the Mishnah *Sanhedrin* are to a considerable degree fantasy courts," these tractates illustrate the leniency that characterized the rabbis' Pharisaic predecessors.[18]

Of course, if the Pharisees were as lenient as has been suggested above, this would explain their popularity with the public, attested by the gospels and Josephus alike. But if they were so lenient and if they believed that repentance led to forgiveness, surely we should expect the Pharisees to welcome back to the fold those "sinners" who demonstrated genuine repentance? But, if they had been willing to reinstate them, there would have been no need for Jesus to tell the story of the Prodigal and his unforgiving brother; indeed there would have been no need for him to found the Church.

There are two possible explanations. The first extends Maccoby's theory about the accusations of Sabbath breaking, so that it was not Pharisees who closed the gates to repentant sinners, but Sadducees; such an attitude is consistent with their harshness as mentioned earlier. The debarring of sinners is mentioned in only two passages: Matt 23:13 and the Parable of the Prodigal Son. Although Matt 23:13 is addressed to the "teachers of the law and Pharisees," it is possible that Jesus has the Sanhedrin in mind; we have established that the evangelists sometimes used "Pharisees" as a nickname for it. Pharisees are not mentioned by name in the Prodigal Son; it is the elder brother's refusal to accept the returned Prodigal that is widely assumed to represent the Pharisees' attitude to "sinners," but it could arguably represent the Sadducees'.

---

18. Ibid., 419f.

Hypocrites or Heroes?

The second allows that it was Pharisees and not Sadducees whom Jesus had in mind, but that it was only certain particularly grave categories of "sinner" whose repentance the Pharisees were refusing to accept; less serious cases received the leniency which Sanders describes. There is evidence that Jesus had a special concern for tax collectors and prostitutes. For example, his call of the tax collector Matthew/Levi was the first recorded action of the second phase of his ministry; it could be regarded as an enacted parable demonstrating that he accepted even beyond-the-pale outcasts such as these. Moreover, in Matt 21:31f Jesus refers to the tax collectors and prostitutes entering the kingdom of God before the Jewish leaders because they had responded to the ministry of John the Baptist, presumably by repentance and submission to his baptism. Similarly, Luke 7:29 refers to tax collectors who had been baptized by John and who now responded positively to Jesus' ministry. Judaism—and presumably therefore the Pharisees—regarded tax collectors and prostitutes as particularly heinous sinners because their sin involved disloyalty to Israel which was considered equivalent to apostasy against Yahweh. The tax collectors worked ultimately for the Romans—even those who worked for Herod were in the service of a king who was a puppet supported by the Roman regime and so this still amounted to serving Rome. The prostitutes' clients would have been primarily Roman soldiers, so they too were regarded as "serving Rome." Pharisaism, which had a strongly nationalist element, would have regarded these two categories of sinner as having violated God's covenant with Israel. Perhaps, therefore, they considered that whereas perpetrators of less serious offenses could be reinstated upon repentance, these particular sinners constituted a special category whose exclusion was irrevocable. On this basis the evangelists depict Jesus as showing greater leniency than the Pharisees, as he insisted that even these, the gravest of sinners, should be restored to the community if they repented. And if the Pharisees refused to readmit them, Jesus would create a new faith community, the Church, in which even they would find a welcome.

Both of the above explanations are credible, but the second is perhaps preferable as it does not require the logical leap of substituting Sadducees for Pharisees; moreover, it accords well with the situation portrayed in the gospels.

WERE THE PHARISEES REALLY HYPOCRITES?

Jesus was an astute observer of human nature and his sense of justice second to none. He surely therefore had good reason for the diatribe in Matt 23:13–36 in which he denounces the *grammateis* and Pharisees as hypocrites six times. His accusation was based in part on the contrast between the piety that they showed and expected of others and their lack of compassion for the "sinners" (see above) whose lives they had ruined.

But this passage and the shorter parallel in Luke 11:47–51 must be balanced against other passages in the New Testament which show the Pharisees in a more favorable light and the fact that the Jewish populace, according to both the New Testament and Josephus, held the Pharisees in high esteem. Abraham Lincoln's much quoted dictum, "You can fool all the people some of the time, and some of the people all the time, but you cannot fool all the people all the time," surely applies here; if all Pharisees had been the hypocritical charlatans implied in Jesus' diatribes, they would certainly not have had the public acclaim that by all accounts they did enjoy. As Deines eloquently expresses it, "How is it, then, that the Pharisees are described as the people's party in the New Testament as well as in Josephus? Why would the people follow their example if they were nothing but hypocrites, eager to burden others with heavy halakhic [legal] bundles?"[19]

Undoubtedly some Pharisees were hypocrites; hypocrisy is inevitable in a religion which demands ethical perfection, since its followers advocate a standard which they themselves cannot attain. Surely some Pharisees were guilty of the particular faults of which Jesus accuses them in Matt 23. Probably, as Maccoby surmises, most Pharisees would have agreed with Jesus' accusations; they were well aware of the dangers of hypocrisy.[20]

It is always, however, perilous to argue from the specific to the general. That *some* Pharisees were hypocrites need not mean that *all* were. Luke records several friendly encounters between Jesus and Pharisees and the fact that the Pharisees apparently withdrew—albeit at the last moment—from the plot against Jesus (see *Jesus' trial and passion: the unexpected twist in the tale*, p. 193) surely indicates that on the whole they were decent people trying to improve conditions for the whole nation.

Deines is surely right in his conclusion:

---

19. Deines, 'Good Guys,' 22.

20. "Thus when Jesus calls the Pharisees 'hypocrites' he was not telling them something they did not know ..." (Maccoby, *Jesus*, 87.)

Hypocrites or Heroes?

> The main problem is that scholars and laypeople alike too often ignore the fact that polemical texts cannot be taken at face value for historical information. They mistake the *polemical* stance of the New Testament against the Pharisees as an *objective* description of the Pharisees, and this is as much in evidence today as it has been in the history of the church. To be sure, polemics can serve as a source for historical understanding, and polemics only work when they contain some truth. But it is also true that polemics have a purpose and quite often point to a more deeply rooted conflict in another sphere. This is clear in Matthew's gospel. He accuses the Pharisees of all kinds of things, but underlying these accusations is the extent of the Pharisees' influence on the Jewish people (in Matthew's terminology, "the crowds").[21]

For further on the use of polemical language in the New Testament see on *Jews accuse Jesus of being demon-possessed*, p. 97.

WHAT WAS JESUS' RELATIONSHIP WITH THE PHARISEES?

The gospels record both friendly and hostile encounters between Jesus and the Pharisees. The simplest and most likely explanation is that Jesus' relations with them changed; as explained in the last chapter, evidence suggests that Jesus' ministry divides into two phases characterized by his vastly different relationships with the Pharisees.

In the first phase he enjoyed friendly relations with the Pharisees. He was himself a respected member of the movement and he observed its conventions. He was, however, aware of its shortcomings and his primary aim during this phase was to reform it.

That first phase came to an end when Jesus came under official surveillance at the healing of the paralyzed man let down through the roof. Criticized by his observers for pronouncing the paralyzed man's sins forgiven, he recognized the impossibility of reforming the movement and switched to an alternative agenda. His aim now was to build a new movement largely from the repentant "sinners," excommunicated Jews, whom the Pharisees dismissed as under God's curse and irredeemable. Partly because he was now associating with "sinners," including tax collectors, and partly because of his alleged breaches of the Sabbath, Jesus now came under

21. Deines, 'Good Guys,' 22.

ever-increasing criticism from the Pharisees and his growing frustration with them is evident in such diatribes as that in Matt 23 and Luke 11.

HYPOCRITES OR HEROES?

If this book were a court of law trying the Pharisees on the charge that they were hypocrites who plotted to kill Jesus, their piety and philanthropy being a mere front, what verdict would it reach? The evidence has been presented, much of it from the New Testament trusted by most Christians as the prime authority for their faith. The judge has summarized the evidence, conflicting though it is. So what is the last word?

So far as the charge that they plotted to kill Jesus is concerned, the evidence does not stand up to careful scrutiny. Pharisees may have been involved in a plot against Jesus, but its intention was to find grounds on which he could be lawfully arrested. That is very different from murder. There was a later plot to have Jesus killed, but the evidence in the New Testament supports Maccoby's suggestion that the principal conspirators were the high priests who were Sadducees rather than Pharisees. So the case against the Pharisees must be dismissed.

The charge that the Pharisees were hypocrites, however, finds some support. But the same charge brought against *any* believer in the God of the Bible could probably be proved; all sincere believers in God purport to obey a Being whose demands transcend human capability; it is the inevitable shortfall that the Bible calls "sin," of which Old Testament and New Testament alike attest that all humanity stands guilty. Inasmuch as all believers advocate that one should serve a God whom they themselves fail to satisfy, all are hypocrites. So, although the Pharisees *were* hypocrites, they were no more so than many other religious groups. Undoubtedly amongst them there were some who made a show of their piety by wearing flowing robes or over-long tassels, deservedly eliciting Jesus' criticism. Their system of oral law may have been unwieldy and burdensome for many Jews, but in some respects it made life easier for them, especially concerning Sabbath observance. Their worst fault was one which Jesus mentions only obliquely although ultimately it is this which underlies his whole ministry. By using excommunication as a penalty for many crimes the Pharisees had consigned a whole underclass, the "sinners," to the margins of society with little or no hope of restoration, even for those demonstrating sincere repentance. That, ultimately, is the message of the Prodigal Son and the reason

Hypocrites or Heroes?

for Jesus' attempted reform of Pharisaism. It was because that failed that Jesus founded the church.

So, if the charges against them are largely groundless, should the Pharisees instead be accorded the status of heroes? Even though the New Testament's agenda makes it reluctant to attribute any merit to the Pharisees, it cannot conceal the trends in the culture it depicts. The Jews as a whole adulated the Pharisees, according them the status of heroes or celebrities. This was partly because their system of oral law did make observance of Torah easier for ordinary Jews, especially on the Sabbath, and partly because the Pharisees were themselves ordinary Jews working to improve the lot of the whole community; in this they stood in sharp contrast with the Sadducees and the Romans. Their past was associated with the heroes of the Maccabean Revolt. It was from the ranks of the Pharisees that the Zealots arose with their quest to overthrow the Romans by violent means and restore national sovereignty to Israel.

Moreover the New Testament does record some genuinely friendly actions by Pharisees towards Jesus or his followers. There were the unnamed Pharisees who advised Jesus to flee Herod Antipas' territory in order to save his life and there was the occasion when Gamaliel persuaded the Pharisee members of the Sanhedrin to spare the lives of Peter and some other apostles. Concealed in what the New Testament fails to say rather than in what it makes explicit is one of the most extraordinary facts about the Pharisees—despite their heated debates with Jesus, when it became clear that the Sadducees were determined to have Jesus put to death, the Pharisees wanted no part in the plot. They were not involved in the arrest, "trial" and execution of Jesus. Some of them were followers of Jesus, but even the others apparently recognized that the movement's persecution of Jesus was unjust. If the Pharisees had had the same influence with the Romans that the Sadducees enjoyed, perhaps they might have intervened and prevented the crucifixion of Jesus.

In conclusion, then, so far as the ordinary Jews were concerned, the Pharisees *were* heroes. Moreover, Jesus adopted and built upon their theology and praxis. In many ways the Christian movement is an enhanced Pharisaism. Historically most Christian believers, like the Pharisees, have attempted to live out their faith within mainstream society and to exert a beneficial influence upon it, being the salt that lends it flavor and the guiding light that shines upon it (Matt 5:13–16). Moreover, many of the ethical principles upon which western civilization is founded, a legacy of its Christian roots, originated within Pharisaism. The Pharisees are the unrecognized and unsung heroes of the western world.

A HERMENEUTICAL POSTSCRIPT

This possibly unexpected conclusion has implications for our interpretation of the New Testament. It is no exaggeration to say that the New Testament's depiction of the Pharisees is biased. Each individual reference can be justified, but nevertheless their combined effect blackens the Pharisees. Like all the best stories, the New Testament needs villains to counterbalance its heroes and polemics has forced the Pharisees undeservedly into the former role. The New Testament's primary purpose, of course, is to promote Jesus, his teaching, and the exploits of the apostles; by making their adversaries more sinister, the heroes in contrast appear more praiseworthy. It is no coincidence that most of those aspects of Jesus' ministry in which the New Testament remains silent, leaving readers to work out for themselves what is happening, concern the Pharisees in some way. A prime example is the two divisions, pro-Pharisee and pro-"sinner," of Jesus' ministry. Others include Jesus' excommunication and the withdrawal of the Pharisees from the plot against Jesus as the passion became imminent.

These silences have repercussions for hermeneutics. Attention was drawn earlier (see *"Reading between the lines" in the gospels*, p. 162) to the need for interpreters to reconstruct the missing pieces of the jigsaw puzzle. The evangelists wrote so economically that readers often need to interpolate. Despite this, even the most erudite scholars sometimes fall victim to the temptation to understand a passage literally where the evangelist has compressed some complex meaning into a single word. A prime example is Keener's comment on Matt 12:1f: "One would not usually expect to find Pharisees in a Galilean wheatfield on the Sabbath."[22] Although Matthew wrote, "When the Pharisees *saw* [*idontes*] this [the disciples plucking heads of grain]," that need not imply that a group of Pharisees was standing there in the field, watching Jesus and his disciples as they made their way through. It is far more likely that the farmer saw them and reported the incident to the delegation known to be investigating Jesus—and they later approached Jesus about it. That surely is what Matthew intended to convey by *idontes*, which is one of the most flexible verbs in Greek and can certainly have the meaning "hear about." With a minimum of interpolation the text could

22. Keener, *Matthew*, 351.

have been rendered, "When the Pharisees heard about this," sparing Keener the incongruity of standing his Pharisees in a Galilean wheatfield on the Sabbath.

If the Pharisees have a lesson for today's Bible interpreters, it is surely the need to be imaginative in the exegesis of God's word, as indeed they themselves were. Sometimes it may even be necessary to recreate the missing pieces of the puzzle.

Appendix
Substitution of Synonyms

THE FOLLOWING TABLE LISTS the instances where the evangelists have substituted one of the keywords (*Pharisaioi, grammateis, nomodidaskaloi, nomikos*) for another or inserted an additional keyword in conjunction with another. Only those occasions are included in which it is reasonably certain that one evangelist was copying the same material as another and has made a substitution or addition.

---

grammateis (Mark 2:6) → *Pharisaioi* and *grammateis* (Luke 5:21)
grammateis tōn Pharisaiōn (Mark 2:16) →*Pharisaioi* (Matt 9:11)
grammateis tōn Pharisaiōn (Mark 2:16) →*Pharisaioi kai hoi grammateis autōn* (Luke 5:30)
grammateis (Mark 3:22) → *Pharisaioi* (Matt 12:24)
heis tōn grammateōn (Mark 12:28) → *Pharisaioi . . . heis ex autōn [nomikos]* (Matt 22:34f)
hoi Pharisaioi (Luke 11:39) → *grammateis kai Pharisaioi* (Matt 23:25)
tois Pharisaiois (Luke 11:42) → *grammateis kai Pharisaioi* (Matt 23:23)

We may summarize the trends as follows:

Where Mark has only *grammateis*, Luke sometimes inserts *Pharisaioi* in addition to it while Matthew amends this to *Pharisaioi*. Where Mark has *grammateis tōn Pharisaiōn* Matthew simplifies this to *Pharisaioi*. In Q passages, where Luke has *Pharisaioi*, Matthew has *grammateis kai Pharisaioi*.

The number of substitutions is too small for reliable statistical analysis, but it would seem that Matthew prefers *Pharisaioi* and deprecates

Appendix

grammateis, although the Q passages run counter to this trend as in these Matthew introduces *grammateis* where there were none before. Luke also favors *Pharisaioi*, but never substitutes it for *grammateis*. Neither evangelist ever deletes *Pharisaioi* in favor of another term. The nature of these changes demonstrates that within those contexts the terms were regarded as synonymous.

Bibliography

Barrett, C. K. *The Gospel According to St John*. London: Society for Promoting Christian Knowledge, 1978.
Beasley-Murray, G. R. *Word Biblical Commentary: John*. Nashville: Thomas Nelson, 1999.
Bernard, J. H. *A Critical and Exegetical Commentary on the Gospel according to St John*. Edinburgh: T. & T. Clark, 1928.
Bright, J. *A History of Israel*. London: SCM, 1960.
Bultmann, R. *The History of the Synoptic Tradition*. Oxford: Basil Blackwell, 1968.
Caird, G. B. *The Gospel of St Luke*. Harmondsworth: Penguin Books, 1963.
Cranfield, C. E. B. *The Gospel according to St Mark*. Cambridge: Cambridge University Press, 1966.
Davies, W. D., and Allison, D. C. *A Critical and Exegetical Commentary on the Gospel According to Saint Matthew*. London and New York: T & T Clark, 1988, 1991 and 1997.
Deines, R. "The Pharisees Between 'Judaisms' and 'Common Judaism.'" In *Justification and Variegated Nomism: Vol 1: The Complexities of Second Temple Judaism*, edited by D. A. Carson, P. T. O'Brien, and M. A. Seifrid, 443–504. Tübingen: Mohr Siebeck/Grand Rapids: Baker Academic, 2001.
———. "The Pharisees—Good Guys with Bad Press." In *Biblical Archaeology Review*, 39.4 (2013) 22, 57–58.
Dunn, J. D. G. *Jesus' Call to Discipleship*. Cambridge: Cambridge University Press, 1992.
France, R. T. *The Gospel of Matthew, The New International Commentary on the New Testament*. Grand Rapids: Eerdmans, 2007.
Gundry, R. H. *Matthew: A Commentary on his Literary and Theological Art*. Grand Rapids: Eerdmans, 1982.
Hagner, D. A. *Word Biblical Commentary: Matthew*. Dallas: Word Books, 1995.
Hill, D. *The Gospel of Matthew*. London: Marshall, Morgan and Scott, 1972.
Jeremias, J. *New Testament Theology: Part One: The Proclamation of Jesus*. London: SCM, 1971.
Johnson, L. T. "The New Testament's Anti-Jewish Slander and the Conventions of Ancient Polemic." *JBL* 108.3 (1989).
Jossa, G. *Jews or Christians?* (WUNT 202). Tübingen: Mohr Siebeck, 2006.
Keener, C. S., *A Commentary on the Gospel of Matthew*. Grand Rapids: Eerdmans, 1999.
Kummel, W. G. *Introduction to the New Testament*. London: SCM, 1966.
Maccoby, H. *Jesus the Pharisee*. London: SCM, 2003.
———. *Philosophy of the Talmud*. London: RoutledgeCurzon, 2002.

Bibliography

Manson, T. W. *The Sayings of Jesus*. London: SCM, 1949.

Martyn, J. L. *History and Theology in the Fourth Gospel*. Louisville: Westminster John Knox, 2003.

Mason, S. "Flavius Josephus and the Pharisees." http://www.bibleinterp.com/articles/Flavius_Josephus.shtml.

M'Neile, A. H. *The Gospel according to St Matthew*. London: Macmillan, 1915.

Morris, Leon. *Luke: An Introduction and Commentary*. Nottingham: InterVarsity, 1974.

Motyer, Stephen. *Your Father the Devil? A New Approach to John and "the Jews."* Bletchley: Paternoster, 1997.

Nineham, D. E. *The Use and Abuse of the Bible*. London: Macmillan, 1976.

Nolland, John. *The New International Greek Testament Commentary: The Gospel of Matthew*. Grand Rapids: Eerdmans, 2005.

———. *Word Biblical Commentary: Luke*. Nashville: Thomas Nelson, 2000.

Przybylski, Benno. *Righteousness in Matthew and his World of Thought*. Cambridge: Cambridge University Press, 1980.

Rivkin, E. *A Hidden Revolution*. Nashville: Abingdon, 1978.

Saldarini, A. J. *Pharisees, Scribes and Sadducees in Palestinian Society*. Wilmington: Michael Glazier, 1988. Republished Grand Rapids: Eerdmans, 2001

Sanders, E. P. *Judaism: Practice and Belief 63 BCE–66 CE*. London: SCM, 1992.

Stanton, Graham. "Presuppositions in New Testament Criticism." In *New Testament Criticism*, edited by I. H. Marshall. London: Paternoster, 1977.

Stendahl, K., "Matthew." In *Peake's Commentary on the Bible*, edited by M. Black, H. H. Rowley, and A. S. Peake. Nashville: Thomas Nelson, 1962.

Sukenik, E. L. *Ancient Synagogues in Palestine and Greece*. Oxford: Oxford University Press, 1934.

Thiselton, A. "Reader Response Hermeneutics." In *The Responsibility of Hermeneutics* by Lundin, Thiselton, and Walhout. Grand Rapids and Carlisle, Eerdmans/Paternoster, 1985.

Wright, N. T. *Jesus and the Victory of God*. London: Society for Promoting Christian Knowledge, 1996.

———. *Paul and the Faithfulness of God*. London: Society for Promoting Christian Knowledge, 2013.

———. *The New Testament and the People of God*. London: Society for Promoting Christian Knowledge, 1992.

Index of Biblical References

OLD TESTAMENT

Exodus

20:5	59n50
20:10	139
20:12	36
22:22	52n42
31:13	199
31:14f	182n45

Leviticus

19:32	113
20:10	77
27:30–32	55

Numbers

18:21	55
35:30	78

Deuteronomy

5:16	36
10:18	52n42
19:15	78
23:25	26
24:1	41
24:17–21	52n42
24:19	26

2 Kings

1:2	32n25
2:11	40n31

Ezra

10:8	157

Nehemiah

13:3	157

Job

34:30	147
36:13	147

Psalms

32:1–5	206
110	48–49
118:22f	190
118:26	42–43

Isaiah

1:3	vii
3:14	188n65
5:7	188n65
27:2	188n65
55	206

Jeremiah

2:21	188n65
3:4	152n25
3:19	152n25
31:9	152n25
31:30	59n50
32:18	59n50

Index of Biblical References

Lamentations

5:7	59n50

Ezekiel

15:1–6	188n65
18:2	59n50
18:4	59n50
34	186

Daniel

9:27	128n15
11:31	128n15
12:11	128n15

Hosea

10:1	188n65
11:1	152n25

Amos

4:1	vii

Micah

5:2	14

Malachi

1:6	152n25
3:1	169
2:10	152n25
4:5	40

DEUTEROCANONICAL LITERATURE

Sirach

50:1	125

1 Maccabees

14:27–48	130

NEW TESTAMENT

Matthew

2:4	13
3:5	15
3:7–12	170
3:7–9	171
3:7	14–15, 60, 94, 145, 203
3:13–17	170n22
4:19	18
4:22	18
4:23	173n27
5–7	174
5:13–16	212
5:17–20	16, 174
5:17–19	16, 166
5:20	2, 12n4, 15–16, 142, 146, 160n1, 174
5:21–48	16–17, 167
5:22	167
5:27f	167
5:46f	165, 175
5:48	16, 148
6:1–18	52, 146–147, 174
6:16	25
7:28f	164, 175
7:29	17
8:19f	18, 20n16
9:1–8	177n32
9:2f	165
9:3–6	180
9:3	19
9:9–13	177n33
9:9	18, 178n36
9:10–13	2, 20, 64, 155n29–30, 160n1, 164n7, 179n37
9:10f	123, 158n35, 167
9:10	158
9:11–13	144
9:11	164, 215
9:13	156, 175
9:14	24, 170n21
9:20	167, 173

Index of Biblical References

9:34	25, 32, 180n42	15:3–6	167
9:36	186	15:11	37
10:5–10	186	15:12	36
10:6	157n33	15:24	157n33
10:33	61	16:1–12	204
11:2–7	170n21	16:1	33, 37, 180
11:14	40n32	16:6	38–39
11:19	64n53, 158n35, 185n57	16:11f	38
11:28–30	51, 85, 187	16:14	185
11:28	167	16:16f	40
11:29	85n68	16:18f	53
12:1–8	199n3	16:18	184
12:1f	213	16:21	13n5
12:2	26, 35, 144, 164	17:3, 9	40
12:9–14	145, 180n41, 183n51, 199n4	17:10–13	40
		18:12–14	192
12:10–13	41n32	18:17	165, 176
12:10	27, 150	19:3	41
12:14	2, 27–28, 44, 83, 148, 168, 205	19:22	18
		20:18	13n5, 42
12:22–37	54	21:15	13n5, 43
12:24–32	181	21:23–27	54
12:24	26, 31–32, 165, 180n42, 215	21:23	45, 183, 187n63
		21:25–27	15, 172n25
12:25–29	32	21:25	187
12:38f	204	21:28—22:10	33, 54n46
12:38	32, 37, 180	21:28–32	188
13:10–51	33	21:31f	159, 189, 208
13:10	33	21:32	22n19, 29, 31, 53, 172n26, 177, 191
13:34	184		
13:36	33, 38	21:33–46	188n64, 189n66
13:51	33	21:45f	45
13:52	33	21:45	45
13:54–58	181n43	21:46	195
14:1f	185	22:1–10	188, 191
14:2	62	22:8–10	191
14:12	170n21	22:15f	164n8
14:36	167, 173	22:15	20, 46
15:1–6	34, 37, 137, 144, 164	22:15–22	180n40
15:1f	20n15, 32, 73n58, 150n23, 155n30	22:23–33	165
		22:34f	47, 164n8, 215
15:1	12n4, 143n18, 145n20, 203n14	22:41–46	48
		23	16, 62, 147, 168, 174, 209, 211
15:2	167		

Index of Biblical References

Matthew (*continued*)

23:1–36	181
23:2–4	49
23:2f	2, 143, 165
23:2	12n4, 51–52
23:2–7	15
23:4	50, 53, 85, 123, 139, 167
23:5–7	51, 82
23:5	146, 167
23:6	50n38, 146n21
23:7	138n11
23:13–36	209
23:13–29	2, 160n2
23:13–15	52
23:13	12n4, 58–59, 65, 159, 177, 184, 191, 193, 206, 207
23:14	51n41
23:15–33	147
23:15	12n4, 54, 143, 153
23:23f	55, 165
23:23	12n4, 215
23:25f	56
23:25	12n4, 215
23:27f	57, 59
23:27	12n4
23:28	57–58
23:29–36	59
23:29–32	58
23:29	12n4
23:31	61
23:32	60
23:33	60
23:34	60–61
23:35f	61
24:23	65
26:3f	68
26:3	13n5
26:6–13	30n23
26:57	13n5, 69
26:59	69
27:1	70
27:12	70
27:41	13n5, 70
27:56	171n23
27:62–66	196
27:62	71, 194
28:19f	54
28:19	185

Mark

1:4	170
1:9–11	170n22
1:13	172
1:21–27	183n51
1:21	173n27
1:22	17
1:41	202n11
2:1–12	177n32
2:6f	19, 180
2:6	215
2:13–17	177n33
2:14	178n36
2:15	158n35
2:15–17	179n37
2:16f	21, 155n29, 164n7
2:16	12n4, 158n35, 215
2:18	24
2:23–28	199n3
2:24	26
3:1–6	180n41, 183n51, 199n4
3:2	20, 27–28, 150
3:6	2, 27, 44, 83n66, 148–151, 168, 201, 205
3:22	20n15, 26, 31, 33, 35, 37, 73n58, 98, 143n18, 145n20, 150n23, 180n42, 203n14, 215
3:23–27	32
4:33f	145, 163, 178, 184
6:1–6	181n43
6:14–16	185
6:17–29	184
7	13
7:1–13	35, 137, 144, 164
7:1–5	20n15, 32, 73n58, 150n23
7:1	12n4, 145n20
7:5	12n4
7:9–13	113
7:14–23	56

Index of Biblical References

8:1	33	4:16–30	181n43
8:11	37	4:16	173n27
8:15	38	5:10	171
8:31	13n5, 39	5:17–26	177n32
9:11–14	40	5:17–21	19, 73, 143n18
10:2	41	5:17	13, 30, 32, 35, 37, 143, 145n20, 150n23, 179, 203
10:33	13n5, 42		
11:18	13n5, 44	5:21	12n4, 215
11:27	13n5, 45	5:27–32	177n33
11:28	187n63	5:27	178n36
11:30–33	172n25	5:29–32	179n37
11:30	187	5:30–32	21, 155n29, 164n7
12:1–12	188n64, 189n66	5:30	12n4, 158n35, 215
12:9	189	5:33	24
12:10f	190	6:1–5	199n3
12:12	45, 193	6:2	17
12:13–17	77, 180n40	6:6–11	180n41, 183n51, 199n4
12:13	46, 150, 184n52	6:6f	30n24
12:28–34	196	6:7	12n4, 20, 27, 145, 150, 205
12:28–32	47, 167	6:11	150
12:28	215	6:32–34	175
12:35	48, 146n21	7:1–10	153
12:38–40	51	7:29f	28
12:38	138n11, 146	7:29	22n19, 53, 159, 172n26, 208
12:39	50n38	7:30	13
13:19	65	7:34	64n53, 158n35, 185n57
13:32	66	7:36–50	30, 155n30, 180
14:1	13n5, 67, 149, 205	7:36	3n5, 56, 63n52, 83n67, 153, 160n1, 179n39
14:3–9	30n23		
14:43	13n5, 68	7:40	164n8
14:53	13n5, 69	9:7	62
14:55	69	9:9	62
15:1	13n5, 70	9:22	13n5, 39
15:31	13n5, 70	10:16	61
16:1	171n23	10:25	47
		11	62, 147, 211
Luke		11:14f	32
1:5–25	169	11:16	32
1:36	169	11:37–54	30
1:57–80	169	11:37–41	56
2:41–52	168	11:37	3n5, 63n52, 83n67, 153, 160n1, 179n39
3:12f	22n19, 172n26		
3:21f	170n22	11:39	215

223

Index of Biblical References

Luke (continued)

11:42	55, 215
11:43	50n38, 51, 138n11, 143n21, 195
11:44	12n4, 57
11:45	36
11:46	49–50, 53, 85
11:47–51	59, 209
11:49	60
11:51f	61
11:52	52, 58–59
11:53f	46, 184n52
11:53	12n4, 46
12:1	38
13:10–17	183n51, 199
13:28f	66
13:31	3, 62, 83n67, 153
14:1–6	30, 63, 183n51, 199
14:1f	30n24, 180
14:1	3n5, 20, 83n67, 153, 160n1, 179n39, 199
14:3	13
14:16–24	191
15	13
15:1f	64
15:1	158n35
15:2	12n4, 64n53, 185
15:3–32	187
15:3–7	64, 192
15:4	157n33
15:8–10	64
15:11–32	64, 188, 191, 206
15:28–30	159
15:28f	64
16:13	65
16:14	64, 113, 136, 201
17:21f	65–66
18:10–14	22n19, 25, 66, 137, 188
18:11	147
18:22	57
19:1–10	22, 185
19:7	185n57
19:10	157n33
19:39f	42
19:47	13n5, 44, 67–68, 149, 151
20:1	13n5, 45
20:2	187n63
20:4–8	172n25
20:4	187
20:9–19	188n64, 189n66
20:19f	46
20:19	13n5, 45, 180n40
20:20f	184n52
20:39	47
20:46	50n38, 51, 138n11, 146
22:2	13n5, 68, 149, 205
22:66	13n5, 69
23:1	70
23:10	13n5, 70

John

1:19–26	75n61
1:19	14, 94, 104, 145, 171n24, 203n12
1:21	75n61
1:24	14, 145, 171n24, 203n12
1:25	75n61
1:29f	170
1:32–34	170
1:35–37	170
1:35f	170
1:40f	170
2:6	92, 104
2:13	92, 104
2:18–20	94
2:18	45, 104, 187n63
2:20	104
3:1f	71
3:1	92
3:10	71
3:22–26	184
4:1–3	72–74, 79, 81–82, 142
4:1f	184
4:1	72n56
4:3	73
4:9	104
4:22	92, 104
5:1–18	145, 182
5:1–16	199

Index of Biblical References

5:1	92, 104	9:13	72n56
5:9f	95	9:14	145
5:10	104	9:15f	182
5:15–18	95	9:16	135
5:15	104	9:18	91, 98, 104, 145
5:16	104	9:22	75n61, 82, 85, 91, 98, 104, 135, 144, 181–182
5:18	95, 104, 149, 152		
6:4	92, 104	9:24	145, 158, 182
6:14	75n61	9:40	79
6:41	95, 104	10:16	178, 181
6:52	95, 104	10:19	92, 104
7:1	95, 104	10:22–27	181
7:2	92, 104	10:24	99, 104
7:11–15	96	10:30	166
7:11	104	10:31	99, 104, 149
7:13	104	10:33	81, 99, 104
7:15	104	10:39f	99
7:21	145, 182	11:8	99, 104
7:32	72–74, 203	11:19–45	90
7:34	97, 101	11:19	100, 104
7:35	96, 104	11:31	100, 104
7:40	75n61	11:33	100, 104
7:45–53	73n59, 74	11:36	100, 104
7:49	201	11:45–47	80–81
7:50	71	11:45	91, 100, 104
8:2–11	30n24, 76, 180	11:46–51	73n59
8:3	12n3–4	11:46	72n56
8:13	78	11:49f	102
8:21	101	11:50	152
8:22	97, 104	11:53	68, 81, 149, 152
8:31–59	9	11:54	100, 104
8:31	97, 104	11:55	92, 104
8:40–44	2, 168	11:57	81, 153
8:40	83n66, 149	12:1–8	30n23
8:44–47	90n1	12:9–11	101
8:44	160	12:9	104
8:48	97, 104	12:11	104
8:52	97, 104	12:19	72n56, 82, 182
8:57	97, 104	12:42f	75n61, 82, 194
8:59	149	12:42	80, 85, 91, 135, 144, 181, 196
9	73, 79	13:33	101, 104
9:1–14	182, 199	16:2	183
9:13–34	73n59, 79	18:3	68, 194
9:13–16	79	18:12–14	102

Index of Biblical References

John (continued)

18:12	104
18:14	104, 149
18:15	73
18:20	92, 104
18:28	90n2
18:31	102, 104
18:33	93, 104
18:36	102, 104
18:38	102, 104
18:39	93, 104
18:58	171n23
19:2f	93
19:3	104
19:7	103, 104
19:12	103, 104
19:14	103, 104
19:19–21	93
19:19	104
19:20	104
19:21	104
19:25	171n23
19:31	103, 104
19:38	103, 104
19:39	71
19:40	93, 104
19:42	93, 104
20:19	104

Acts

1:6	75n62
4:5	13n5, 83
5:17	207
5:27–41	3
5:34–41	116, 196, 207
5:34	13, 83, 138
5:36–39	83
6:7	viii
6:12	84
9:1	135
13:14f	182n47
14:1	182n47
15:5	185n56
15:10	85n68, 123
15:5–10	84
17:1f	182n47
17:10	182n47
18:1–6	177n31
18:4	182n47
19:1–6	170
19:8	182n47
19:35	85
22:3	86
23:1–10	155
23:6–9	86, 88
23:6	120n24
23:8	123
26:5	86, 88, 120n24

Romans

15:26	182n46

1 Corinthians

1:20	87
16:1–4	182n46

2 Corinthians

8:1–9:15	182n46

Philippians

3:4b–7	87
3:5	86, 120n24

1 Timothy

1:7	88

Titus

3:9	89
3:13	89

Hebrews

11:32–38	59

Index of Names and Subjects

Aaronide priesthood, 126, 128
adultery, 12n3, 17, 30n24, 76–78, 167, 174, 180
am ha-aretz, 118–19, 155, 186
Antiochus Epiphanes, 114, 127–28
Antitheses, 16–17, 167, 174
Apollonius, 128
Apollonius of Tyana, 98
apollumi, 44, 64, 68, 150–151, 157, 186–87, 189–90, 205
association, 106, 108, 117–18

baptism, 15, 28, 53, 60, 72, 170–172, 184–85, 187, 189, 206n16, 208
Barrett, C. K., 182
Beasley-Murray, G. R., 72, 178, 183
Ben Sira, Jesus, 125–27, 131
Bernard, J. H., 178
bias, 12, 83, 108, 152, 180, 195, 213
boundary extension, 140, 198
Bright, J., 128n16–129n17
Bultmann, R., 142–43, 161, 192

Caird, G. B., 192–93
Chasidim, 37
chief priests, 13–14, 21, 39, 42–46, 67–71, 74–76, 80–81, 83, 93, 100–101, 105, 113, 136, 140, 149, 151, 194, 196–97, 203–5
Common Judaism, 6–7, 154, 206
Cranfield, C. E. B., 190n67

Davies, W. D. and Allison, D. C., 155–56n29

Deines, R., 3, 7–8, 14–15n7, 24, 133, 154, 166, 179, 209–10n21
delegation, 6, 20–22, 26–27, 29, 41–42, 45, 63–64, 73, 94–95, 143, 145, 171n24, 174, 177, 203, 213
demons, 25–26, 31–32, 97, 110, 165, 180, 186
dinner, 3, 20, 22, 29–30, 56, 62–63, 101, 153, 158, 160n1, 179
diversity, 119, 136
Dunn, J. D. G., 156–57

elders, 13, 34–35, 39, 42, 45, 68–70, 83–84, 113–14, 130–131, 140, 144, 153, 157
Eleazar, 114, 129, 130, 132, 207
Essenes, 6, 86, 89, 108–12, 115, 121, 123, 125, 128, 136, 142, 153–57, 166
excommunication, 24, 53, 75n61, 79–80, 82, 85, 135–36, 142, 144, 157–59, 168, 178–79, 181–83, 185, 187, 191, 199, 210–211, 213
exorcism, 25–26, 31–32, 41, 165
Ezra, 124, 126, 157

fasting, 24–25, 66–67, 138, 174
form criticism, 161
France, R. T., 14, 18, 39, 155n30, 169, 174–75, 185n55, 186n58, 187, 190n67, 198n1, 200, 203

Galilee, 3, 6, 16, 18–20, 22, 26, 30, 41, 63, 72–74, 95, 135, 142–43, 145, 148, 150n23, 171, 173–74, 176–77, 180, 203–4

227

Index of Names and Subjects

Gamaliel, 3, 83–84, 86, 116–38, 140, 144, 196, 207, 212
Gentiles, 18, 42–43, 54, 84–85, 88, 93, 140, 143, 153, 156, 158–59, 171–72, 175–78, 183, 186
greetings, 51–52, 138, 146
Gundry, R. H., 40

haberim, 118, 155n30
Hagner, D. A., 53, 186, 190n67
Hasmonean, 5, 117n17, 124–25, 129, 131
healing, 19–21, 27–28, 31, 41, 63–64, 79, 94–95, 145, 149–51, 153, 158, 177–79, 181–83, 186, 199, 201, 203, 205, 210
Herod, 13–14, 22, 27, 38, 59, 62, 66, 132, 133, 141, 153, 208
Herod Agrippa, 86, 88, 153
Herod Antipas, 3, 62, 184–85, 212
Herodians, 27–28, 46, 148–51, 201, 205
Hill, D., 186
Hillel, 34n26, 41–42, 54, 65, 113, 116, 165, 201
hoi Ioudaioi in John's Gospel, 1, 10, 13, 90–106, 134–35, 194
hyperbole, 29, 51, 55, 153, 175
hypocrite, 2–3, 10, 34, 36, 38, 52, 55–59, 136, 146–48, 153, 159–60n2, 165, 172, 174, 209, 211
Hyrcanus, Jonathan, 109, 114, 132, 207

idontes, 22, 26, 213

Jeremias, J., 156n30
Jerusalem, 6, 14–15, 19–20, 31–35, 39, 42–43, 45, 72–74, 82–83, 85, 90–92, 94, 100–101, 105, 122, 127–29, 132, 141–43, 145, 149–52, 169, 171n24, 174, 176–77, 182, 185n56, 203, 205
Joarib, 129–30
John the Baptist, 14–15, 20, 24–25, 28–29, 31, 37, 40, 53–54, 60, 62, 63, 72, 94, 143, 145, 158–59, 166, 169–73, 176–77, 179–80, 183–85, 187, 189, 203, 205–6, 208
Johnson, L. T., 98

Josephus, 5, 7–8, 10, 15, 16n8, 76, 107–16, 120, 123, 125, 131–32, 136, 138–42, 200, 207, 209
Jossa, G., 5, 170n20
Judas Maccabeus, 129

Keener, Craig, 50, 53–55, 153, 155n30, 213–14
keys, 52–53, 79
kingdom, 15–16, 32–33, 52–54, 58, 65–66, 75n62, 102, 142, 159, 165, 174, 186, 189, 208
Kümmel, W. G., 74n60

M'Neile, A. H., 191
Maccabean Rebellion, 128, 131, 197, 212
Maccabees, 129, 147
Maccoby, H., ix–x, 2–3, 6–8, 16–17, 24, 27, 34–35, 37, 41, 48, 50, 52–53, 83, 86, 113, 133, 138n9, 148, 151–52, 154, 160–161, 165–66, 168, 184, 194–95, 199–205, 207, 209, 211
Manson, T. W., 49–50n36, 191–92
Martyn, J. L., 182–83n49
Mason, S., 108–9n4
Mattathias, 129–30
minim, 166, 183
Mishnah, 5, 117, 120, 207
missionary, 54, 89, 143, 153
Morris, L., 192–93
Moses, 17, 34, 37, 49–50, 52, 76, 84, 87, 115–16, 130–131, 143
Motyer, S., 9, 80, 90, 105–6
murder, 17, 44, 150, 167, 174, 211

Nehemiah, 157
Neusner, Jacob, 117
Nicodemus, 70–74, 76, 82, 84, 92, 101, 148, 196
Nineham, D. E., 162n6
Nolland, J., 19, 21, 57, 62, 65, 158, 186, 190n67, 193n73
normative Judaism, ix, 5, 7, 8, 24, 88, 113, 118–21, 133–34, 136, 141–42, 154, 157, 164, 168, 173, 179

Index of Names and Subjects

officials, 6, 14, 19–22, 25, 32, 63, 68–69, 86, 88, 91, 94–96, 98–106, 135–36, 142–43, 151–52, 157, 173, 177, 179, 201, 205
oral law, 8–9, 23, 32, 35, 50, 123, 130, 139, 141, 145, 164, 167, 187, 211–12

parables, 22n19, 23, 25, 33–34, 38, 45–46, 54, 60, 64, 66–67, 137–38, 145, 147, 159, 165, 174, 178, 183–84, 187–93, 195, 206–8
paradosis, 85, 131–32, 135, 145, 164, 167, 200
Paul, 4, 6, 8, 11n1, 85–88, 120, 133–35, 137n5, 143, 155, 166, 176n31, 182
perushim, 116, 119, 122, 131
Peter, 3, 40, 53, 73, 83–85, 123, 184, 196, 207, 212
phylacteries, 51–52, 146
Pilate, Pontius, 44, 46, 70–71, 75, 93, 102–3, 151, 194, 197
plots against Jesus, 2–3, 27–28, 37, 44, 67–68, 70, 81, 83, 95–98, 100, 148–53, 160, 168, 177, 180, 193–96, 198, 205–6, 209, 211–13
polemical parables, 33, 46, 54, 60, 188, 191
polemics, 9, 11, 98, 106, 165, 210, 213
power, 19–20, 22, 25–26, 32–33, 37, 46, 62, 109–10, 117, 127, 130–133, 135, 139–41, 144, 146, 165, 180, 197, 201
Prodigal Son, 64, 159, 188, 191–93, 205–7, 211
prostitutes, 29–31, 157, 159, 172, 189, 208
Przybylski, B., 16, 167
purity, 23, 38, 57, 106, 112, 117–20, 137, 155n30

rabbi, 5, 7, 17–18, 26, 34n26, 51, 55, 71, 99, 107, 115–16, 123, 148, 166–67, 174, 200, 207

rabbinical literature, 3, 5, 7–8, 10, 17, 107, 113, 115–22, 136, 142, 161, 165–66, 196, 198–201
repentance, 21–22, 28–29, 31, 53, 61, 159, 163, 170–171, 173, 175, 177, 179, 188–89, 191–93, 206–8, 210–211
righteousness, 2, 15–16, 20–21, 23, 57–59, 61, 66–67, 87, 111–12, 114, 132, 142, 146–47, 156, 160n1, 173–75, 189
Rivkin, E., 8–9, 105, 108, 116, 123–27, 129–31, 133, 135, 165–67
robes, 51–52, 93, 146, 211
Romans, viii, 11, 43–44, 66, 68–69, 75, 77, 84, 86, 103, 106, 112, 117, 133, 137, 140–141, 146, 149, 151, 153, 157, 176, 180, 182, 194, 197, 202, 205, 208, 212

Sabbath, 17, 26–28, 32, 53, 63–65, 79, 94–95, 103, 117, 128, 139–40, 144–46, 149, 151–52, 158, 164–66, 171, 182–83, 198–201, 203–95, 207, 210–214
Sadducees, viii, 5–6, 8, 13–14, 21, 27–28, 37–39, 43–44, 46–47, 60, 63, 65, 71, 75–76, 78, 81, 86, 88, 95, 108–11, 113–15, 119–20, 123, 125, 128, 130–132, 136–37n6, 140–143, 151–54, 157, 165–67, 171, 180, 189, 196–97, 200–208, 211–12
Saldarini, A. J., 5–8, 72, 105, 115–21, 135, 137, 142–44
Salome Alexandra, 109, 132
Sanders, E. P., 6–7, 132, 136–37, 154, 194, 198, 200, 206–8
Sanhedrin, 3, 13–15, 19–21, 24–27, 29, 31, 33, 35, 37, 39, 42, 45–46, 63, 68–71, 73–75, 79–84, 86, 88, 91, 94–95, 100–103, 105, 116, 131, 135, 140–141, 143–45, 151–54, 157, 171, 176–78, 180, 184, 187–88, 193–97, 203–5, 207, 212
Sanhedrin (Mishnah tractate), 207
Seleucids, 126–29

229

Index of Names and Subjects

self-righteousness, 1, 10, 64, 67, 147–48, 188, 192
Sermon on the Mount, 15, 17, 52, 146–47, 173–74
Shammai, 41–42, 65, 113, 116, 165
sign, 32–33, 37, 71, 74, 79, 81, 84, 93–94, 180, 187
sinners, ix, 2, 20–24, 29–31, 53, 64, 66–67, 79–80, 82, 119, 123, 136, 144, 155–59, 163–64, 167–68, 172–73, 175–79, 181–93, 206–11, 213
Soferim, 124, 126, 131
Stanton, G., 12n2
Sukenik, E. L., 50
surveillance, 3, 20, 25, 30–32, 35, 56, 62–63, 72, 143n18, 145, 150–151, 163, 177–80, 182, 184, 187, 205, 210
synagogue, 17, 26–28, 30n24, 50–52, 58, 61, 79–80, 82, 84, 92, 98, 130–131, 144–46, 153–55, 157–58, 166, 171, 173, 178, 180–183, 199

Talmud, 5, 7n23, 116, 120, 166, 200
tassels, 51–52, 146, 167, 173, 211
tax collectors, ix, 2, 20–23, 25, 28–29, 31, 64, 66–67, 119, 123, 137–38, 144, 147, 155–59, 164–65, 167, 172, 175–79, 185, 187–89, 193, 208, 210

Temple, 7, 9, 43–46, 48, 59, 66–67, 74–76, 78, 85, 91–94, 96–100, 105–6, 112, 120, 127–29, 131, 134, 149, 154, 158, 165, 170, 181, 183, 187–88, 194, 196–97, 200, 206
Thiselton, A., 184n53
Torah, 14–16, 20, 23, 25–26, 35–36, 44, 50, 52–53, 55, 58, 62, 67, 77, 88, 106, 123, 130, 132, 135, 138–39, 141, 144–45, 150, 154, 155n30–157, 161, 164, 166–67, 173–74, 177, 180, 199–201, 206n16, 212
tradition, vii, 15, 17, 20, 25, 34–37, 50, 74, 85, 106, 115–16, 121, 142, 145, 161, 166, 177, 180, 183–84, 186, 204
twofold law, 8–9, 86, 88, 123–27, 131, 135–36, 142, 173, 187

washing, 34–35, 37, 56, 79, 92, 137, 144, 164, 167
Wright, N. T., 2, 4–5, 11, 21–22, 137, 141, 156–57, 165, 169, 206

Zadok, 130
Zealots, 113, 141, 212

www.ingramcontent.com/pod-product-compliance
Lightning Source LLC
Chambersburg PA
CBHW062018220426
43662CB00010B/1375